SHATTERED LIVES

The Story of Advocate BARBIE

LIEZL THOM | LAURIE PIETERS

TCB
PUBLISHING
Taking Care of Business

First published in 2011 by TCB Publishing, a division of TCB Group

TCB Publishing
343 Lynnwood Road, Menlo Park, Pretoria
P O Box 11273, Hatfield, Pretoria, 0081

www.tcbgroup.co.za

Publisher: Bernard Hellberg
Editor: Bernard K. Hellberg
Layout & Cover Design: Aneska Meintjes

Typeset in Palatino (Text) & Alternate Gothic (Headings)
by Virtual da Vinci Creative Room

Printed by Business Print, Silverton, Pretoria

ISBN 978-0-620-51152-0

For Irma Labuschagne, who believed there is good in every person...

To protect the victims of "Advocate Barbie" and her consort, the names of the women and children affected have been changed, with Jeannine du Plessis being the exception. Jeannine never had a problem with being identified while she was alive and we believe she would not have wanted her name to be forgotten in death.

PROLOGUE

The tall blonde woman stares impassively ahead of her, as her name is taken up in the national register of sex offenders. Even though the public cannot access the document freely, Cézanne Visser is one of the few entries that will not slip by unnoticed. The implication of her details being entered into the register is that she will never be allowed to work with, or be a custodian of, children. Ironically, even the judge who convicted and sentenced her, concluded that she would probably never lay another finger on a child.

Visser's demure appearance is very different from the stereotypical paedophile who, according to common perception, is a scruffy middle-aged man who drives a beaten up, faded green or orange Datsun and skulks outside school grounds, looking for his next victim. The image of intelligent, educated professionals does not come to mind when one first thinks of a sex offender. Even less so are advocates, who are supposed to uphold the law – which is, amongst other things, supposed to protect children. The idea that a sex offender can be found in the guise of a beautiful woman, underscores the incongruity that Visser – who had a bright future as an advocate ahead of her – betrayed everything she undertook to safeguard.

Wearing a black leather jacket and a purple blouse, the woman dubbed "Advocate Barbie" by the media looks significantly different to the Barbie doll lookalike arrested almost eight years ago. Gone are the massive DD-sized breast implants and super tight clothing she used to sport. Her long, bleach blonde tresses have been chopped off in favour of a softer, straw-coloured bob. Even her face looks softer – the harsh make-up replaced by subtle pastels. The fact that she's gained some weight and now resembles the average woman on the street also adds to the sense that she is trying to shake off the image responsible for the moniker.

This last, humiliating formality behind her, the unlikely sex offender is escorted to the holding cells, from where she's transferred to the Pretoria Central Prison's female section to start serving her 7-year prison term. Clutching a tote bag, a pillow and a duvet, she finally succumbs to the tears she had been fighting the entire day during a final, private farewell with her mother.

Her fall from grace is complete – and in the full glare of the public eye, which has been following her for almost a decade.

1.
WOLF IN SHEEP'S CLOTHING
DIRK PRINSLOO

Although this book is about "Advocate Barbie," her story is intrinsically linked to that of Dirk Prinsloo. At the onset, we have to stress that, regardless of our own personal feelings, regardless of what Cézanne Visser says and most importantly, regardless of what his accusers say, Prinsloo has not yet been tried on the sex charges against him.

While in other countries the onus might be on the accused to prove his/her innocence, under South African law, a person remains innocent until proven guilty. As much as we acknowledge that there are people – mainly Visser and her sympathisers – who want Prinsloo convicted without him having the opportunity to defend himself, we cannot, by law, make any claims of criminal behaviour on his side. What we are allowed to do is to repeat the allegations against him – but we stress once again that those are untested accusations. We also repeat what Visser claimed during her trial – but it has to be noted that the High Court in Pretoria rejected her testimony in totality. In fact, Acting Judge Chris Eksteen called Visser a blatant liar in his judgement.

Visser had only one goal in mind when she levelled her accusations against Prinsloo – to stay out of prison. With this objective, she subjected herself and her mother to hours of scrutiny in the witness stand. The two women must at times have been mortified while giving evidence. As an observer, I cringed on their behalf as they testified about sado-masochistic practices I had never even heard of. I also have to say that

I do not believe Visser made up all the bizarre incidents she related to the Court, and as I a firm believer in the adage that smoke inevitably means fire, I have my suspicions about the type of man Prinsloo is, but those remain only opinions based on what I've seen and heard. Unless expressed by a judge in a court of law, opinions and suspicions do not equate to a conviction. Judge Eksteen rightly said, when he convicted Visser, that he would like to hear Prinsloo's reaction to the accusations she had levelled against him.

Much about Prinsloo remains hidden. Most of what has been said about him in the media was an orchestrated attempt by his former mistress to cast all aspersions on him and to deflect blame from herself. Through interviews with former colleagues and schoolmates, and from personal anecdotes related by Laurie (who worked for the couple and remained in contact with them long after she resigned), we have tried to capture an image of the man behind the public persona. We will also admit that, for the most part, Prinsloo and his motivations remain an enigma.

Similar to his co-accused and former mistress, Prinsloo also views himself as a victim. Through his correspondence with me and other members of the media before he was caught in 2009, Prinsloo painted himself as the injured party. In the words of a colleague with whom he corresponded, *"he sees himself as a victim and has blamed everyone, except himself and Jesus, for his circumstances."* The fact that he is a self-confessed atheist, probably removes Jesus from that equation – leaving only himself as blameless, the innocent victim of circumstances and conspiracies.

The first time he was arrested, Prinsloo contended that he was being prosecuted to either remove him from society or to exact revenge upon him. he claimed to be a champion for justice who stood up for the downtrodden. Prinsloo argued that this made him a *"thorn in the side"* of those he exposed as corrupt and unjust. He claimed that the police officials who investigated the case against him acted out of revenge because of previous altercations he had had with them.

Both Laurie and I take issue with the fact that the experts Visser turned to in order to support her *"battered woman"* defence, diagnosed Prinsloo with a number of personality disorders based solely on her description of him, without ever having met him in person. We do not suggest for a second that he is a saint, but one shudders to think what might happen to our democracy and hard-won human rights, if people can be classified as deviant based solely upon another's say-so. The whole idea is reminiscent of Dark Age tales of people with uncomfortable views or sensitive information being shipped off to mental institutions. Nevertheless, we have highlighted the two basic personality disorders ascribed to Prinsloo – *Narcissistic Personality Disorder* and *Antisocial Personality Disorder*.[1]

---

1 Described at the back of this book.

I have spoken to several women who knew Prinsloo before the charges against him first came to light. Their reactions varied from *"the hair on my neck stood on end every time he'd walk past me"* to *"he was exceptionally charming and went out of his way to help me."* The truth lies somewhere in the middle, I guess.

Most of the women interviewed in our attempt to gain a better understanding of Prinsloo's personality, agreed that he could be extremely polite and charismatic. According to one of them, he was highly skilled in the subtle art of flirtation and could play the social game very well. The words used most often to describe him included, *"very slick," "a manipulator of note"* and *"a charmer."*

From the different perspectives, I've gleaned that Prinsloo would start any of his attempts to either exact a favour from a particular woman or *"connect"* with her socially by paying her a compliment. This pattern apparently repeated itself after he fled the country. His Russian mistress, Anastasia, testified during his trial in Belarus that the first words he spoke to her after establishing that she could speak English were to tell her she had *"beautiful hair,"* which showed she was *"high class."*

Journalist Hanti Otto had a similar experience during her coverage of the trial in Belarus. When Prinsloo saw her in the courtroom, he immediately complimented her on her hair – saying her new style suited her – notwithstanding the fact that Hanti has had more or less the same hairstyle for years.

Another favourite strategy of Prinsloo was to compliment women on their hands and nails. A former female colleague related how he would often remark on her well-manicured hands and rings. She said she had the feeling he was opening the field for a potential flirtatious interaction – but never pursued it when she failed to act on his signals. It seems Prinsloo is a keen observer with an eye for detail. He also, apparently, has an eye for a beautiful woman, but that only puts him on par with the majority of heterosexual men.

While he noticed and commented on the physical attributes of the women he came into contact with, Prinsloo also took immense pride in his own physical appearance. He favoured designer clothing and, from what I've been told, even the running shorts he regularly wore sported some or other brand name. Being of average height, Prinsloo spent hours in the gym sculpting his physique. Hanti says he was really hurt when, after his arrest, a Sunday newspaper reported that he was overweight and unkempt.

When he perceived a flaw, in anything, Prinsloo would try to fix it – once again putting him right on par with the majority of men. Most people, but men in particular, deal with problems by fixing them. What sets Prinsloo apart, is the extent to which this tendency manifested itself in the way he treated his female partners, improving them by enforcing a regime of strict dieting, many hours at the gym and often more than one visit to the plastic surgeon.

What Prinsloo probably failed to recognise was that these women might not have been as resilient as he was, and that his need for perfection would take a serious toll on their self-confidence and self-image. After all, no woman likes to be told that she is fat, ugly, in need of bigger boobs or needs to lose some cellulite – even if it happens to be true. A smart man is the one who always and immediately answers an emphatic *"NO!"* to the question *"Does this dress make me look fat?"* He doesn't say: *"No, it's not the dress, it's your big arse that makes you look fat!"* Bearing this in mind, it is debatable how smart Prinsloo really is. On a more serious note though, his tendency to reconstruct the women in his life to his own idea of beauty, is indicative of his controlling, manipulative personality.

It is also quite possible that Prinsloo saw his partners as an extension of himself. Imperfections in them reflected badly on him, making them unworthy of his love. In contrast, when they were complimented, he revelled in the attention they received. He could then be proud of them, show them off and bask in the glow of the perfection that he had created. This is exactly what he did with Visser – who seemed to enjoy being thrust into the limelight and who revelled in the attention showered on her. He wanted other men to be jealous and to covet what he had, because in his mind it proved his superiority to the masses.

Another possibility is that Prinsloo acted out of genuine altruism and did not intend to hurt anyone. Maybe he had a vision to improve the women in his life for their own sake, to make them perfect, into an ideal persona that everyone would desire.

Throughout their relationship and even after their arrest, Prinsloo took obvious pride in his creation – "Advocate Barbie." He would often ask questions like, *"Isn't she perfect? Isn't she beautiful? Isn't she the most amazing thing that you have ever seen?"* He created the impression that he loved Visser very much and worshipped the ground she walked on. He provided everything she asked for, catering to her every whim – materially and financially anyway. He always appeared to be very proud of her, showing her off to anyone who displayed any interest, much like a boy would show off a shiny new toy.

As a teenager, Prinsloo was obsessed with bodybuilding and spent hours with his friends at the local gym. Apart from his close friends, he did not make much of an impact on his classmates. Very few of the *Hoërskool Eldoraigne* alumni I questioned even remembered him – and those who did struggled to recall any lasting impression he had made on them. If indeed he *is* the egomaniac that he is made out to be, the lack of impact he had had on his classmates must be a bitter pill for him to swallow.

According to those who knew him as a youngster, Prinsloo did not really date much while in high school or during his university days. When he did, he dated fellow students and had ordinary relationships – there were never any claims or allegations of abnormal sexual behaviour.

Prinsloo's father, Johan, never really opened up about his eldest son – except to Hanti who broke the news to him that his child was arrested in Belarus. Laurie, however, managed the almost impossible; to have a telephonic conversation with him. She writes:

"What Johan told me briefly about his children, aligned with what I had experienced when I met Gerhard, the youngest of the three Prinsloo boys. Gerhard was a talented musician working in the USA at the time that Dirk and Cézanne were together. I met him during one of his visits home. Gerhard and I had a very insightful conversation one afternoon when Dirk asked me to keep his brother company while he finished off some work. We chatted briefly about his life in the States. I had also spent quite a bit of time in New York and loved the city. He was animated and charismatic as he related tales of his life there. He enjoyed his time abroad and seemed happy with the path his life had taken.

I experienced him as a very pleasant guy who was easy to talk to and fun to be around. He did not always agree with his brother and didn't seem to be too comfortable with the pornographic magazines left lying around the house, or with Dirk's apparent obsession with them. Gerhard indicated that his brother had always been a little eccentric, yet he was driven, and tenaciously pursued his goals until he had reached them. Dirk liked to win. He enjoyed success and he enjoyed power. Dirk's desire to become an advocate was so strong, that at high school he already began marking his underwear as "Advocate Prinsloo."

Both Dirk and Gerhard were stubborn. Both were strong dominant personalities and it was this strength of character and stubbornness that ultimately drove them apart. The brothers had different opinions about life, neither would bend in the face of adversity and they realised that it would probably be in both their best interests if they agreed to disagree about certain things, and just kept their distance from each other."

An apparent animal lover, Prinsloo was extremely concerned about the fate of his dogs after he had fled. In the staggered conversations he had with Hanti during his Belarusian trial, he asked her to try and determine the animals' whereabouts and facilitate their transfer to his father. Hanti says this softer, considerate side of Prinsloo also came out when he and Visser were first arrested. She told me: *"I got the impression that he was more concerned about Cézanne's welfare than his own. He described her as a lady – not fit for prison. He created the impression that she was a delicate flower by describing her as someone who needed sunlight."* I chose to view the latter statement more literally and cynically wondered if she would survive if her all-over tan started to fade.

My impression of Prinsloo – derived both from the interviews I did, as well as the limited exposure I had to him during the first sex crimes trial – was of a suave, charming manipulator with the gift of the gab. He has been described as extremely intelligent and very well spoken. In Hanti's words: *"People mustn't think he's a poephol (asshole). He is very, very clever."*

Laurie is quick to agree with Hanti about Prinsloo's intelligence – however she adds that: *"Although he probably has a superior IQ, I believe that he has very low emotional intelligence, specifically when it comes to reading, identifying and understanding the feelings and needs of others."*

As far as I could establish, Prinsloo had in the past defended several convicted paedophiles and sex crimes accused. In some of the cases where he lost, the perpetrators won on appeal and were released back into society. One is tempted to ask if this is where his alleged predilection for child pornography and under-aged prostitutes was fostered.

Fellow advocates had very little time and respect for Prinsloo – whom they often described as an embarrassing stain on their profession's reputation. I was told how Prinsloo, after resigning as a prosecutor, apparently over claims that he had become aggressive towards an accused, sent out laminated copies of his CV to just about every reputable attorney in Pretoria in an attempt to solicit work. As bizarre as I find the fact that anyone would go as far as to laminate their CV, it did land him quite a few plum jobs – even though I could not find any attorney who was willing to admit that they had referred work to the notorious Dirk Prinsloo. His business cards were also virtually indestructible, as he did not want people to be tempted to throw his name in the dustbin.

Laurie has far better insight into Prinsloo. She writes, *"Dirk believed that he was an exceptional advocate and always fought hard for his clients. I ran into one of his former clients recently and he described Dirk Prinsloo as flamboyant and brilliant. He instilled a sense of confidence and trust in those he represented in court. He told me that he found Dirk to be an immensely likeable chap and he found it very difficult to reconcile all the deeds that he was accused of with the advocate who had represented him very successfully!*

He really did go out on a limb for his clients. I remember one day when he sent me off to the Conciliation Commission to secure a report that could win his client's case. It was a report that the Commission claimed had been misplaced. When I asked how on earth he thought I could accomplish this he told me to use my assets, find a dirty old man, flash some skin and a dazzling smile and do whatever it took to secure the report. He added that I was a beautiful woman and he was sure I would succeed in my mission. He really could be very manipulative, and I returned a few hours later, having briefly transformed myself into Erin Brokovich, proudly clutching the report. Needless to say, Dirk was impressed and extravagant with his praise. He really knew how to make people feel good about themselves, when it suited him.

I also remember a day when he came back to the office after successfully suing Telkom – and more specifically the Yellow Pages. He bounced into the office like a "Duracell Bunny," proclaiming proudly that he had destroyed his wealthy opponent's "powerful" and "overpriced" lawyers. He felt vindicated that they had tried to "take him for a ride" – a feeling he did not take kindly to.

I found court testimony, that Dirk was both verbally and physically aggressive towards women, completely out of tune with my own experience. I will agree that he flew into rages, would rant and rave and could appear aggressive, but I always found that if I stood my ground and pointed out the logical facts in a given situation, he would back off and listen.

I don't think he liked confrontation terribly much. He did tend to bully people in order to bend them to his will; however, I never found him to be a tyrant who had to be obeyed without question. I questioned him quite a bit through the years and am still here – alive and uninjured – which is why I came to the conclusion that his bark was worse than his bite. In the entire time that I knew Dirk I never heard him swear at anyone."

Another anecdote Laurie shared with me might shed more light on what was going on in Prinsloo's mind:

"Dirk was also rather paranoid about his privacy. He was preoccupied with security. People weren't allowed onto his property without an appointment. So there were few surprise visits – like the time he told me to refuse the Sheriff the Court entry because he didn't have an appointment.

One afternoon he asked me to accompany him on an errand, the nature of which I cannot remember. At one point, Dirk stopped the car at a telephone box and proceeded to tell me a really bizarre story about how the National Intelligence Agency had bugged his telephones and were monitoring his every word. Apparently he was a threat to the "authorities," as he was not afraid of them and challenged them when he found their conduct dubious. He was worried about being abducted or even murdered by operatives. He really was a bit paranoid – or maybe he was grandstanding. Perhaps, in his own mind, he was important enough for the National Intelligence Agency to spy on. For me, the experience was very peculiar, but then again, with Dirk peculiarity was commonplace."

It remains a mystery how the seemingly ordinary boy from an ordinary family turned into a man accused of sex crimes against children. One theory will have it that the work he did which involved paedophilia, may have triggered some deep-rooted predatory behaviour.

This does not, however, explain the obsession with pornography and all the other paraphilias[2] that he allegedly exhibited.

In his conversation with Laurie, Johan Prinsloo pondered what had gone wrong in his eldest child's life. She got the sense that he was wondering – even if he wouldn't verbalise it – whether he had had any role to play in his son's criminal behaviour, both the crimes which he has been convicted of and those of which he is still only accused. The embattled father described how hard it was to live with the knowledge

2 Listed at the back of the book.

that his son was a convicted criminal in a foreign country and that he would be tried for horrific crimes when he was finally extradited to South Africa.

Like any parent, he loves his son deeply and wants him to be treated fairly, although he is not blindly insistent that his child is innocent. He also refuses to say anything against his son's former mistress – in sharp contrast to her mother, Susan, who does not let an opportunity to vilify Prinsloo pass by.

2.
INNOCENCE LOST
CÉZANNE VISSER

L istening to her evidence during her trial, one would be forgiven for thinking that Cézanne Visser was a spineless jellyfish without moral grounding. During her testimony in court, she was at pains to emphasise to what extent she was under Prinsloo's control and that she had no mind of her own. The words *"it was like his brain was transplanted into my head"* were uttered repeatedly as she tried to shirk all responsibility for her actions, blaming Prinsloo for her criminal behaviour.

I do not doubt for one second that Visser was, at least to some extent, under Prinsloo's control, yet out of millions of women across the globe who are trapped in abusive relationships, I've not heard of a case where another woman had gone to the same extent as Visser as a result of that abuse. The case of Joey Haarhoff, common law wife of paedophile Gert van Rooyen, may carry similarities – but because the pair was never brought to justice, the facts of her situation will never be known.

To me, Visser is the confluent product of several factors, mainly her Christian upbringing in a Nationalistic Afrikaner environment and her mother's particular emphasis on keeping the peace at all cost, combined with an unusually sadistic and controlling partner. As a product of our previous government's programme of indoctrination that prepared Afrikaners to serve a misguided doctrine, young men were prepared for National Service, while young girls were surreptitiously taught that their role, as the next generation of *"volksmoeders"* (mothers of

13

the nation), was to support their men at all cost. This, combined with the church-endorsed paternalistic view that a woman's needs are secondary to the need of a man, could have reinforced the submissive role Visser had already learnt from an early age.

Afrikaner children who were schooled in the heyday of Apartheid were also taught not to question authority. The adage that children should be seen and not heard was commonly used as a reason to shut up any challenge to the *status quo*. If the child persisted with an argument, the good old rod (or wooden spoon or slipper – or whatever else was at hand) was hauled out and any dissent and insubordination was beaten out of him or her.

Visser is described as extremely submissive by Clinical Psychologist, Micki Pistorius – who evaluated her and testified in mitigation of sentence. According to Pistorius' report, Visser respects authority unreservedly. She also describes her as someone who takes life very seriously, lacks a sense of humour and spontaneity and who keeps a tight rein on her emotions, especially her suppressed anger.

To the casual observer Visser seems to exude a quiet confidence – although she can, at times, come across as very intimidating and unapproachable. This standoffishness has always been part of her personality, but it seems to have escalated since her arrest, serving her well as a defence mechanism.

Visser is also an undeniable arch-manipulator – an art she learnt from a young age and one which she honed over the years. In an e-mail Prinsloo sent me before his arrest, he claimed that Visser's entire defence is a thinly veiled attempt to manipulate the judicial system, public opinion and, ultimately, the judge. He felt that the only reason this feeble attempt was not rejected outright was because she is a beautiful woman.

The one personality trait that did not manifest during the trial was the sense of responsibility ascribed to Visser by the experts who evaluated her. The impression she created – most probably inadvertently – was that she was shirking responsibility, trying to lay all blame at Prinsloo's door. When one reads carefully between the lines of her testimony and the reports by Pistorius and Forensic Criminologist Eon Sonnekus, a picture of a woman racked by guilt emerges. Yet, I always had the impression that this was not something she would easily admit to. Admitting to feelings of remorse would indicate accepting responsibility, which might be seen as renouncing the control she claims Prinsloo had over her.

The debate over where the coercive control over Visser ended, and where her personal liability began, was never settled by Acting Judge Chris Eksteen's judgment – and it would not have been his intent to draw that line. When the defence argued its case, Visser was portrayed as a naïve, mindless little girl who blindly obeyed orders. This was not the impression she created with the prostitutes she regularly picked up. They saw her as just as much of a hunter – and in some ways even more predatory – than any man who used their services.

3.
CORRUPTING A VIRGIN

For years, the media's fascination with Visser, and her lover Prinsloo, proves to be insatiable. Literally thousands of centimetres of column space is devoted to her physical appearance alone. The charges against them and Prinsloo's antics in the courtroom play second fiddle to detailed descriptions of Visser's hair colour and style, skimpy outfits and chest size. She is probably one of only a handful of women on earth who gets a newspaper mention every time she cuts her hair.

Friends who knew Visser before she met Prinsloo described her as introverted, gentle and caring with a deeply entrenched sense of right and wrong. A dedicated scholar, she was deputy head girl in primary school and a prefect when she matriculated at *Die Hoërskool Montana* in the north of Pretoria. Her mother remembers her as a shy girl who never had a boyfriend. In fact, she did have a relationship with a boy in grade 9 (one of her classmates) – but the young man felt smothered when she started taking the liaison too seriously and broke up with her.

During her school years, Visser concentrated on her academic performance – although she also took a keen interest in sport and cultural events. She and her friends regarded the act of kissing as the epitome of intimacy.

Her father's job at the South African National Intelligence Agency meant the family had to move several times, causing the young Cézanne to attend no less than five different primary schools. Throughout her childhood years, her parents' marriage was characterised by conflict, tension and physical violence. Although Visser's father allegedly often vented his frustration and aggression on her mother, the girl would only see the results of the abuse afterwards. She rarely witnessed him beating her mother, but was fully aware of the assaults.

Visser's parents were high school sweethearts. Her mother, Susan, was a first-year student when she fell pregnant. She was devastated at the time and battled to come to terms with her pregnancy. Her proverbial shotgun wedding to Johan – and her parents' unambiguous disappointment – contributed to Susan's unhappiness and probably also to the cracks that soon appeared in their marriage: the same cracks that would later develop into an insurmountable crevasse.

Cézanne's response to the constant discord was to try to placate her father. She generally sided with him – possibly as a ruse to calm him down. She also feigned earaches and other imaginary complaints to diffuse the situation. Although she underwent multiple surgeries to her ears, she would often abuse her condition as a ploy to stop her parents from arguing. It is quite possible that, in her view, medical problems and procedures could bring about certain benefits.

Both Cézanne and her mother put on brave, happy faces to hide the reality of their conflict-ridden home life. Despite her father's alleged threats to commit family murder, the young girl and her mother refused to publicly acknowledge the problem. Her mother's response to the situation ingrained in Cézanne the idea that a woman had to do everything in her power to keep her man happy, even at her own expense. It also taught her that a cheery outward appearance could mask the bitter truth of domestic violence – a lesson she later had cause to put to very good use.

Visser's father eventually lost his job and subsequently battled to find employment, abandoning his family on several occasions. When Cézanne was 9 years old her parents divorced – but they decided not to tell their only child about it. They continued to live under the same roof for years – with their daughter blissfully unaware of their true marital status. She only found out about the divorce when she applied for a student loan and was devastated by the news. She threw a number of violent tantrums manipulating so upset that her parents re-married for her sake.

After matriculating, Cézanne enrolled at the University of Pretoria to follow her dream of studying law. From a young age she wanted to help other people. Her compassion was probably fuelled by the constant vulnerability and powerlessness she experienced as a child. Obviously intelligent, she passes both her BLC and LLB law degrees with distinction. The recently qualified advocate enrols at the Pretoria Bar Association to complete her six-month practical as a pupil – a requirement to register for the Bar exams. This exam is the last hurdle before being entered on the Roll of Advocates of the General Council of the Bar of South Africa. By all accounts, she is on the cusp of what promises to be an illustrious career.

Visser's private life is less rosy. Her parents' stormy marriage is on the rocks again and the constant arguments and bickering are taking their toll on the young advocate. Once again she has to bear the brunt of their marital conflict – having played intermediary and peacemaker between the two of them for most of her life. She hates the thought of another divorce, which she can see looming on the horizon, yet there is very little she can do about it.

Visser's first real attempt at romance is also less than stellar. During her pupilage, she falls hopelessly in love with one of the two mentors assigned to her. Fortunately, or unfortunately, the brief fling – which she sees as a potentially serious relationship – does not extend to the bedroom. At 24, Visser is still a virgin and extremely naïve. When the divorced tutor realises the extent of his acolyte's feelings towards him, he makes it clear that they are not reciprocated, leaving Visser bruised and unsure of herself. She suffers the crushing humiliation of rejection at the airport one day, when he conveniently forgets to collect her and she has to find her own way home.

Shortly after this introduction to heartbreak, Cézanne sits for the all-important Bar exam. For the first time in her life she meets another one of life's unpleasant surprises, when she fails. She is thrown a lifeline but subsequently fails that exam as well. The experience leaves her even more confused, vulnerable and less than prepared for the outrageous rollercoaster ride her life would become in just a few short weeks.

Visser's failed romantic relationship did little to equip her for life with Dirk Prinsloo. Having lived a sheltered existence until now, she knew very little about ordinary heterosexual relationships – let alone the array of sexually deviant and perverse practices she would soon come to regard as normal. The submissiveness she internalised as a child, combined with her bruised ego and broken heart, would have made her susceptible to any garden-variety psychopath. Unfortunately for her, her path crosses that of Dirk Prinsloo when she is least able to offer any resistance.

Visser and two friends, who also failed their Bar exams, join the Independent Bar Council of South Africa (also known as the Rogue Bar) – which is chaired by Prinsloo. He regularly meets the members of the Independent Bar, as his *Pro Deo* work is divided among them, and soon takes notice of the pretty but naïve Visser.

Prinsloo, a debonair and successful Advocate with a predilection for impressionable young women, invites Visser and her two colleagues to a *braai* at his house. The homestead – which he calls *Inner Circle Castle* – is situated on a smallholding in the prosperous suburb of Raslouw,

Centurion. He soon singles Visser out and lavishes his attention on her, giving her a tour of the house and lush, immaculately kept garden. She leaves with her classmates, deeply impressed with Prinsloo and his imposing residence.

After this first meeting, Prinsloo regularly invites Visser to *Inner Circle Castle*, from where he runs his office. Soon a relationship starts to bloom despite the fact that Prinsloo is eight years her senior and still married. The older man's compliments and fervent attention is like salve for Visser's shattered self-esteem. He showers her with expensive gifts, enchants her with fairytale-like pet names like *"Princess,"* declares his undying love and devotion to her and ensures her that he will always take care of her.

Visser, who has never had any actual suitors, thrives on the adoration. She has finally found Prince Charming who would rescue her from her turbulent parental home and help kick-start her career. Nothing is too much trouble for Prinsloo, who tries hard to woo his future mistress and panders to her every need and whim. Befitting of a romantic hero, he promises her the earth, the moon and the stars. Visser, who had never been taught that promises like these are nothing more than a combination of good intentions and good old-fashioned sales technique, laps it up.

The saccharine sweetness soon becomes less innocent, as Prinsloo's ferocious sexual appetite rears its head. During one of her visits to *Inner Circle Castle*, he pulls off his pants and demands oral sex. When the inexperienced woman reveals that she has no idea what to do, he uses the cult pornographic movie *Debbie does Dallas* as an instructional aid. Prinsloo impresses on her that a woman's worth – in his eyes – is measured by her ability and willingness to perform fellatio. Afterwards, he lets Visser know that he is very impressed with her first attempt.

Although they have not had intercourse yet, the sexual innuendo and tension continues to mount. Once, while on a trip to a shopping centre, Prinsloo takes Visser to the lingerie section of a department store and takes a G-string off the shelf. Visser, who has never worn anything but full briefs before, nervously tries it on while Prinsloo, who slipped into the change room, watches on. She tags along rather sheepishly as he pays for the scant underwear, telling her he cannot wait to see her wearing it – and nothing else. A few weeks later, he convinces her to move in with him.

Cézanne loses her virginity the first night she spends with Prinsloo. He penetrates her after a hurried and somewhat clinical attempt at foreplay and leaves her feeling cold, empty and vaguely disappointed – she was living the dream, so why did fireworks not accompany the sex? A disillusioned Visser later describes the sex act as almost brutal, yet – not knowing any better and trying very hard to please Prinsloo – she pretends to enjoy it.

Prinsloo continues to spoil Visser with an incessant stream of gifts, revealing clothes, surprises and cash. He persuades her to highlight her mouse brown hair – ostensibly because she has potential to become an international fashion model and her natural hair colour is too dowdy. Visser's legal work dries up. Prinsloo tells her that she should not continue with her chosen profession, as it would interfere with his plans for her. In reality, he demotes her to the performing of menial tasks. She basically becomes his gofer, driver and delivery service. Despite the obvious waste of her talents, Visser gladly complies – blinded by her ambition to become a celebrity. She would tell the media personality Rian van Heerden a few months later that she would do anything to become famous.

At *Inner Circle Castle*, sex becomes an all-pervasive theme – the more graphic and lewd, the better. Prinsloo masturbates, or has his mistress go down on him most mornings while he watches porn movies with his breakfast. The entire house is filled with explicit books and magazines and Visser is tasked with opening these books and magazines on a different page each day. Apart from the morning interlude, Prinsloo also demands oral or penetrative sex several times a day.

Visser's remodelling begins. Prinsloo convinces her that she is an uncut diamond and he would polish her into a fashion supermodel. Upon his insistence, Visser gets the first of several tattoos – a small Chinese symbol on her lower back. She also undergoes her first breast enlargement because Prinsloo tells her it would advance her career in front of the camera. When she comes home after the procedure, he makes it blatantly clear that he's not satisfied with the results and orders her to have even bigger prostheses inserted. The second procedure turns her former B-sized breasts into a pair of DD's.

The sex gradually becomes more taxing and demanding. Foreplay is virtually non-existent and consists mainly of Prinsloo ramming his penis down his mistress' throat. Yet, despite the fact that he can't satisfy her sexually – or couldn't be bothered to – Visser pretends to be deeply gratified. The training she received as a child – putting up a brave, happy face – comes in handy as she convinces concerned friends and family that she is truly happy.

Shortly after she moves in with Prinsloo, Visser obtains a domestic violence protection order against her parents. Her mother has voiced several objections and reservations about the blooming relationship – and even goes as far as doing an interview with *Huisgenoot* magazine in which she accuses Prinsloo of being a monster who has stolen her daughter. Prinsloo convinces Visser that her parents are trying to sabotage her happiness and are jealous of their relationship. The added strain to the already fragile marriage causes it to deteriorate rapidly – Visser's parents get divorced for a second, final, time.

The transformation of her face and body continues relentlessly. She starts wearing blue contact lenses to change her Bambi-brown eyes into unfathomable orbs. Prinsloo notices cellulite deposits on her thighs and butt and spends hours scrubbing the areas with all kinds of anti-cellulite concoctions. He also convinces her that her lips are not pouty enough and that she needs to have them enhanced. During several surgical procedures, fat is sucked out of her buttocks and injected into her lips. The synthetically engineered material *Gore-Tex* is also inserted under her lips to make them fuller. She is starting more and more to resemble the plastic doll with which she would be associated for the rest of her life.

Her new life as the trophy girlfriend of a wealthy, influential man sees Visser take on the running of his household. Her skills in the kitchen are put to good use as she cooks exquisite meals for him – food that she is not allowed consume herself. She is also tasked with finding personal assistants for her lover. Prinsloo's behaviour towards his employees has resulted in an exceptionally high staff turnover rate and an advertisement for an assistant to a successful advocate becomes almost a monthly fixture in the classified section of the local knock-and-drop newspaper.

4.
BLURRING THE LINES
MERCIA JACOBS' STORY

One of the women who answered the ad was Mercia Jacobs.[1] Mercia was about 20 years old when Prinsloo employed her as his secretary – a position she stuck out for exactly seven working days. Her last day – the one which caused her to resign – would change the course of her life forever. For a large part of that fateful day, she had found herself working alone in the office. The housekeeper and the gardener were around but no one else was present on the property. When he returned from court, Prinsloo tossed his toga at Mercia, instructing her to take it to the bedroom.

As she walked into the room, she was surprised to find Prinsloo already there. When she stopped in her tracks at the door, he told her to come in and hang up the robe in the walk-in closet on the opposite side of the room. Despite every instinct telling her to flee, Mercia entered the room and headed towards the other side to hang up the toga. Even when Prinsloo warned her that everything she saw in *Inner Circle Castle* was highly confidential and that she may not discuss anything that happened there with anyone, Mercia continued to ignore her deepening sense of unease.

The young secretary was a little taken aback by her employer's warning. She had always believed that anything that happened in the office, especially the office of an advocate, should be kept confidential. Unfortunately, Mercia had no idea of the type of man she was dealing

1 Not her real name.

with – and that he certainly was not referring to legal matters.

When she walked into the cupboard, she baulked at the array of pornographic material that assaulted her eyes. There was no end to the buffet of porn on offer. Everywhere she looked she saw lewd and graphic images on magazines covers, videotapes and boxes that held a vast number of sex toys. Horrified by what she saw, Mercia couldn't help but wonder about the advocate couple's blatant lack of restraint. She hung up the toga, eager to get out of the bedroom.

According to Mercia's evidence, Prinsloo moved quickly to block her path as she tried to move past him. With the alarm bells no longer only ringing, but tolling deafeningly in her ears, she froze in terror and remained rooted to the spot. She would describe to the court years later her absolute disbelief and horror when Prinsloo raised his hands and reached for her breasts. His unwelcome hands continued their journey as he removed her jacket and the dress she was wearing. Mercia shrank from his touch – he made her skin crawl and she wished desperately that he would leave her alone.

The shocked personal assistant testified how Prinsloo continued to fondle her breasts and then pushed her head towards his erect penis, forcing it into her mouth. He ordered her to suck his throbbing member and continued to ram it down her throat. Too frightened to oppose him, Mercia did as she was told, hoping that it would be over soon and that she could make her escape. Because she had seen an extremely aggressive side to him in the short time that she had worked for him, she genuinely feared for her safety and was too afraid to resist.

Satisfied, her employer pushed her aside. The young women grabbed her clothing and ran to the nearest bathroom, where she dressed before returning to her office. She had to get out of there and she had to do it fast. Mercia was having difficulty controlling her rapidly beating heart and breathing, and she did not know how much longer she could fight the waves of nausea that were washing over her.

Fortunately for her, Prinsloo had already left the property and was heading out to the Virgin Active for a workout. He was fanatical about his body and enjoyed his physical strength – a physical strength that was useful in the role he seemed to enjoy most in life, that of dominating women. Prinsloo seemed to view women primarily as sex objects, there to fulfil his needs, needs that were insatiable.

Mercia hurriedly gathered her personal belongings. She found her personnel file in his filing cabinet and removed her CV from it, determined to take it with her. She did not want Prinsloo in possession of any of her personal information. She even ripped her phone number off the telephone apparatus to which it had been fixed with a piece of tape.

Making a beeline for her car, she prayed she had left nothing behind that this man, who masqueraded as an advocate, could use to track her down. Mercia knew that if she ever saw him again in her life it would be too soon.

Her emotions bubbling to the surface, she managed to steer her car out of the property for the last time, passing Visser at the entrance. She vowed to never willingly return to this house of horrors, this *Inner Circle Castle*. Despite being severely shaken up by what had happened, she was grateful that her fears that Prinsloo would rape her had not materialised.

Sobbing uncontrollably as she drove out, Mercia felt isolated and ashamed. She didn't know where to turn for support and whom she could trust enough to unburden her traumatised soul. Feeling humiliated and dirty, Mercia phoned a friend and told her exactly what had happened to her that afternoon. The older woman was shocked but she knew that, for the sake of the traumatised woman, she needed to remain calm. It took her a while, but she eventually managed to calm Mercia down enough to listen to her advice. Mercia's friend firmly believed that there was no way on earth that a sexual predator should get away with it and she told Mercia to immediately open a case of indecent assault. If she didn't stop him, the woman said, he would just find himself another victim. In hindsight, her words were prophetic.

Mercia drove to her boyfriend's office where she told him everything that had happened to her that afternoon and begged him to drive her to the Silverton police station, where she opened a case of indecent assault against Prinsloo.

From there, they drove to Wilgers Hospital for a medical examination – by this time it was already 21h30. Mercia was examined by the physician on duty, a Dr De Vos, who was looking for signs of injury commensurate with the claims of indecent assault. Mercia explained to the doctor how she had been forced to perform fellatio on Prinsloo and how he had pawed her breasts. The physical examination that the doctor performed did not yield any results – everything appeared to be normal physically.

Dr De Vos was, however, struck by the young woman's emotional state. She was obviously traumatised and displayed many of the symptoms associated with shock – including nausea and a violent headache, while her hands were also sweating profusely. These symptoms are common in victims of sexual assault and other violent crimes.

The physician was so worried about Mercia that he offered to admit her for the night, thinking that it would be important to keep her under observation. Because the young woman was so distressed, Dr De Vos asked her if she needed protection while in the hospital.

By now, Mercia was exhausted. All she wanted to do was to go home, crawl into her own bed and sleep, preferably for a really long time. Dr De Vos decided to respect Mercia's feelings and wrote her a prescription for medication to calm her nerves and assist her to get the sleep she so obviously needed.

He also gave her a medical certificate, excusing her from work indefinitely and/or permanently. Once she had faxed the note to Prinsloo, there would be absolutely no reason for her to return to work. Mercia was very grateful that Dr De Vos understood her position and was making things as easy for her as he could.

The next morning, she faxed the doctor's note to Prinsloo. He responded by sending her a letter in which he indicated that he would pay her what he owed her for the time that she worked for him and that he was dismissing her on the grounds that she had not returned to work.

A few days after the incident, Prinsloo phoned Dr De Vos, stating that he was Mercia's employer and required some information. He asked the doctor for the MAS number linked to the case and the name of the investigating officer. Thirdly, Prinsloo wanted to know why there had been no mention of a diagnosis on the medical certificate.

Dr De Vos responded by saying that he had already given the J88 form (the legal document on which injuries are noted) to Mercia, and that, to the best of his knowledge, the investigating officer's surname was Spies. The physician said that he unfortunately had absolutely no idea how to get hold of Spies.

He then explained to Prinsloo that any diagnosis made by a medical practitioner was confidential information and protected by doctor-patient confidentiality. If the patient wanted the diagnosis to be reflected on the doctor's note, the patient could authorise the doctor to do so.

He added that he was not prepared to give Prinsloo any information about his patient. As he was talking, the doctor became aware that the advocate at the other end of the line was not particularly happy.

When Prinsloo realised that he might be in a tight spot, he decided to act proactively in order to discredit Mercia as a witness. He rushed off to the Wierda Bridge Police Station and opened a case of theft against her – claiming she had stolen R10 000 from his practice the previous day, after waiting for him to leave the premises.

The investigating officer from Wierda Bridge informed Mercia of the charges against her and asked for her side of the story. He even went so far as to take a warning statement from her. Quite some time went by before she heard anything about either case again. She had imagined, eventually, that both dockets had ended up in the proverbial file 13 at the police stations involved in the investigations.

When the case eventually came before the High Court and Mercia finally had the opportunity to take the stand against Prinsloo and Visser, State Prosecutor, André Fourie, showed her two statements written by Visser. The first one was in response to the indecent assault case that she had opened against Prinsloo. In it, Visser stated that she was at home on the day in question and that she was present in the room when Mercia had had oral sex with Prinsloo. She stated categorically that Mercia had been a willing participant in all sexual acts and that Mercia had performed all the acts voluntarily, willingly and without being coerced.

The second statement formed part of the docket of the theft case that Prinsloo had opened against Mercia. In this statement, Visser affirms the contents of the previous statement, but adds that after she and Prinsloo had left for the gym that afternoon, Mercia had stolen about R10 000 from the practice before disappearing.

It became obvious, in the course of the Prinsloo/Visser trial, that their tactics hinged on trying to discredit the witness. Prinsloo often did this by soliciting false statements from whomever he could convince to make one. Another tactic that he used regularly was to open cases against his accusers. He charged Mercia, Riana and Jeannine with theft in an effort to discredit them as witnesses long before they would be called to testify against him.

Through hard work and therapy, Mercia was able to move on. She went on to marry a man who supported her throughout the trauma of testifying in the sex crimes trial. Finally, once she had delivered her testimony, she was free to continue her life. Mercia was lucky to be able to put Prinsloo and Visser firmly where they belonged – in the past. For her, justice was served and the pair got exactly what they deserved.

5.
THE MAKING OF "ADVOCATE BARBIE"

Despite her conservative upbringing, Visser blindly accepts her lover's insistence on frequent oral, vaginal and anal sex – several times a day. Prinsloo forbids her to wear clothes around the house – saying he constantly wants to look at her naked body. He also buys her a whole arsenal of vibrators and other sex toys. He loves watching as she uses these to masturbate while he incites and instructs her.

Within weeks of her rather disappointing introduction to sex, Prinsloo brings home a black prostitute and tells Visser he found a *"friend"* for her. On his instruction, the two women kiss and fondle each other, while Prinsloo photographs them. After this first encounter, threesomes become a frequent ingredient in their sex life – as do prostitutes.

Visser even compiles a database of Prinsloo's favourite call girls and streetwalkers for future reference. She becomes a regular visitor to the brothels in Pretoria and Johannesburg in order to find sex workers to satisfy her boyfriend's needs. Several of the prostitutes admitted years later that they enjoyed going to *Inner Circle Castle* because they were very well paid.

Soon the couple's sex life changes from slightly kinky to decidedly sadomasochistic. As their relationship develops, Prinsloo's behaviour towards Visser changes. At first it is a gradual change, but his behaviour deteriorates rapidly as he goes from being loving and considerate, to violent and controlling. His temper is sparked by seemingly trivial incidents and flares up often and unexpectedly.

Although their physical relationship can hardly be described as loving and gentle, when Prinsloo is in a rage he becomes brutally violent in his penetration – regardless of the sensitivity of the chosen orifice. Sex becomes a tool for punishment and humiliation if Visser does not comply with, or even anticipate, his every whim. As part of her atonement, Visser often has to bring one or several prostitutes to their home for sex with either Prinsloo, or with herself.

There's no longer even a pretence of gentleness or foreplay and Prinsloo starts hitting Visser against the head if she gags during oral sex. The act is often so rough that her soft palate is left almost permanently bruised – damage that he would even photograph. Verbal abuse is also thrown into the mix, re-activating the apprehension and anxiety Visser had known in her parents' home. She's no longer Prinsloo's *"Princess"* – instead, he calls her a *"stupid slut."*

He also uses an array of objects to penetrate Visser, including a revolver which he keeps under his pillow at night. On the odd occasion when sex is less brutal, he takes photographs of her and so documents some of the bizarre and degrading acts she performs for his pleasure. Mimicking her boyfriend's proclivity for sticking all kinds of objects into her vagina, Visser often inserts vegetables or other items into herself to humour and pacify him during his temper tantrums.

The disdain and entitlement with which Prinsloo treats Visser's body grows as his stranglehold on her psyche intensifies. He orders her to go to the gym twice a day, six days a week, as she's too fat to be considered beautiful. Naturally slim to begin with, Visser soon melts down to a size six. Body hair also does not conform to Prinsloo's idea of beauty and he instructs Visser to wax her private parts, her legs, arms and underarms. On his insistence, Visser undergoes nose reconstruction surgery, has permanent make up applied and pierces her navel, nipples and genitals.

Food becomes another tool in Prinsloo's growing arsenal against Visser. He often eats hearty meals in front of her, while she is allowed only a protein shake, supplemented by a handful of vitamin tablets. If the couple goes out to a restaurant, Prinsloo orders himself steak, but Visser has to have a salad without any dressing, as it is fattening. He also chooses her outfits – skimpy, revealing clothes which leave very little to the imagination.

The relatively conservative residents of Centurion are scandalised as Visser accompanies her lover to the Centurion Mall wearing a see-through, black lace dress, with only a teensy thong and microscopic bra underneath. He had bought the ensemble at a sex shop and insisted on her wearing it to the shopping centre. Prinsloo loves showing off his "Barbie doll" in public and brags to his friends and colleagues about his beautiful girlfriend. The remodelled woman revels in the attention she is getting, not only from her lover, but also from the other men he flaunts her to.

Four months after Visser moves in with him, Prinsloo books a table at a coastal hotel where they intend to usher in the New Year. Here he tells her that they are now husband and wife, and she changes her surname to his, despite the facts that there was no ceremony to sanctify their union legally, or that he was still legally married to someone else. Although she started using his surname months before, Visser's sophisticated legal training completely fails her as she blindly accepts Prinsloo's word that their marriage is now legally binding under Common Law.

At Prinsloo's insistence, Visser has his name tattooed just above her private parts, while he documents the entire process through his camera lens. Prinsloo also shows her a picture of two naked women fondling each other and convinces her to have the image tattooed on her stomach. He tells her that her body is his canvas and he will create art on her skin to make her pretty. His idea of art seems to centre around his own name, which is also tattooed on Visser's back. A picture of a woman licking her own breast, and a dragon, complete the artwork on her body.

Visser's ascension into the eye of an eager public gets a boost when the first South African version of *Idols* hits the screen. Prinsloo encourages his girlfriend to participate, even going so far as sending her for singing lessons. He selects a Tina Turner hit for her to perform and she spends hours practicing the song. Despite not having the greatest singing voice, she makes it through to the third round of the competition – probably because the judges were somewhat amused by the caricature.

"Advocate Barbie" is born when Visser is interviewed by *Huisgenoot*. Shortly after the *Huisgenoot* article appears, the couple is also interviewed on the Afrikaans TV programme, *Voorblad*. In the pre-recorded background footage, "Advocate Cézanne Prinsloo" initially appears in her advocate's toga before stripping down to little more than a scant bikini. During the actual interview, she wears a tight-fitting patent leather outfit, with the zipper straining against her massive breasts. Host Ferdinand Rabie incredulously asks her if she's not concerned about people's reaction to her sexed-up look. *"Dirk allows me to be myself,"* she replies. She smiles seductively as she tells Rabie how much she enjoys her new look and how Prinsloo supports her in everything she does.

Rabie shot to fame as a reality television star when he notoriously defecated in the garden of the *Big Brother* house. Despite this, he went on to win the first series of the South African version of the internationally syndicated reality series. He is known for his uncouth and boorish behaviour – which he promptly displays by pawing Visser's breasts on the set before signing his nickname, *Boesman*, on the one and drawing a heart on the other. He also asks Prinsloo if he would object if Visser kissed him. To the obvious delight of "Advocate

Barbie," Rabie steals a kiss. Prinsloo beams as the camera focuses on him, looking every inch the supportive husband.

A slew of interviews with several radio stations and newspapers follow – turning the couple into self-styled celebrities. Visser is asked to adjudicate a children's talent competition and the subsequent media attention feeds into her image as an attractive, well-to-do, if slightly burlesque, philanthropist with a soft spot for children. This image comes in handy later, when she convinces a children's home to let two girls go home with her to *Inner Circle Castle*.

The interview with Rabie – or, more specifically, the fact that she wore a toga during the insert – gets Visser into trouble with the Independent Bar Council of South Africa, which wants to take disciplinary action against her and Prinsloo for bringing the profession into disrepute. Prinsloo would later be removed from the Council's roll, while Visser would voluntarily have her name deleted. The threatened action from the Bar is the precursor to the storm of controversy and allegations that would break over the couple's heads in the near future.

Apart from the temper tantrums and subsequent mental, physical and sexual abuse, and the relentless efforts to mould Visser into his idea of the perfect woman, life with Prinsloo is pretty good. The couple lives in absolute luxury and there's nothing Visser wants for materially. Prinsloo supports her financially, pays for the maintenance of her vastly altered physical appearance and – after he had isolated her from just about her entire support system – becomes the centre of her world. Visser is left fluctuating between complete adoration and intense fear. The one or two girl friends who remain in touch with her quickly disappear over the horizon when it becomes clear that Prinsloo wants them to become sexual playmates for his girlfriend.

6.
WORKING FOR THE PRINSLOOS
LAURIE PIETERS' STORY
PART I

Sitting at my desk at home one Thursday afternoon in mid October 2001, I was wondering what I was going to do with the rest of my life. Having just finished a project for a client, I was feeling unchallenged and unfulfilled. I had always wanted to complete the law degree that I had started early in the 1990s and was seriously considering giving it another go.

The local *Rekord* newspaper is regularly delivered on a Thursday afternoon. For lack of anything better to do, I picked it up and scanned the jobs section. I came across an advertisement for a personal assistant position at the office of an advocate. On a whim, I reached for the phone, deciding to give the advocate a call. At the time, I thought it might be worthwhile to work for a legal professional before making a decision about returning to my studies. It was a decision that would change my life or at least alter its course for the next few years.

My call was taken by a young woman. She identified herself as Cézanne Prinsloo invited me to come for an interview with Mr Prinsloo at 18h00 the same evening. She explained that he was too busy during normal working hours to interview candidates for the advertised position. I agreed, and was told to bring along my *Curriculum Vitae* and any other documents or references that I deemed pertinent to the interview. She gave me the address in Raslouw as well as some basic directions.

Excited and looking forward to meeting the advocate, I found the practice easily, since it was barely two blocks and less than one kilometre from my home. As I am not fond of driving on the best of days, I considered the short distance from home to be a perk. Arriving five minutes early, I pressed the buzzer. There was a large sign at the gate that read: *Inner Circle Castle*. I stated that I was there for the interview as arranged with Mrs Prinsloo, and with that, the large steel gates swung open.

The driveway leading to the house was long and winding and flanked by beautiful gardens and trees. Directly in front of the gate a gorgeous water feature and a large pond sported an array of birdlife, including two swans. I noticed a tiny antelope under one of the trees as well as a little black rabbit scampering off through the bushes. The grounds were very scenic and tranquil and created a very favourable impression. It seemed to be the ideal setting in which to be employed.

The door was opened by a tall, long-legged and striking platinum blonde who introduced herself as Cézanne Prinsloo. My eyes were immediately drawn to the huge, fake breasts that jutted from her very slim frame. She was extraordinarily out of proportion and I wondered how on earth her spine supported her bulging breasts. To me, she resembled a comically overdone Baywatch babe. 'Pamela Anderson with a twist,' popped into my mind.

Smiling with cosmetically enhanced lips, she invited me into the room and asked me to take a seat, saying that Mr Prinsloo would be with me shortly. With that, she disappeared down the passage and into what appeared to be the kitchen. I could not contain a little smile. My curiosity was definitely piqued and the words "curiouser and curiouser" came to mind.

I didn't wait long for the arrival of Mr Prinsloo. In contrast to the leggy blonde I had just met, he was a short, muscular man, sturdy, to say the least. He moved with confidence, greeted me warmly and invited me to take a seat on the couch from which he proceeded to interview me for the advertised position. He outlined the job requirements, stated what he was looking for an assistant and perused my CV and my references. He seemed content that my qualifications and experience were adequate.

It was a standard, straightforward interview until he asked me what I considered to be a rather odd question for an interview – especially if you were not seeking a position in a brothel. He asked me about my attitudes concerning sex, as if he was trying to determine if my sexual views were liberal or conservative. I almost choked, but stated that what consenting adults did behind closed doors was pretty much their own business, as long as no one got hurt in the process.

He then introduced the blonde bombshell who had initially greeted me, as his wife. Prinsloo told me that she was also a practicing advocate and that they worked together. Should I succeed in my application for employment at his practice, I would essentially be working for both of them.

They were one of the strangest looking couples I had ever seen together. She was at least a head taller and quite captivating. She seemed gentle and sweet and came across as almost submissive in his presence. By contrast, he seemed a little man with a powerful and dominating personality who obviously suffered from a severe case of *Napoleon Syndrome*. I got the impression that he craved power and liked to impose his presence on anyone in a room with him.

Apart from the bizarre question about sex, I felt that the interview had gone well and was not surprised when Cézanne called the next day to inform me that my application had been successful and if convenient, they would like me to begin working for them on Monday. I agreed, even though it was the last week of October 2001 and I had not planned to start before 1 November 2001.

My employment at the Prinsloo home began on the Monday. Initially, the work atmosphere and environment were very pleasant. I worked alone in the reception area which doubled as an office. It didn't take me long to learn the ropes and within a week or so I felt confident in executing the tasks assigned to me. I took my responsibilities seriously and sought to learn all I could about the day-to-day running of the practice.

On the first day of my working for the Prinsloos they were kind enough to prepare lunch for me. I was surprised that the meal included a generous glass of red wine – not really the average office luncheon beverage. I hoped everyone in the house could hold their liquor. The whole event was unexpected and unusual. When I mentioned the lunch to my father, he was stunned and reacted in typical fashion. He asked what kind of establishment Prinsloo was running, immediately saying that things couldn't be on the level. I had to agree with him although I did so reluctantly at first. Deciding to keep my guard up and my eyes open, I eventually experienced many business firsts with the Prinsloos – incidents that would reshape many of my views.

From the first day, some of Dirk's personality traits concerned me. Being controlling and domineering, he resisted, sometimes violently, any opposition from the people who surrounded him. For instance, he insisted that any person who was allowed onto the property had to have an appointment with him.

One afternoon, the Sheriff of the Court buzzed the intercom, requesting entry so that he could deliver a summons. I called Dirk and informed him that the Sheriff was at the gate. He barked at me to *"tell that asshole to fuck off and come back when he has an appointment."* I thought that his instruction bordered on ridiculous and opened the gates, allowing the official to enter the property. Dirk was really angry with me. He went ballistic, for about half an hour after the Sheriff departed, calling me names, none of which bear repeating and all of which were highly derogatory. I just let him rant and rave, smiled sweetly at him and said, *"I am so sorry, I must have pressed the wrong button and inadvertently let the guy in."* In any case, there was no way that I was going to be caught in the middle of a war between Mr Prinsloo and the Sheriff.

For me, Dirk Prinsloo represented a conundrum. On the one hand he could be kind, gentle, considerate and insightful and on the other hand he could be downright mean, narcissistic, aggressive, manipulative and controlling. I would wonder every morning for which Dirk Prinsloo I would be working on that particular day. However, I was never afraid of him. At no stage did I feel that I couldn't stand up to him or defend myself against his tirades. There were times that I even found his behaviour amusing, similar to that of a spoilt child.

Perhaps I was fortunate in that I didn't really need the job as his Personal Assistant and was quite capable of supporting myself doing graphic design work. My reason for deciding to take the job with him was merely to decide whether I wanted to go back and study law at UNISA or whether I should focus on a different field of study – a decision that the Prinsloos greatly influenced.

One aspect that became clear early on in my employ at the Prinsloo home was that they had a fairly bizarre sex life. This was obvious from the fact that during the day when they were not expecting clients, the clothing worn by the couple was sparse, to say the least. Cézanne usually left early for the gymnasium, returning at around eight o' clock in the morning just after my arrival. At this time Dirk Prinsloo was normally still in bed. Often she would return to the bedroom and the two of them would not emerge until eleven o'clock or until Mr Prinsloo had an appointment.

I found this behaviour more than a little odd. I did my best to ignore the sounds that travelled down the passage and into the kitchen through the quiet house. The stone floors only heightened the acoustics. When one entered the kitchen to make coffee in the morning, you were often subjected to the sounds escaping the Prinsloo bedroom. It wasn't pleasant and definitely not musical either.

Emily, the Prinsloo's domestic worker, was also highly disturbed by the goings-on in the bedroom. On one particular occasion, when things were noisier than usual, she wandered into my office. She seemed really distraught and I asked her what was wrong, to which she replied: *"Ms Laurie, I don't understand Ms Cézanne. She is screaming and he is using those machines when he is having sex with her. Those machines he puts inside her they are so big, I am telling you, big like a baby. I don't know how you even put something so big inside the woman. And afterwards me, I have to wash these machines. I don't like it, I really don't like it. They are crazy."* It seems that her sentiments were similar to mine. But Emily was well paid and couldn't afford to lose her job so I suggested that she should do her best to ignore the situation. In the meantime, however, if she was really uncomfortable, I told her to start looking for other employment, which she did.

Another really odd occurrence was the appearance of a very disturbing couple alternate Thursday evenings. To this day, I have never managed to find out who these people were – all I knew was that they gave me the creeps. The man, especially, made the hair on my neck stand on end. There was something about him which triggered every instinct in me to flee. Yet he was always very pleasant. Anyway, they arrived at the house three times during the time that I was employed at the Prinsloo home. I wondered what they were doing there and one day, with my curiosity getting the better of me, I asked Emily, who simply told me that they came for sex. From her answer I could only deduce that the Prinsloos were swinging – another thing no employee should know about her employer.

I never got the impression during my period of employment with them that Cézanne was unhappy. Like any other couple, she and Dirk had their squabbles, arguments and screaming matches. There were days when they fought like cat and dog, after which she would dissolve in tears. It seemed to me that Emily was frequently the person that Cézanne turned to for comfort. Occasionally, and usually on the days when Dirk was particularly bombastic, nasty and aggressive, she would turn to me. There were days when it seemed Dirk Prinsloo's sole intention was to hurt the people around him. He appeared to take great pleasure in belittling both Cézanne and me – chastising us mercilessly for the smallest transgression, or for what he on that particular day considered a transgression of his rules.

Dirk viewed himself as Lord and Master of everybody around him and was fixated on the idea of control. He simply couldn't bear the thought of anybody disrespecting or disobeying him. In reality, he had no-one's respect, not mine and certainly not Emily's. She thought he was an idiot and I shared her feelings. I often wondered how he went through life so convinced of his own self-importance when, in my view, he was just an awful little man. I don't know if Cézanne respected him but I am sure that she feared him. Yet she was constantly claiming how much she loved him. I never did get that either. She was besotted with Dirk, catering to his every whim.

Looking back, it is easy for me now to identify the narcissistic, sadistic and manipulative traits that formed the core of Dirk Prinsloo's twisted personality. At the time, to be honest, I just thought he was a jerk. I often wondered how Cézanne put up with his behaviour. Then there were other days where Cézanne and Dirk simply couldn't keep their hands off each other. They would touch each other – often very inappropriately – in my office. He would ask me questions like, *"isn't she just the most gorgeous creature that you've ever seen?"* or, *"doesn't she just have the most amazing body that you've ever seen?"*

She would often refer to him as her *"sex god."* He would kiss her, holding her tightly against him, forcing her lips apart, while he explored her mouth with his tongue, his hands dropping down to either her buttocks or between her legs. There appeared to be no limits to their hands-on behaviour and they honestly didn't seem to care whom was there to witness their antics – at least not when it came to me.

The Prinsloos seemed to lack basic morality and had absolutely no shame. The whole situation was very awkward for any person forced to witness it, and I found it extremely uncomfortable. I tried to put on a brave face but after about three weeks of working for them I realised that this environment was just not for me. Their whole lifestyle was unsavoury and I started to get a really bad feeling that things were not going to end well.

This feeling was amplified one morning when I received a phone call from Cézanne's mother. She wanted to speak to her daughter and when I informed her that Cézanne was out of the office, she asked to leave a message. She requested that I ask Cézanne to call her back as soon as she could. Dirk, who had heard the phone ring, called me into his office, wanting to know who had called.

When I told him about Susan's message he exploded and started yelling at me. He launched into a tirade about how evil Cézanne's mother was and how she did not approve of their relationship. He told me that she was doing everything in her power to break up his relationship with his beloved Cézanne. He then went on to say that Cézanne's father was no better than the mother and they had harassed him and Cézanne to such an extent that they had been forced to take out a Domestic Violence Protection Order against Cézanne's family in order to set boundaries and stop them from perpetually interfering in their relationship.

He added that should Susan ever phone again, I was to tell her to never call again and that her daughter did not wish to see or speak to her ever again. I was fairly surprised at the venom in his voice. It was clear that he felt highly threatened by Cézanne's mother. Furthermore, he insisted that I was not to relay Susan's message to Cézanne. I had never seen him quite so beside himself and immediately knew that there was a lot more to this story than met the eye.

After Cézanne returned, I overheard her and Dirk having a heated conversation in his study. It was clear that the topic was Cézanne's mother and the recent phone call that I had received. The next moment, I was on the wrong end of another tongue-lashing – this time from Cézanne. She pretty much repeated everything that Dirk had said earlier. She told me how her mother constantly interfered, and how she had undermined their relationship.

Cézanne repeated that the interference was so bad that she had been forced to take out a protection order against the woman as she could no longer put up with her constant meddling. She also told me that she didn't want to have any contact with her mother and that, should she call in future, I was to make sure that I gave her no information about either Dirk or her and that I should tell her not call the office again. If she did, I was to report the situation to Dirk. I agreed, but my curiosity was growing. What had the poor woman done to enrage both advocates to this degree? It was a mystery I simply had to solve.

Susan called me again the next day. I relayed to her the events that had transpired the previous day when I had been forced to give her message to Dirk. I also asked her not to call the office again and gave her my home number – telling her to call me at home that evening so we could talk. I felt really sorry for this woman who gave the impression that she wanted to protect her daughter and also wanted to be part of her life.

Throughout the years she never wavered in her role as her daughter's protector. Where she found her strength is a mystery to me and I will always have a measure of respect for her. I did not necessarily agree with all her methods, but I still feel that her motives were pure. She was the lioness protecting her wayward cub.

For a while, I gave Susan what information I could about the welfare of her daughter, in the sincere hope that she would be able to reach Cézanne and assist her when necessary. Unfortunately, this was not to be. Although Emily, Susan and I were all concerned for Cézanne's welfare, she herself seemed completely oblivious to the perilous turn her life appeared to be taking.

Cézanne Prinsloo was living the high life, the adored ornament on Dirk Prinsloo's wealthy arm. He flaunted her publicly, showing her off to the world and basking in the attention she generated. He had created her and he was enjoying her.

To all intents and purposes, she appeared to be enjoying the limelight just as much, if not more, than him. She often boasted about the gifts that he gave her, the wonderful lingerie and clothing and jewellery with which he showered her. If she needed money she merely had to ask and, just like God, he would provide. Cézanne milked the situation for all she could; she took full advantage of what he had to offer and she revelled in it.

One day at work she showed me photographs of her, dressed up in a very revealing black mini. She and Dirk had gone out to the movies at Centurion Mall. She told me how she had worn this skimpy little outfit and how wonderful she had felt wearing it, walking across the paved terrace towards the escalators at the mall on Dirk's arm. She had watched people's jaws drop at the sight of her, men and women alike, but mostly the men – who had looked at her with open desire and lust.

For the first time in her life, she said, she felt powerful. Through her sexuality she could manipulate and exert control over other people. It felt good, like nothing she had ever felt before. She was a sex goddess and it was a feeling she never wanted to give up. Cézanne craved the attention, she wanted fans and when she made this known to Dirk the idea was born to turn her into a celebrity by launching her as a TV star or as a model.

The first step in her TV campaign was to enter the South African *Idols* competition – and what a stir that created. Although she had absolutely no singing voice to talk of, her DDs caused quite a sensation on national television. Gareth Cliff, one of the judges, seemed quite unable to control himself, his eyes almost popping out of his head at the sight of her as he sat at the judge's table, grinning from ear to ear.

Needless to say, she advanced much further in the competition than her singing warranted.. The prospect of seeing her again would spur many a young man to return to their TV screens for a second helping of the busty blonde advocate Cézanne Prinsloo's talents – and I don't mean her voice.

By then, fortunately, I had already left their employ. Dirk was proud as punch of his "Barbie" and was basking in the attention she was receiving from the media.

From the onset of my employment with the "Prinsloos" I had been under the impression that Dirk and Cézanne where legally married. However, this was not the case, as I found out when Dirk one morning asked me to fax a divorce settlement agreement to lawyers in Pretoria who were at that stage representing his wife Elsie. He wanted to settle his divorce so that he could move on and marry Cézanne. He was in quite a rage about the settlement conditions.

Dirk felt that Elsie was taking him to the cleaners and that the settlement was unfair. From the names that he called his soon-to-be ex-wife it was clear that he felt nothing but contempt for her. I was more than a little surprised at this revelation. I had been working for the "Prinsloos" for almost a month now, only to find out that morning that they were not a married couple after all.

In a subsequent conversation, he revealed that he had married his previous legal secretary and that, although they had been separated for quite a while now, she refused to accept his previous settlement offers as she was a "nasty, greedy little bitch." He further indicated that he wished her dead and had seriously considered making arrangements for her to end up that way.

When Cézanne returned to the office, I asked her about Elsie. Cézanne's reaction almost precisely mirrored Dirk's earlier reaction. She seemed to perceive Elsie as a money-grabbing bitch and a huge obstacle to her realising her dream of becoming Dirk's wife. She went on to say that she really wished that Elsie would accept Dirk's latest settlement offer so that they could all finally get on with their lives. Years later, when I heard her testify in the High Court that she thought she was legally married to Dirk, this conversation with her came to mind and I knew that the testimony she was giving was far from the truth, the whole truth and nothing but the truth... 'So help me Dirk.'

Later that day, I was summoned by Dirk and asked to type up a letter while he dictated. One of the pictures on his screensaver was of a beautiful blonde, with an amazing figure who, at first glance, was the spitting image of the American country singer Faith Hill. I commented that she was a very pretty girl and he replied: "*Yes, she is. That's Elsie, my ex-wife. I made her, believe me; she didn't always look like that.*" He added that she had cost him quite a bit in surgical enhancement procedures.

Looking at the photograph of Elsie it struck me that he had created Elsie's looks, much like he was creating Cézanne's look. Dirk Prinsloo was building the woman that he fantasized about, first Faith Hill and now Barbie. He was living out his sexual fantasies in these women – they were simply sexual objects he had created for his own pleasure, props in his fantasy world and nothing more. This was the strangest man I had ever encountered.

For most of the time that I was employed in the Prinsloo home – besides the rather bizarre behaviour that they exhibited towards each other – I was largely unaware of their sexual preferences, which they kept hidden. What I did know was more speculation and deduction than confirmed fact. The first confirmation of my suspicions came late in November 2001 when Dirk was running late for court and asked me to fetch a jacket hanging in his cupboard for him to wear. This was the first time that I had entered their bedroom…

I had quite an education the morning I first entered the Prinsloos' lair. It was a crash course in pornography, as there were literally hundreds of pornographic magazines lying around open in the bedroom and even more in the closet. I had to push them out of the way in order to get to the jacket that I was supposed to fetch. With my jaw literally hanging open I managed to get the jacket off its hanger. The situation was pretty disconcerting and I think I was a little in shock from the assault on my senses.

My initial thought was to just get out of that room. I composed myself, walked down the passage to his desk and calmly handed Dirk his jacket, which he took while clearly scanning me for a reaction. I decided not to give him the satisfaction of knowing that I was even slightly rattled by what I had encountered.

I smiled and wished him good luck in court. In truth, I had just lost the last tiny fragment of respect that I initially had for him – respect which had already been whittled away by his behaviour during my employ at his practice. Frankly, it didn't seem to be much of a practice at all.

His clients were a motley crew at best, at least those few that I laid eyes on. They seemed, for the most part, to be Chinese. He appeared to spend a lot of time obtaining visas and work permits for these clients and often boasted that these clients were members of the Chinese mafia. I couldn't, of course, verify these claims, save to say that they were a rough bunch.

The handful of clients I personally came in contact with often caused me to wonder how Dirk was making sufficient money to sustain his lavish lifestyle. By the balances on his books he was definitely financially secure. However, most of this money was tied up in trusts.

When I initially heard that he had fled South Africa, I thought that he was heading for China and that perhaps these same clients would be his final destination providing him with a safe haven. I could never quite figure out the Russian angle, save that Russia is fast becoming known as the porn capital of the world and, as such, it occurred to me that he would be very comfortable there.

I was to celebrate my 33rd birthday on 2 December 2001. I arrived at work on the last day of November at quarter to eight as usual. I made some coffee and prepared for the day's work. Dirk showed up while I was still having coffee. It was highly unusual for him to be up quite so early, unless he was going to court. In his hand he carried a gift packet with a card attached to it, which he presented to me, saying that he hoped I would have a wonderful birthday. He was grinning from ear to ear as he handed over the package. I took it from him and thanked him for the gift. He left my office saying that he was going out for a short while.

Obviously curious, I had to see what Dirk had bought me for my birthday. I suspected that it was going to be something just a tad over the top. Praying that whatever it was it wouldn't bite me or vibrate, I unwrapped the gift. To my complete and utter surprise or shock, I found a very, very, very skimpy G-string and bra set. Actually it was rather beautiful and would have been a perfect gift for a man to present to his lover, but for an advocate to present to his personal assistant was perhaps not such an appropriate idea. I had only been his PA for about five weeks at the time and I was wondering about the possible implications of this gift.

At about lunchtime, when both Dirk and Cézanne were home, they popped into my office and asked me if I was happy with their gift. Dirk proudly boasted how he and Cézanne had seen the underwear while they had been shopping at the *Hustler* store and that Cézanne had suggested that he bought this lingerie set for me because she felt that it would improve my confidence and make me feel more like a woman. At this point he could have knocked me over with a feather. I had never felt that I lacked confidence or indeed had any need to feel more like a woman than I already did. I said that I was sure that it would be a confidence booster and thanked them once again for the gift. It seemed they were content with my answer and floated out of my office, hand-in-hand on their way to the gym.

As I heard the vehicle leaving down the driveway I felt an uncontrollable bout of giggles coming on. I simply could not stop laughing. The tears were streaming down my face at the absolute absurdity of the situation. It took me a while before I could pull myself together, gather my things and put them in the car. The entire situation was just becoming way too weird for my tastes and too many alarm bells were sounding every day. I felt unsafe and knew that time was of the essence. If I stayed and something bad happened to me I would only have myself to blame. I had always had good instincts and knew that listening to them now would be in my best interests.

I had to pass by my mom's home to pick up my son. I ran the scenario past my mother and grandmother in order to get their take on what had just transpired at the office. *"Guess what my boss just gave me for my birthday?"* My mother responded that she was surprised that he would give me anything as I had been working there for such a short period of time. She finally took the bait and asked me what the gift was.

I grinned, slipping my finger through one of the tiny straps and hoisting the lingerie out of the packet. My mother took one look at the revealing ensemble and exclaimed, *"Oh, good God, no!"* *"Oh yes!"* I replied," *Told you he was weird! What you think this means?"* Knowing full well what the answer would be, I asked the question anyway.

Meanwhile, my grandmother was overcome with laughter in her rocking chair in the corner. Gran has always had a rather disturbing sense of humour and she asked me when last I had bought myself a really good pair of *takkies* (running shoes). She went on to explain that I was going to need them to run down that rather long driveway when one day I found myself running for my virtue, if I didn't extricate myself from the situation immediately.

Never had a truer word been spoken and I often wonder what would have become of me and my future if, on that day, I had ignored my gut feeling, as well as my mother and very wise grandmother's advice. Fortunately, I did listen and got out. Well, perhaps not completely out but well to the side and out of range of flying shrapnel that was the Prinsloo relationship which, a year later, was to explode like a bomb – leaving total devastation in its wake.

On the Monday morning I resigned on fairly amicable grounds, citing the volume of graphics work in my company. However, I indicated to Dirk that I would be more than happy to assist him for the duration of the time that it took him to find a replacement for me. He seemed happy with the arrangement and advertised once again for a personal assistant, a position which was filled by a young woman named Riana Brink[1]. I left Dirk Prinsloo's employ a little wiser than when I arrived there.

---

1 Not her real name.

A few weeks later the first call from Dirk came. He wanted photographs of Cézanne retouched and edited. These pictures were destined for *YOU* magazine and would form part of an article on Cézanne in that publication. He also had a set of professionally taken photographs of both Cézanne and himself which required retouching. He desperately wanted to use these professional photographs to launch her international modelling career.

Later that afternoon Cézanne Visser arrived with three CDs at my complex. She explained that the first disc contained images of her handing out prizes to young children at some or other event in Johannesburg. The other two, she said, contained professional photographs of her. On these CDs she and Dirk had chosen a number of photographs which they wanted me to retouch and distribute per e-mail to a list of addresses which Dirk would supply. I told her it wouldn't be a problem and that my standard rate for retouching would apply. She agreed and we chatted for a while before she received a call from Dirk, telling her that he needed her at the office.

It was fascinating to see how, in an instant, Cézanne's entire attitude changed from a relaxed, happy person, to that of a very nervous, flighty, almost panicky individual. She choked down her coffee and ran for her car. The old blue Honda she usually drove was nowhere to be seen. In its place was a rather large maroon and grey Mitsubishi Colt double cab. When I asked where the Honda was, she replied that Dirk had bought her this Colt because she was finally stepping up in the world and hoped her dreams would soon become a reality.

Strangely, when I asked Dirk about the vehicle he said that it was his and that he allowed her to drive it as it pleased him to see his woman driving a car that befitted her ever-growing stature. His celebrity girlfriend deserved a flashy ride. He simply couldn't have her driving around in the beaten.up old Honda as it was not in line with her new image and didn't reflect well on him.

By this time, her *Idols* performance had already resulted in her acquiring a measure of notoriety. She said that she was being asked to attend functions as a *"personality"* and that she now had a base of thousands of fans. Cézanne was enjoying all the media interest. When I asked her if she didn't feel that a lot of the media attention was critical and negative, she said that there was no such thing as bad publicity – that any attention was positive. With that, she gunned the engine of the large Colt and sped off. Today I have to wonder if her sentiments are still the same.

I walked into my kitchen, made some coffee and then headed up the stairs to peruse the photos that Cézanne had just delivered. I opened up the disc in order to clean up the light and focus on the photographs of the awards function so that I could forward them to *YOU* magazine. If it was only the light and focus that needed adjustment, I thought, it wouldn't take long at all. What I saw on that disc was an eye-opener. Photographs depicted Cézanne lying naked on a bed, next to an equally naked Dirk Prinsloo while their feet were being massaged by two similarly naked young women.

These two, later identified as Monja and Marzanne[2], were living on the streets of Sunnyside at the time. Dirk's penis was in his hand, the head exposed as he masturbated. Not much was left to the imagination. I found the image repulsive but, if nothing else, the images finally confirmed my suspicions about the Prinsloos' private lives. Here I had visual confirmation and evidence of their delinquent sex life. I scrolled through the images. The disc contained other similar images as well

---

2 Not their real names.

as a set of photographs depicting Cézanne in a gold and black corset, posing in some of them on Dirk's arm, who was clad in blue jeans and a blue shirt.

There were further images of Cézanne lying on a leather couch, presumably the one in his office in front of the TV in a black lacy bra, an unbuttoned mauve cardigan, blue jeans and black boots. Her jean-clad legs were spread apart and her right hand was positioned suggestively over her pubic area. Her now over-enhanced lips formed into a sultry pout. The images were bizarre, repulsive and fascinating, all at the same time.

Towards the end of the CD I found photographs of Cézanne handing out certificates to children at some or other function. She seemed carefree and appeared to be thoroughly enjoying the occasion and the attention. There was very little adjustment needed to correct the lighting and focus on these few images and soon the job was done and ready to be e-mailed to *YOU* magazine. With the first job out of the way I inserted the second CD into my computer.

To be honest, I was more than a little apprehensive of what I would find on the next CD. I was not to be disappointed. There were a large number of photographs of Cézanne on the second disc. The photographer had done a pretty good job for the most part and generally the images were of a good quality. Some blemishes needed to be removed from Cézanne's skin, but the work was doable.

It was while I was retouching these photographs of Cézanne that it became clear to me just how bad the surgery was that had been performed on her breasts. The skin was stretched and had a blueish tinge, with the veins clearly visible. There were large and ugly indentations on her breasts where the implants had been inserted. It looked like the second prosthesis had simply been dumped on top of the first – making her breasts appear noticeably fake and really disfigured. They looked completely ridiculous and I struggled to understand how any person could allow themselves to be butchered into looking so appalling. In my opinion, the surgeon who performed the procedure had been irresponsible and did not have the best interests of his patient at heart.

During the time I worked for the Prinsloos, I took Cézanne for what I believed would have been her third breast enlargement. From her testimony in court, I've had to revise my assessment as – according to her evidence – she only had two augmentations done. During the 30-minute drive I practically begged her to reconsider her decision to go ahead with the procedure, but to no avail.

Nevertheless, Cézanne had often complained of severe back pain and I couldn't understand why she would put her health at risk in order to fulfil Dirk's fantasies. When I asked her about it, she responded that she would do *"anything that he demanded, including surgery."* She expressed the hope that it would further improve their already *"incredibly satisfying"* sex life.

Cézanne wanted Dirk to be happy and when he was happy so was she. She smiled, saying the enlargement wasn't going to be much anyway, only about a wineglass in each breast. I asked her, *"If Dirk really loves you, would he expect you to endanger your health?"* It was not a question she wanted to answer and she withdrew defensively from the conversation. Looking at the result, I felt both guilty and sad over the part I had been ordered to play in her deformation.

Scrolling through the photographs, I noticed that Cézanne had a large number of rings both through her nipples and in her labia. She was also sporting a couple of tattoos on her pubic region, on her back and around her ankle, only one of which was legible to me while I was retouching the photographs. This one was the word 'Dirk' running down her stomach beginning just under her navel and disappearing into the various g-strings she donned for the photo shoot. Another notable feature was her finger- and toenails which were each brightly painted in a different colour.

It was pretty obvious that, should Cézanne pursue a modelling career, it was not going to be in the area of fashion. Her enormous breasts would immediately exclude her from any runway or photographic work. Effectively, it appeared to me that the only part of the industry that would have any use for a woman of her exaggerated dimensions would be photographic and film work in the pornographic industry. Magazines like *Hustler*, *Loslyf* and such would always have use for a model with Cézanne's qualities.

Although I had told Dirk and Cézanne that I would forward the photographs to associates and acquaintances of mine in the modelling industry once the images had been retouched – I honestly had no contacts in the world of porn. I knew that my contacts would be of no use, besides, I sincerely had no wish to have my name associated in any way with the porn industry and with what was obviously transpiring in the Prinsloos' home. I resolved to get the work done for Dirk and get the discs back to him as soon as possible.

Cézanne's life was taking some very ugly and destructive turns. It was around this time that I began to seriously worry about her and her future. Dirk was steering her life resolutely down a path from which there would be no return. Cézanne seemed to be a happy and oblivious passenger on a sordid freight train, driven by an overzealous lust for publicity and an underdeveloped sense of morality. It was only a matter of time before it would derail. When it did, her survival would depend on her street smarts, which she seemed to lack.

To me, the really sad part was that she didn't seem to have a clue as to how bad things could get and where she could eventually end up – which turned out to be Pretoria Central Prison. From the photographs I deduced that she was becoming increasingly entangled in their seductive lifestyle. Dirk Prinsloo's fantasy world was becoming Cézanne Visser's reality. I truly wish that I had done more to encourage Cézanne to extricate herself from his web. I feared that it was most probably, too late by now, yet decided to talk to her about it the next time that I saw her.

Around this time I again heard from Susan Lemmer. I felt so sorry for this poor woman who was desperately trying to reach her daughter to offer her the support she so obviously needed. I told her what I knew of Cézanne's life and the dangers in which I thought she now found herself, hoping in vain that her mother could help her regain some sense of normality before her life imploded. Unfortunately, this was not to be.

After I finished retouching the photographs and e-mailed them off, I compiled an invoice for the work done. I called Dirk and Cézanne to let them know that the photo-retouching work was complete, and asked them to come over and see if they were happy with the results. They undertook to come around that evening and, since we were already cooking a fairly large meal, my mother asked me to invite the couple to stay for dinner.

During the meal, I paid careful attention to how carefully Dirk controlled what his girlfriend ate. When we had finished our meal my mother offered everybody a second helping and Cézanne said she would love some more. Smiling, she handed my Mom her plate. Dirk shot her a killer look. Obviously he had already decided that Cézanne had had quite enough to eat. Upon catching sight of his obvious displeasure, she quickly changed her mind about seconds. He did not have any such qualms and happily handed his plate for a second helping.

While working at their home, I noticed that Cézanne seemed to live almost exclusively on meal replacement formulas, protein shakes and vitamin pills. Until that evening, however, I hadn't realised just how anal he was in controlling her food intake. By his own admission, Dirk Prinsloo detested fat people. In his rulebook, cellulite was sinful and had to be obliterated – even if he had to spend fortunes on anti-cellulite creams and hours rubbing it away. I assumed that was why poor Cézanne was spending so much time working out. It must be said that Cézanne did have an amazing body during her time with Dirk, even if her proportions were a bit out of balance.

Shortly after I left Dirk Prinsloo's employ, another advertisement appeared in *Rapport* for an assistant to replace me. A chill ran down my spine when I thought of what horrors awaited the woman who would replace me. I hoped that whoever she was, no harm would come to her at the hands of the Prinsloos.

7.
IN THE NAME OF LOVE
RIANA BRINK'S STORY

Laurie's fervent wish that her successor would survive her tenure at *Inner Circle Castle* unscathed, was to be in vain.

Riana Brink* worked at the Pretoria Bar when she met Visser in 2000 after the latter enrolled to do her pupilage. Riana regarded Visser as a friend and they often went out together with the other young advocates, spending quite some time in each other's company. Shortly after Visser left the Bar – having failed her exams – Riana resigned to start up a typing business. Initially it went well, with approximately 40 advocates who made use of her services. However, when the Bar relocated its offices, it became difficult for Riana to collect work from her clients at short notice.

Before long, Riana found herself in financial difficulty, leading to her seeking fulltime employment, preferably in a legal practice. When she noticed an advertisement in the classifieds for a personal assistant to an advocate, she thought her prayers had been answered. She was ideally qualified for the job and immediately arranged an interview. When she arrived at the address in Raslouw, she was shocked at the sight of the woman who greeted her at the door. The blonde standing before her barely resembled the girl she remembered from their days together at the Pretoria Bar.

Riana couldn't fail to notice the huge increase in Visser's bust and her now platinum blonde hair. She was also markedly thinner than the woman who had failed her Bar exam the year before. As was the case with Laurie, the interview went as would be expected – except for a question on her opinions regarding pornography. Riana told Prinsloo that if it was his hobby, she did not have a problem with it, as long as he didn't try to involve her in his pastime.

At the time, Riana was embroiled in a violent battle for custody of her daughter who, at that stage, was with her ex-husband because of her precarious financial position. She desperately wanted her daughter back, but in order to accomplish this, she had to improve her financial status and she had to do so fast. After being told by Visser that her job application was successful, she explained to Prinsloo that she still had a few odds and ends to complete for some of the advocates at the Pretoria Bar. He, in turn, made it clear that he expected her to be available on a 24/7 basis, including weekends and evenings, and that no overtime would be paid. Despite these conditions, Riana was desperate and accepted the position.

Initially Riana was very happy working for the couple. She was well acquainted with the legal environment and found her work challenging, stimulating and satisfying. It wasn't long before Prinsloo's aggressive and abusive mannerisms began to surface. His self-control was poor on the best of days – but he took it to a whole new level with Riana and was incredibly aggressive towards her.

It wasn't long before Prinsloo's aggressive and abusive mannerisms began to surface. His self-control was lax on the best of days – but he took it to a whole new level with Riana and was incredibly aggressive towards her. Taking full advantage of her precarious situation, he insisted, for instance, that she stand at attention behind her desk when he entered the room. Prinsloo demanded respect even though he had done nothing to earn it. He would often yell at her and called her all kinds of names – telling her she was *"dumb," "stupid,"* an *"idiot"* and *"retarded."* Within days of her arrival at *Inner Circle Castle*, Riana's working days had changed into a complete nightmare. Prinsloo afforded her no respect at all and belittled her at every opportunity. This fed his narcissistic self-image and he revelled in the power he wielded over her.

Riana felt trapped in Prinsloo's employ as she had been told by the Family Advocate that if she left, she would be seen as financially unstable and unable to hold down a job – which would seriously prejudice her chances of getting her daughter back. Instead of using its resources to assist Riana, the Family Advocate compounded her situation and left her vulnerable to the likes of Prinsloo. It cannot be in the best interests of any child to live with a parent who is under this amount of stress in her work situation.

Riana was terribly unhappy but she decided to bite the bullet and continue to work for Prinsloo until she was able to bring her daughter home. Because of the threats made by the Family Advocate, she stayed even after she was granted custody.

Prinsloo forced his new assistant to work long hours of overtime without remuneration. One Saturday morning, after she had won her custody battle, Riana had to move to a new home, which could accommodate her child. She was overjoyed that her daughter was finally coming home and wanted to give her a homecoming that she would never forget. But her employer had other ideas. He ordered her to report tot the office after she had moved her belongings into her new residence. When she objected – saying that she had to look after her child – he insisted that she come in. Riana was left with no option but to leave her daughter with her ex-husband until the evening. Prinsloo had effectively ruined the reunion she had planned.

Riana was expected to perform tasks not normally associated with the position of a PA – such as repairing garage doors. On one occasion he instructed her to phone the pool maintenance company to repair the swimming pool vacuum cleaner. Assisted by Klaas, the gardener, she took the cleaner apart, removed some debris and got it working perfectly. On his return, Prinsloo wanted to know if she had phoned the technician. When she answered that she hadn't, he flew into a rage. Before she could explain that she and Klaas had fixed the problems themselves, he smashed the glass pane on her desk and with one foul swoop wiped everything off it – all the time screaming obscenities.

Soon he started assaulting her physically, slapping her against the head when he felt that she had been negligent. He also frequently threatened that he would *"bliksem"* her to death if she as much as whispered a word to anyone about the goings on at *Inner Circle Castle*.

Before long, the assaults started taking on a sexual undertone. From day one Prinsloo had insisted on hugging her upon both her arrival, and before departure from work. As he became bolder and more obnoxious, he began grabbing and feeling her breasts whenever she stood next to him. He would slip his hand between her thighs and under her skirt. Riana's skin crawled as she endured his touch, determined to hang on to her job as it was the key to retaining custody. When she told her boss to stop, he would flash her a sinister smile and ignore her. Riana was often severely rattled by the growing brazenness of the harassment – which seemed to amuse her employer no end.

One afternoon, while Riana was sitting outside her office smoking, Visser approached her – apparently at Prinsloo's request – and asked her if she would be interested in joining them in a threesome. Visser added that her lover had been fantasizing about having sex with more than one woman at a time – and wanted Riana to be that woman. Of course, this was no fantasy but behaviour the couple regularly participated in with prostitutes and other willing parties.

Riana was shocked but managed to retain her composure and politely turned down the offer. Prinsloo was not present when Visser approached Riana with this proposition. However, this was not the first time that he had suggested a sexual encounter and he was less than thrilled with Riana's refusal.

One afternoon, Visser arrived home accompanied by a young girl named Jeannine. To Riana she appeared to be very young – a pre-teenager. The child seemed shy and reserved and apart from greeting Riana, did not speak to her. Visser told Riana that she and Prinsloo were mentoring the girl, who did not have any family and was living in a children's home in Pretoria. Jeannine helped Visser offload groceries from the car. Among the goodies in the packets, were clothes, sweets and bubble bath for Jeannine. Visser told Riana that she had plans to pamper the orphan as she had nowhere to go over weekends and they wanted to improve her life.

Riana thought her employers were amazingly thoughtful and compassionate to open their home to a poor orphan. She saw Jeannine twice after their first meeting and noticed that the child was completely enamoured with the blonde busty woman whom she obviously regarded as her benefactor and saviour. From what Riana would tell the High Court in Pretoria years later, Jeannine doted on Visser and hardly ever left her side. The advocate seemed to enjoy the girl's company in return and the two spent hours together in light-hearted chatter.

One of the computers in the office at *Inner Circle Castle* was connected to the internet. Visser and Riana often used it to send and receive e-mails on behalf of Prinsloo, who would later claim that he was completely computer illiterate and could not have downloaded anything from the internet. Riana found it disturbing that the password for the PC was *"Slet100"* – but like with everything else at her workplace, she bit her tongue and kept her opinions to herself. She noticed that Visser, in particular, used the computer for hours to access the World Wide Web. While working on the machine, Riana came across large volumes of pornographic material stored on the hard drive. Shortcuts on the desktop were also linked to a number of Internet porn sites.

The advocate couple did not even try to conceal their obsession with internet porn from their secretary and tried to involve her in their favourite daytime pastime. On several occasions, Visser and Prinsloo called Riana to the side office, where the Internet computer stood, to get her opinion on some of the genitals on display – either on the computer or the magazines that were on display throughout the house.

On more than one occasion Riana would be asked whether she thought the *"poesie"* in the image was beautiful – with Prinsloo waiting patiently for her to reply. Although completely sickened by the images, she would put up a happy face and mumble something in the affirmative. She could not afford to lose her job and the thought of losing her daughter again was far worse than anything Prinsloo could dish out. Every night when she got home, Riana would take a shower in an attempt to wash away the filth to which she had been subjected at work.

On the odd occasion when her employers left town, they expected Riana to look after their vast property and animals. She would find herself surrounded by a multitude of opened pornographic magazines, displaying graphic images of nude women in sexually explicit positions. When she asked Emily if she could move the magazines out of the way, the housekeeper fearfully informed her that it was forbidden to move, close or even touch the magazines, as each one had been placed exactly where Prinsloo had wanted it.

Although she had grown numb to the piles of magazines and images across the house, Riana found the couple's bedroom especially unsavoury. No matter where she looked, she could not get away from the thousands of pornographic images that defiled the room. They were everywhere, on the floor, on the bedside tables, on the Jacuzzi and in the cupboards. Added to this there were a number of photographic albums containing pornographic photographs of Visser and Prinsloo involved in numerous sex acts with unknown persons.

Then there was the child pornography displayed in the room – an entire album depicting photographs of a young girl with long blonde hair. The magazines made Riana very uncomfortable and she simply couldn't reconcile herself with the idea of sleeping between all those naked people displayed so lewdly on the glossy pages around her. When she saw Riana's distress, Emily helped her pack away the magazines – to give her at least some respite from the assault on her senses. The next morning the two women carefully replaced them exactly as they had been.

Neither Visser nor Prinsloo made any effort to hide from Riana the fact that there was child pornography in their home. One day, in an incident the PA found particularly disturbing, Visser showed her photographs of a young girl, filmed with her genitals exposed and clearly visible, with a disused train acting as the backdrop. The image had obviously been downloaded from the Internet and had been printed in full colour on an A4-sized paper. Visser pointed out the similarities between the little girl and Riana's sister's child. She had seen her assistant's niece one weekend when she had to come in to work while her sister and the child were visiting. Ironically, it was true what Visser had said about the child in the photo – she looked almost exactly like Riana's niece who was only nine years old at the time. Riana was shocked to the core yet, again, she did her best to keep her composure.

No one will know what could have been running through Visser's mind when she showed Riana that particular photograph. If her trial testimony is to be believed, she was merely noting a fact – the two girls looked eerily similar. Although a more sinister motive – that she viewed the child as a potential gift to Prinsloo – cannot be overlooked. By her own admission in court, Visser was permanently on the prowl for potential sex partners for her seemingly insatiable lover.

Another aspect of the couple's sexual behaviour that Riana found extremely distasteful and disturbing was Dirk's fascination with pornographic videos. It seemed to her that Prinsloo simply could not get enough. He would watch pornographic movies for hours on end. Even when he was supposed to be working, pornographic material would be constantly playing in the background.

Occasionally, he would call Riana into his office to give her orders or dictate a letter. At times like this he would use the opportunity to fondle her breasts or run his hands up her skirt between her thighs. Reminding herself why she was enduring this constant humiliation and harassment, Riana would simply bite her lip and get out of his office as fast as she could.

She would often arrive at work to find Visser giving Prinsloo a blowjob. He must have had a very short memory – or felt that his girlfriend needed constant evaluation – as he made it abundantly clear that a woman's value is determined by her ability to perform fellatio. It was not unusual for him to call Visser during working hours for an appraisal of her skills. Incredibly, he would also call Riana to the office while his mistress was going down on him. She was expected to stand there and watch while he gave her instructions on what he wanted her to do at work that day.

Wherever she went in the Prinsloo home, Riana felt she was confronted by either pornographic images or sex toys, an array that included masks, lubricants, handcuffs and an astonishing assortment of vibrators. They were all shapes, colours and sizes.

She experienced the Prinsloo home as a house of sexual horrors and tried her best to ignore her surroundings and do what she had to, in order to remain employed. This was one of the most difficult times of her life, and what she had been exposed to in that house would haunt her for the rest of her days.

In the time that Riana worked for Prinsloo and Visser, several prescriptions for a range of medication were faxed from the office of a Dr Wannies Janse van Rensburg. The doctor, who was a friend of Prinsloo, would arrive at the house, from time to time, in a red sports car. Riana considered it rather strange that prescriptions were being issued without any consultations. The drugs most commonly prescribed by Van Rensburg were *Viagra* and *Rohypnol*.

On her way to the beauty salon one morning, Visser told Riana that she was going for her usual Brazilian wax, manicure and pedicure. She invited her along and indicated that she would pay for Riana's treatment. Only too happy to escape Prinsloo and the office, Riana accepted and went with Visser – even though she had never been to a salon before and had absolutely no idea what to expect.

Upon their return, Prinsloo asked the women how they had enjoyed the morning and if they were satisfied with the treatments that they had received. Visser assured Prinsloo that they were very happy and told him that Riana had a beautiful *"poesie."* Prinsloo demanded to see the results of the hair removal he had, in effect, paid for. Riana tentatively lowered her trousers, exposing herself for his inspection, all the while wishing for the earth to open up and swallow her, while he took his time inspecting her pubic area.

Later that afternoon he insisted that Riana again expose her genitals – posing with Visser while he took photographs of the two women standing together. Initially, he ordered her to drop her pants to the floor. She refused and lowered them only to slightly above the knees. Overcome with humiliation, she wondered how much more of this abuse she would be able to take. She realised that she had to get out of there as soon as possible.

Riana had won her custody battle and had her daughter back with her, thanks in part to Prinsloo, who had lent her R1 000 for her legal expenses. He had also lent her another R1 000 as deposit for her accommodation. It was very difficult for her to reconcile the kind Prinsloo with the tyrannical one. Often she felt her loyalties divided as on the one hand, she felt she owed him while on the other, she was terrified of him.

Her emotions were in constant turmoil, tossed about from one extreme to the other. Despite her misgivings Riana continued to work for the Prinsloos, as she felt she was beholden to them. She also felt that Visser needed her and held their friendship in high regard.

Like Riana, Visser often also found herself on the wrong end of a tongue-lashing from an intolerant Prinsloo. They spent many hours crying together and comforting each other in their shared misery. These highly charged emotional exchanges with Visser made the beleaguered secretary highly conflicted about resigning and leaving the blonde woman alone at the mercy of Prinsloo.

As part of her punishment for her many so-called misdemeanours, money was often deducted from Riana's salary. These deductions were accompanied by written warnings, which she would be forced to sign – whether she agreed with the accusations or not.

One particularly awkward incident occurred on the day that either Prinsloo or Visser drove over one of their Jack Russells, killing the dog. They wrapped the carcass in a duvet and took it to the veterinary surgeon for cremation. When Riana went to collect the ashes, she was told that the bloodstained duvet had been cremated with the dog. This enraged Prinsloo to such an extent that he deducted an amount – either R300 or R400 – from her salary.

Riana managed to endure the intolerable situation for almost six months. It would take a seemingly insignificant incident to finally break the proverbial camel's back.

Riana's father, with whom she had little contact, was working in Mozambique and she wanted to see him. She also wanted her daughter to spend some time with her grandfather. He was coming home for the weekend and Riana felt it would be the ideal opportunity to catch up at his home in Standerton. When she approached Prinsloo on the preceding Friday afternoon and asked to leave work early, he flew into a rage once again. Prinsloo demanded that she report at work the Saturday – telling her that she could leave early that afternoon but that she had to be at work the next morning. Riana stood firm and told him that she would not be coming in.

It was his violent reaction to her request to have the weekend off to spend with her family that finally pushed Riana Brink over the edge. She decided there and then to pack her bags and never return to that dreadful place.

Prinsloo forced Riana to work hours and days of unpaid overtime. He treated her with contempt and disrespect and had absolutely no respect for her boundaries. If he wanted something done or needed information at midnight, he would call. If his call went unanswered, he would fly into a rage and leave derogatory and highly offensive messages on her cell phone.

Instead of going to work on Monday morning, she called an advocate friend and begged him to help her draft a letter of resignation – on the grounds of constructive dismissal. On learning about her ordeal of the past six months, the friend was only too happy to assist. That same day, she faxed the letter to Prinsloo, who retaliated with a barrage of phone calls. Riana refused to take his calls, which further enraged him. He began calling her sister in Kriel, asking where Riana was and demanding that she return to work immediately.

Having finally scraped together the courage to get out, Riana stuck to her guns and refused to return. Her brave decision came at a tremendous cost, though. Unemployed and not being able to pay her debts, her car was repossessed. As it was October and close to year-end, the job market was not exactly thriving. The only position she could find was part-time, and earned her the royal sum of R2 100 per month. With this, combined with the child maintenance her ex-husband paid, she could at least keep a roof over her daughter's head but on many days there was barely enough food for the both of them.

Prinsloo didn't pay Riana for her last month of employment. She had bought furniture from him and owed him approximately the same amount on the furniture that he owed her in remuneration. She decided to keep the furniture in lieu of her salary, figuring the one debt would simply cancel out the other.

Never one to leave well enough alone, her former employer opened cases of theft and *crimen injuria* against Riana after her resignation. He claimed she had not paid him in full for the furniture. The *crimen injuria* charge was based on the statements of two private investigators hired by Prinsloo to obtain a statement from Riana that he could use as future leverage against her. 'Robert' and 'Norman' masqueraded as police officers who interviewed Riana about the theft charges her former boss had opened against her. During the conversation, they also asked her about the circumstances of her leaving Prinsloo's employ.

Riana was in a panic. Despite her regular dealings with legal professionals, she herself knew very little about criminal law. When an officer from the Wierda Bridge Police Station phoned her to inform her of the charges against her, she naively asked the officer if he was going to arrest her, telling him that she would have to make arrangements for her child if he was going to take her into custody. The officer informed her that he was going to refer the case for a decision to Advocate Retha Meintjies at the National Prosecuting Authority.

Strangely, Prinsloo waited a long time to open criminal cases against Riana. In fact it was not until after the couple's arrest in December 2002 that he decided to press charges against his former secretary. Perhaps they were worried that Riana could turn state witness against them. The spurious criminal charges were aimed at discrediting her and portraying her as a potentially biased witness. Of course, obtaining a statement under false pretences by impersonating a police officer would have nullified the document and 'Norman' and 'Robert' should have been charged with impersonating police officers. This angle was never pursued, though, and the two thugs never had to answer for their less than ethical behaviour.

Riana was to face more adversity in the years to come. She was attacked in her home by armed robbers who held her daughter hostage while their accomplices forced her into her car and dragged her all over town to withdraw cash from various ATMs. Her family was left traumatised by these events. As far as can be established, a group of men were arrested in connection with the robbery, although charges against them were later withdrawn due to lack of evidence.

Prinsloo's former secretary's financial woes seem to continue to this day and apparently she has been unable to fully recover emotionally. Recently, a law firm where she was employed opened a theft docket against her after she allegedly stole money. The case is still pending.

8.
CRIMINAL GAMES

An increasingly temperamental Prinsloo oscillates between treating Visser like a princess and abusing and degrading her. The punishment he metes out becomes more brutal and peculiar. On at least two occasions he drugs her and ties her up with leather straps and a collar. During both incidents she suspects she was sexually assaulted, yet she has no recollection of what happened apart from Prinsloo's comments – and the photos he took of her tied up, naked and bruised body. On one of these photos the couple's Jack Russell is seen licking Visser's private parts and Prinsloo laughingly informs her she also *"played"* with their two mastiffs.

The abuse she suffers is offset by the opulence he generously shares with her. Her battered old car has been replaced by a luxury SUV. Although the vehicle is never registered in her name, he tells her she is free to use it anytime she wants. Prinsloo keeps the money from the sale of Visser's car – presumably he uses it as a deposit on the 4x4. Apart from a little respect and some genuine warmth and tenderness, she wants for absolutely nothing in the world.

Like the majority of Afrikaners, Visser was raised and schooled in the Christian religion. Before her involvement with Prinsloo, she considered herself to be a devout Christian. Prinsloo, who is an atheist, enjoys abusing this fact to make his girlfriend squirm. He tells her he will be her only 'god' and she has to address him as such. She, in turn, was Prinsloo's goddess – on the rare occasions when she was not degraded. His caller identity on her phone was *"God,"* while her's was *"My Slut."*

During a holiday outside Mossel Bay, they come across a chapel and Prinsloo orders his *"slut"* to undress and lie on a table which serves as an altar. He violently penetrates her while pulling her hair and spitting in her face and orders her to blaspheme against her former God. As part of her conversion to 'Dirk-ism' he gives her a sadomasochistic book, *The Story of O*, telling her that, from now on it would be her only bible.

The Story of O is a sadomasochistic tale about a Parisian fashion photographer, who is blindfolded, chained, whipped, branded, pierced, made to wear a mask and expected to be constantly available for oral, vaginal, and anal intercourse. Prinsloo makes Visser read passages of the book and often re-enacts the indignities and humiliations suffered by *O*.

While reading *The Story of O*, I tried to compare *O's* treatment with that of Visser and, although I could definitely see some parallels, I also noticed stark contradictions. *O* grants permission beforehand for everything that occurs and her consent is consistently sought. This, for me, meant that she was acquiescent out of choice – while Visser continually emphasised her lack of choice during her testimony. Another discrepancy is the fact that *O* was employed and earned her own money – her bondage was not out of financial necessity, but out of choice. Visser, on the other hand, referred to the fact that she was financially dependent on her lover. Her repeated argument that she was acting out of love and fear is also in contrast to the character, *O*, who was solely motivated by love. Another clear difference is Prinsloo's act of giving Visser his name when he supposedly married her, as opposed to *O* who remained almost completely without any identity and, by the book's conclusion, is treated as an inanimate object.

By Visser's own testimony she is often forced to have sex with one or more women while Prinsloo watches and takes photos, yet he never allows another man near her. One of his favourite passages from *The Story of O* describes how *O*'s master covers her face with a mask before allowing several men to have intercourse with her. Prinsloo tells his own personal sex slave that he would like to watch as ten black mineworkers take turns in raping her. Fortunately for Visser, this is one of only a few of his fantasies that is not enacted.

Prinsloo's sexual predilections become more brazen and risqué. During a trip to a nature reserve near Graaff-Reinet, he beckons two young black women standing by the side of the road. He asks them if they want to *"play"* and once they consent, orders them to strip. Prinsloo photographs them in several sexually explicit poses with his naked girlfriend, before giving them each R100 and a can of cold drink. For Visser, posing naked with other women has become a normal part of life with her lover – as has oral sex whenever, wherever he demands it.

Keeping a detailed visual record of his conquests seems to be very important and Prinsloo regularly sends reels of film to a photo development centre in the Centurion Mall. It is absolutely incredible that the photos he took of his mistress and their bizarre sex games were never reported or – even more mind-boggling – that authorities were not alerted to the images of possible child pornography between the pictures. While I appreciate the tacit confidentiality agreement between service providers and their clients, no bond of confidence should prevail when a crime is suspected. Besides, confidentiality apparently did not mean too much to the developer in question, as explicit photos of Visser were leaked to school children in the area. While I cannot unequivocally say that the photo company was responsible, I seriously doubt whether Visser and Prinsloo would have released their homemade porn into the hands of a bunch of horny teenagers.

9.
A FAVOUR RETURNED
SAMANTHA OLIVIER'S STORY

Samantha Olivier[1] was only 20 when she first encountered the Prinsloos. She worked as a technician at the photo development centre Prinsloo regularly used to copy documents as well as to develop and print the photos he was so fond of taking. During one of his visits to the store he offered Samantha employment at his legal practice. She accepted his offer, on a trial basis, however she did not resign from her job at the development centre. After working for Prinsloo only one Monday morning in December 2002, she had to ask her former bosses to take her back – as she felt extremely uncomfortable in *Inner Circle Castle*.

Shortly after this, Visser arrived at Samantha's workplace to have some documents ring-bound. Samantha assisted her with this and – because of a glitch in the billing system – waived the charges. To thank her, Visser and Prinsloo offered to treat her to dinner. Samantha accepted and on a warm summer evening that same month, Visser picked her up and took her to their home. The couple showed Samantha to the kitchen area where Visser was still preparing the meal. The busty blonde had opened a bottle of wine which the three of them consumed in the kitchen. When the food was ready, they moved to the lounge area to eat.

At some point, Prinsloo suggested that the two women drink some shooters. Visser agreed and immediately jumped up to pour them. Samantha wanted to assist, but her host intercepted her – telling her to

---

1 Not her real name.

relax and keep him company while his girlfriend poured the shooters. Samantha didn't have much of a choice and sat down, waiting for Visser to return with their drinks. When she returned to the lounge, Visser handed one of the shot glasses to Samantha. The women flung back the alcohol before the three of them had their meal. When they had finished eating, Prinsloo took their plates back to the kitchen. This was when Samantha began to feel really strange.

When Prinsloo returned from the kitchen, he sat next to Samantha on the couch and started kissing her. At the same time, Visser reached for Samantha's hand and placed it on her own enormous bosom before caressing the young woman's breasts. Samantha couldn't understand what she was feeling. She had no idea of knowing that her symptoms correlated with the effects of the date rape drug *Rohypnol* or *Flunitrazepam* (a **benzodiazepine**), a very potent tranquilliser similar to *Valium*, but many times stronger. The drug has an immensely strong sedative effect and causes amnesia, muscle relaxation and a slowing of psychomotor responses. When she testified in court Samantha described feeling weird and disjointed and said that to date she struggles with memory loss of that evening.

Rohypnol became (in)famous as it could cause memory blackouts; periods of memory loss that follow ingestion of the drug with alcohol. Victims who have been raped while sedated with *Rohypnol* have reported waking up in strange rooms, with or without clothing, sometimes with a used condom on the bed, occasionally with bruises on their body, but without memory of the previous night, much like the events described by Samantha. She knew what she was feeling could not be ascribed to the alcohol as alcohol had never had this effect on her before and – although she wasn't a heavy drinker – she was used to drinking in social settings.

Samantha's few and very vague memories include Visser reaching down between her legs and penetrating her with two of her fingers. After this, there is a massive and all too common gap in her memory.

The next thing that Samantha clearly remembers is that she woke up in the Prinsloo home and suddenly felt very panicky. She was desperately running around looking for her clothing which had been removed. She was really worried about what had happened to her as she had no recollection of removing any of her clothing. The next thing she recalled was sitting in the maroon Colt, but she could not remember leaving her hosts' home or how she got into the vehicle. She had an uneasy feeling that something was terribly wrong but had no concrete idea of what it was.

Samantha woke up in her own bed the next morning. She was crying uncontrollably although she had no idea what was causing her tears. She knew something terrible had happened to her the previous evening but couldn't remember anything more than flashes of the evening. She felt panicky, nauseous and very confused. These are all common symptoms associated with the consumption of *Rohypnol* in combination with alcohol. She thought that the events of the previous evening may well have been a dream. If only that had been the case.

Because she could not remember what had happened to her in *Inner Circle Castle* she did nothing – like so many other victims of perpetrators using drugs to commit their crimes. How could she approach the South African Police Service to open a case against the couple when she could not even provide them with a statement on which to base an investigation? She would just be made to feel like a fool and in her present state she really could not face the idea of another ordeal. She decided to put the incident behind her and do her best to forget about it.

Some of the gaps in Samantha's memory were filled in when Visser testified in her own defence years after the incident. It bears repeating that Visser's version of events was aimed solely at minimising, or even negating, her own responsibility and amplifying Prinsloo's role.

According to this testimony, Samantha and Prinsloo had a discussion about how much the photo technician admired Visser and her burning desire to have sex with the voluptuous advocate. In Visser's account of the events, it was Prinsloo who went to pour the two women shooters – and she had absolutely no idea that he put anything other than alcohol in it. The court heard that she pulled down Samantha's panty and fondled her private parts upon which she realised the younger woman had a vaginal discharge, which she assumed was an infection. This is when the couple seemingly decided not to continue with their plans – although Visser refused to admit that there was a concerted effort to rape their guest.

A few weeks after that elusive evening at the plot in Raslouw, Visser arrived at the complex in which Samantha lived with her father. In a strange twist of fate, Susan Lemmer lived in the same complex as the Oliviers. This was after the Prinsloos arrest and Visser had re-established contact with her mother.

Samantha noticed the female advocate and cornered her, hoping to question her about the night that was still haunting her. During the conversation Visser told Samantha that she and Prinsloo were no longer together. She neatly sidestepped Samantha's efforts to learn the truth about the incident she still could not remember.

When she returned home after speaking to Visser, Samantha's father noticed that his daughter was very distressed. He asked her what the matter was and why she was so upset. She was very embarrassed and could not bring herself to discuss the situation with her father. Out of sheer desperation he phoned Samantha's mother and she eventually cajoled the truth out of her daughter. When he realised what had happened to his child, Samantha's father insisted that she open a case of indecent assault against the two advocates.

It took Samantha many hours of therapy to work through the events that had taken place that evening in Prinsloo's home. It is doubtful whether she will ever recover completely from what had happened to her but at least the conclusion of Visser's trial and sentencing afforded her some measure of closure. Like all the other victims in the "Advocate Barbie" case, she holds Visser largely responsible for the events. After all, it was the female advocate who had lured her to the property, who had drugged her and who had indecently assaulted her. She was her lover's co-conspirator, his accomplice and his obedient servant, dedicated to the fulfilment of his sadistic sexual needs. To the victims she selected for Prinsloo, Visser was every bit as dangerous as he was – if not more.

10.
SLIDE INTO PERDITION

Although the intervals between them become greater, Prinsloo still regularly spoils his mistress with gifts and surprises. One of these less pleasant surprises, is the sexually transmitted Human Papiloma Virus. The surgery to remove the warts only offers a temporary respite as the STD is, as yet, incurable and will, in time, probably lead to cervical cancer. Apart from the discomfort it causes, it has also rendered Visser sterile. She will never be able to have her own child – and the option of adoption was obliterated when her particulars were entered into the Sex Offenders Register.

Either Visser really is as stupid as Prinsloo claims, or he is impossible to satisfy – which seems to be the more logical option. Be that as it may, he regularly berates her for not pleasing him and punishes her with brutal sex, verbal abuse and drags her around the house by her hair.

One of his favoured methods of punishment is to order Visser to catch his faeces while he squats and to rub it into her skin – or eat it – whichever takes his fancy that day. He also regularly urinates in her face and on her body and forces her to drink it. Once again he captures the degradation on camera.

Having learnt from a young age that appearances are everything and family secrets belong behind very tightly shut doors, Visser does not complain about the treatment she receives. In fact, the few people she has contact with would later describe how she bragged about their amazing sex life. In all the photos he takes of her (apart from those in which she appears to be drugged), she's smiling, the content, pampered girlfriend/wife of a rich and influential man.

Her daughter's physical transformation appals Susan to such an extent that she runs to *Huisgenoot* magazine, describing how Prinsloo, whom she labels a monster, has stolen her daughter and turned her into a cheap looking whore. She calls her daughter *"Miss Milk Jugs"* in the article (*Vernedering van my melklorriekind*) – to which Cézanne retaliates in an interview with *Beeld* newspaper. She tells the newspaper that her mother's threats of suicide and the verbal abuse she's had to endure from her, has prompted her to apply for an arrest warrant, as the interview contravened the family protection order she had obtained against her parents

Cézanne tells the *Beeld* reporter that she is happy and finally looks the way she's always wanted to look. She says in the interview that she decided to change herself and for the first time in her life, she has found someone who supports her and allows her to make her own choices. The Barbie Doll lookalike also decries the fact that people think she does not have a brain because of her physical appearance.

Visser would tell the High Court in Pretoria years later that Prinsloo forced her to change her looks and that she followed his instructions blindly because she was not thinking for herself. Her response when the discrepancy between her answer in court and her interview with *Beeld* was pointed out was that her lover worked out all the answers beforehand and gave it to her to memorise.

From interviews we did with sex workers frequently hired by the couple, it appears there were a number of children among the prostitutes Visser had to regularly pick up for her boyfriend. Although the issue of child prostitution is an uncomfortable one, which is largely denied by authorities, it is an unfortunate reality of the murky sex trade in which Prinsloo and Visser became fixtures. As the sexual experimentation continues to spiral out of control, Prinsloo's appetite seems to turn towards increasingly younger girls. In fact, one of the young women, who was fourteen at the time, claimed that after he was done with her, Prinsloo pushed her towards Visser, telling her to get a younger one as the girl was no longer tight enough to please him.

It would not be long before Visser's path would cross with that of 14-year-old Jeannine du Plessis – a street child who was on the brink of pulling herself out of a web of prostitution and drugs, before meeting the predatory "Mrs Prinsloo."

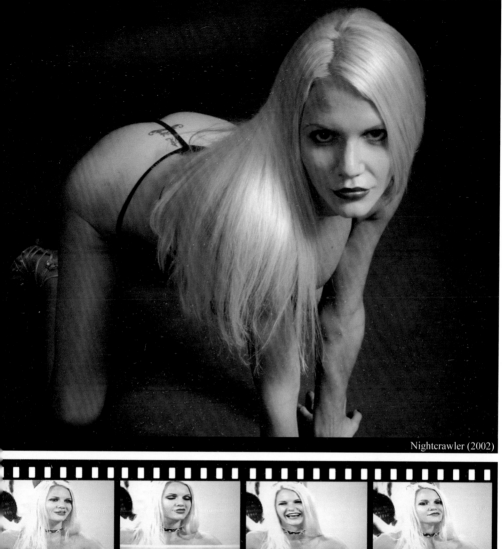

Nightcrawler (2002)

CÉZANNE PRINSLOO

DIRK PRINSLOO

Scenes from the magazine programme, *Voorblad*,
where Cézanne and Dirk appeared with Ferdinand Rabie (2002)

One of the more conservative outfits from The Hustler Shop. Grrr (2002)

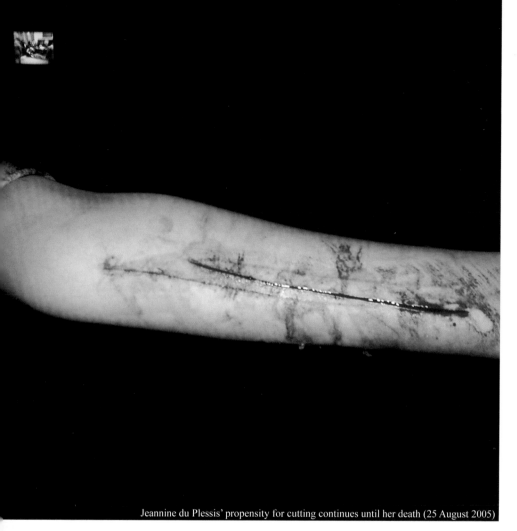

Jeannine du Plessis' propensity for cutting continues until her death (25 August 2005)

Left: Jeannine as a street child (2002)
Right:Jeannine back at school at the time of
meeting Cézanne Visser (2002)

Notorious games at Inner Circle Castle (2001)

Cézanne Visser sporting yet another new hairstyle outside the Pretoria High Court (18 May 2004)

Cézanne looking quite content as Dirk gives her the lick (2002)

A leggy "Advocate Barbie" (2002)

Still an advocate, Cézanne Visser learns that her case is postponed to the following year (25 November 2008)

Not quite the battered woman, Cézanne and Dirk look content (2002)

Jeannine du Plessis as a pre-teen living in a Children's Home (Pre 2002)

After returning from Zelza Rehabilitation facility, Jeannine begins to rebuild her life (August 2006)

In one of many suggestive poses, "Advocate Barbie" shows her assets (2002)

11.
LIFE ON THE STREET
JEANNINE DU PLESSIS' STORY
PART I

The Prinsloos left a trail of destruction in their wake – but most of their victims were able, to some extent or another, to recover from the havoc the two advocates had caused them. Even Visser – who was at pains to emphasise that she too was a victim – can, to some degree, rebuild her life. With her mother's help and support, there is a very real possibility that she can make a significant contribution to society once she comes out of prison. Although the road to recovery is long and without doubt extremely painful, the hope that tomorrow will be better is one of the strongest motivators of human endurance.

For one of the advocate couple's victims, the flame of hope was doused too soon. In fairness, the Prinsloos were not solely to blame, but their contribution was undeniable and very destructive. Ironically, Jeannine du Plessis shares a birthday with Visser's mother, Susan. The second child of four, Jeannine had been prepared in the school of hard knocks almost from the moment she drew her first breath.

Her father Pieter was, at the time, a self-confessed heroin addict and alcoholic, while all indications are that her mother Marie was a heavy drinker who abused several substances, including heroin.

Jeannine was extremely close to Roelien,[1] her older sister by just a year, who was her friend, confidante and protector. At very young ages both Jeannine and Roelien were forced out onto the streets of Sunnyside

---

1 Not her real name.

to beg for food. It is believed their mother became a prostitute to support her habits and to put food on the table. According to friends of Jeannine, Marie and Pieter resorted to stealing during the daytime in order to support their ever-growing drug habit. While they were prowling the streets looking for targets, they left their children in the care of their grandmother.

A confidante of the two sisters claims the grandmother's new husband molested the pre-pubescent Jeannine. It's unclear whether the same fate befell Roelien. After she had run away from home, Jeannine confided in a friend that she *"just didn't want to be raped by that disgusting old man anymore."*

Marie deliberately chose to turn a blind eye – ignoring the tell-tale signs of child molestation, and when Jeannine finally scraped together the guts to confront her parents with the sexual abuse, Marie apparently told her they couldn't take action against her step-grandfather as he knew how they "earned" a living. She warned her daughter to keep her mouth shut about the molestation as the old man would spill the beans on their own criminal activities if he was arrested.

Basically, the nine year-old girl was told to "grin and bear" whatever her step-grandfather would dish out to keep her family safe from the law. For Jeannine, this betrayal by her mother was almost worse than the sexual abuse itself. Shortly after this conversation, the two sisters started running away from home.

It's worth noting that street children do not merely run away from home and never return. They run away for an hour and then perhaps half a day and then a day, followed by a weekend, a week and eventually a month. It's a gradual process and the length of time spent on the streets grows as the children get braver and bolder and learn to survive.

Marie and Pieter were getting divorced as Marie apparently found that she preferred women and had developed a lesbian relationship. Pieter, too, had become involved with another woman whom he had met through social networking channels. Like in all too many divorces, the children were taking a back seat and their emotional needs were playing second fiddle to their parents' conflict and turmoil.

Living in Arcadia with their mother and her new girlfriend, conditions were even worse for the girls than before. There was little parental supervision or care and they were neglected in just about every way imaginable. Marie's girlfriend simply did not want the children around and told them they were not welcome. If they did visit it was to be for short periods of time only. The four Du Plessis children were, for all intents and purposes, totally abandoned by their parents except for the odd occasion when they did feel like seeing them. In fact, a close friend of Jeannine's described the girls as having been *"thrown away by their mother who did not care about them at all."*

The sisters realised they would have to fend for themselves or starve. Being the eldest – and having the stronger personality – Roelien took the lead and Jeannine followed. Initially, the girls were inseparable and Jeannine relied heavily on her sister for comfort and guidance –where the one was, the other was certain to be not too far away.

One afternoon, when Roelien and Jeannine were begging for money on a street corner, they met a woman who was to play a significant role in their lives. Sue van der Merwe stopped at the traffic light and caught sight of the two emaciated street kids who, she estimated, were about her daughter's age. When Roelien asked Sue for money she told her she would not give them cash but would help them if they needed her. She showed them where she lived in Sunnyside and told them they were welcome there if they needed help or food. Just before sunset, the sisters arrived at her home, asking for food.

Sue took the girls in, fed them and gave them a place to stay. It wasn't difficult for her to take in two more children as she was already caring for a number of teenage drug addicts. Jeannine and Roelien stayed over that night, sleeping under Sue's roof in relative safety. By the next morning they had disappeared.

She searched for the children and found them living in a seedy bar with extremely unsavoury characters. Sue approached the South African Police Service for assistance – but officials shrugged their shoulders and told her they were powerless to help. The two girls told their worried benefactor that they were in contact with their mother and, while Sue was trying to get assistance from the authorities, Jeannine and Roelien contacted Marie and her lover, who came and took the children away to an unknown location.

Welfare officials were openly hostile towards Sue when she approached them for help. She was lambasted for trying to interfere and her motives were questioned – with one official, suggesting she had sinister intentions, wanting to know what she wanted to do with the girls and why she had an interest in them. Sue explained that, as a mother herself, she couldn't turn a blind eye to their plight.

Despite her best efforts, for some inexplicable reason, authorities continually thwarted Sue's attempts to help the street kids. A Children's Court official told her the children were living outside the law and the Children's Act no longer applied to them because they had been on the outskirts of society too long. The message she got was that there was nothing that they could – or would – do for them.

Years later, Sue would describe her absolute frustration over the way in which the system had let Jeannine and Roelien down. The courts were not concerned or interested in assisting them, the magistrates seemed to have given up and even Wellington, their case worker, described them as difficult and said that he could not work with them.

Drug abuse is a normal part of life for kids living on the streets – and Roelien in particular was being sucked into a downward spiral of heroin addiction. Eleven year-old Jeannine was using marijuana (dagga) on a daily basis. However, she didn't really consider dagga to be a drug. Everyone on the street smoked it and it was laughingly referred to as "Vitamin Green."

The effects of marijuana greatly eased the mental and physical hardships that are part and parcel of life on the street. But even this supposedly "soft" drug cost money and the sisters did whatever they deemed necessary to scrape together enough cash to feed themselves and pay for their anaesthetic of choice. Roelien, at that stage of her life completely averse to selling her body, begged on street corners. Jeannine had been prostituting herself since the age of nine – not permanently, but if and when the need arose.

Their lifestyle led to the girls being placed in various children's homes and places of safety. They didn't like to be locked up and were used to the freedom of the streets, coming and going as they pleased. No curfews and – as far as they were concerned – definitely no rules. Any attempt at discipline resulted in them returning to the streets. If Jeannine wasn't running away from Tutela or another place of safety, she would be running away from the Louis Botha Children's Home in Queenswood, where her younger siblings had been placed.

Living on the run had become a way of life for the now 12-year-old Jeannine. She was comfortable on the streets – she knew the game and played it well. Jeannine was very manipulative and sly as a fox with street smarts aplenty, and it wasn't long before the girls came to live with Sue again – an on and off arrangement that would continue until Jeannine's death years later.

Sue had only one condition for the children whom she helped. They had to attempt to remain drug-free or, if they couldn't quit, at least reduce their drug intake. She did not tolerate deceit in her home and insisted that if the kids were using, they should do so in front of her – reducing their narcotics by at least half each time. In desperation, Sue hoped that this would eventually lead to their entering a rehabilitation facility and, hopefully, escape the prisons of their addiction.

As if living on the streets and prostituting herself from the age of nine was not enough, Jeannine also had other problems. She had been diagnosed with Borderline Personality Disorder[2] by Weskoppies Hospital. The realities of her young life had put her at great risk of developing such a disorder.

In an attempt to raise money and acquire resources with which to assist the children, Sue registered a non-profit organisation and began to approach donors. She also did her best to keep the children interested in schoolwork. The Du Plessis girls were in Grade Seven and struggling. Sue refused to give up on them and did everything in her power to help and educate them:

"Educating the kids was exhausting – no, actually it was virtually impossible. They could not let a lesson continue without interjecting expletives and ending their contribution with dirty songs they thought were very funny. Most of the boys took to the road as soon as they saw books appear. Group discussions turned into fits of anger, tears and destruction. Eventually we gave up. Hope fled and we had to accept that fact. Although education is important, I also know this to be true – to be encouraged to learn, you have to

---

2 A brief outline of this condition can be found at the back of the book.

see some kind of future for yourself, because if you're not loved, how could you dare to believe in yourself?"

When Jeannine and Roelien came to live with her more permanently, Sue encouraged them to maintain contact with their little brother and sister at the *Louis Botha Children's Home*. Sue had managed what few others were capable of with street children. She had gained their trust and friendship – not an easy task. Most of these children had had a long history of abuse, were rejected by their families, hated authority of any kind and had bad experiences with professionals and probation officers who were meant to help them.

Self-mutilation was one of the coping mechanisms Jeannine devised to deal with the cards life had dealt her. She started cutting herself from a very young age – inflicting horrendous damage on her arms and legs with all kinds of instruments, none of them sterile. She would predominantly use razor blades as they were sharp and cut deep, inflicting maximum pain with minimal effort. The cutting left her terribly scarred. She never gave up the habit, slicing herself up until the day she died. When self-mutilators cut themselves – especially if they go really deep – the physical pain is excruciating. Not so much during the act itself but later, when the adrenalin wears off and the effects of the narcotics dissipate. The pain is all consuming and the mind cannot focus on anything else. For a short while, at least, this relieves the emotional and psychological torments the kids endure daily, making life a little bit more bearable.

While she was living with Sue, Jeannine had a few really good days and a sense of normality would often set in. During this brief period she could imagine that she was an ordinary kid taking part in ordinary childhood activities. One day Sue took Jeannine and her own daughter shopping. When the two girls misbehaved Sue sent them to the car to wait for her. It was very warm that summer's day in the car and the two youngsters were unimpressed.

To express her displeasure, Jeannine left a note on Sue's car seat which read, *"I am a human bean."* When she found the note, Sue burst into a fit of laughter and giggled all the way home, the kids soon joined in giggling away. *I am a human bean* has been a long-standing joke in Sue's home ever since.

Unfortunately, these brief spells of normality never lasted long and Jeannine was not allowed to stay with Sue for more than eight months at a time. She could never fully settle in before welfare officials, her parents or the police would come and take her away. On one occasion, the Welfare arrived at Sue's home and insisted on collecting all the children, who then ended up in *Tutela*. According to the street children, this so-called place of safety was extremely dangerous. They reported having to fight for basic necessities like blankets and a bed. Food, however, was plentiful because it was so awful that no one was prepared to eat it.

The children who resided there were often armed with knives and other weapons which they did not hesitate to use on the younger, weaker children. When they did not behave in accordance with management's rules and regulations, they were often *"locked up in the basement in cells for random periods of time."* According to the kids, *"you would not want to send your worst enemies to Tutela…"* Jeannine hated every moment spent in *Tutela*. Her biggest fear was losing her freedom – she detested being locked up.

Roelien, who was a rebellious and defiant child, decided that she and Jeannine should run away as soon as they got the chance. The staff of *Tutela* did not approve of Roelien's lifestyle. She was involved in a lesbian relationship which, of course, was not seen as conformist behaviour. Jeannine, too, was leaning towards the lesbian lifestyle as it seemed the norm in her bizarre little family.

To the kids, anything was better than having to live at *Tutela*, even dying on the streets. As soon as they could, the girls made a beeline for the streets of Sunnyside. Once again they survived by whatever means they could – stealing, begging, prostitution, it didn't really matter. It was a hand-to-mouth existence with no hope and no future.

In 2000 Jeannine met Nesta, who was, by her own admission, a little monster. She was into everything that a child her age should not be into – the one exception being that she did not use drugs. Nesta was a confirmed lesbian and she had always preferred women or, at that stage of her life, girls.

Taking one look at Jeannine's innocent face and big blue eyes, Nesta fell hard. It really was love at first sight for her. Although not homeless, Nesta's relationship with her mother and stepfather was strained and very difficult, resulting in her running away from home on a regular basis. When she saw Jeannine she realised immediately how vulnerable the child was on the streets. She wanted desperately to protect her and to provide her with the comfort, the love and security that she so obviously needed.

Meanwhile, Sue ran into some difficulties. No-one wanted her unusual family in their neighbourhood as the street children were involved in criminal activities. An eviction notice duly arrived and, in a panic, Sue found a house in Roseville which would become home to the kids for the next few months.

With the children behaving badly, dressing inappropriately and generally causing havoc in the once quiet neighbourhood, the community soon began mobilising against them. Petitions were signed, aimed at forcing them out. It wasn't long before the house was closed. Once again, Jeannine was homeless. Out of options, Sue was forced to move the kids back to her home in Walker Street – where she was immediately served with a 24-hour eviction notice, forcing the children to move to the De Villiershof building in Sunnyside.

Nesta accompanied Jeannine to the building where she did her best to protect her. The children's newfound home was a vacant derelict building in Sunnyside. Seventeen street children, including Jeannine and Roelien du Plessis and the little group of runaways that had escaped from *Tutela*, moved into the De Villiershof building – calling it their new home. Others in the disused college hostel included a few adults and at least two pregnant women who claimed that they were taking care of the children. There was plenty of space and, finally, each child had a room they could call their own.

The Sunnyside Police were now facing a classic socio-economic problem in the apparent illegal occupation of the building. Soon, the children were renting out rooms to vagrants and criminals. Once it came to the owners' attention that it was infested with the homeless, conditions in the building deteriorated rapidly. They disconnected electricity, running water and sewage systems, forcing the squatters to live in squalor. A prominent Sunnyside policeman, Inspector Owen Musiker, expressed concern about the children being exposed to illegal and regulated substances inside the building. He added that the presence of minors in the building placed the police between "*a rock and a hard place.*"

The street kids were terrified of the police and ran from them. They claim SAPS officials would terrorise, abuse and torture them on the odd occasions when they did manage to catch one of them – which was not terribly often as they were truly adept at avoiding our men in blue. Inspector Musiker was quoted in the *Pretoria News* early in 2000 as saying that "...*what you had in the De Villiershof building was a classic example of grime and crime.*" To a large extent this was the truth, but according to Nesta, the people who lived there respected each other and it was uncommon for them to target each other.

Sue continued working with the children, feeding them and encouraging them not to do drugs. She desperately wanted the building to be a drug-free environment – but the best she managed to achieve was to get the kids to agree that they would only do drugs in one particular room. In return for this undertaking, she promised to continue feeding and providing for the kids to the best of her ability.

Despite several meetings with a whole string of role players, the situation remained unchanged. What did in fact emerge from these meetings was that the systems in place did not seem to make provision for extraordinary situations such as the one in the De Villiershof building.

The minutes of a meeting between the different departments clearly illustrate the complete ineptness of the system:

Police:

"...*either we do something about these children now, and prevent them from becoming criminals, or we will pay for the bed and boarding when they end up in jail."*

Welfare:

"Sue, you do not have permission to look after these children. You have to be registered."

Sue:

"I tried to register, but you would not allow me to. What do you want me to do with these 35 children? Leave them without food so that they have to steal?"

Police:

"But they cannot stay on in De Villiershof. They are now renting out rooms to people looking for accommodation. This gives them money for glue."

Metropol Safety:

"We will look for a building belonging to the Council and we can move them into that."

Sue:

"Who will look after them? If you're willing to give me R4 000 per month, I will close my two businesses and I will take care of them."

Welfare:

"You are not registered."

Child Abuse Action Group:

"How long will it take to register her?"

Welfare:

"Six months to one year."

Sue:

"So what can you do in the meantime to help them?"

Welfare:

"Our facilities are full and they will run away in any case."

It seems the people who want to help are prohibited from doing so because of almost insurmountable amounts of bureaucratic red tape created by the State, and the state departments are staffed by people who are quite willing to shout the odds but when the chips are down do absolutely nothing of value to assist.

Sue, who had a long-standing relationship with these children, continued to make daily trips to De Villiershof to feed the kids. For all her efforts, she became a target, being constantly harassed by police officers and Welfare officials who did everything they could to ruin her reputation in the community. Sponsorships dried up and she was forced to distance herself from the street kids in order to protect her own four children who were becoming more and more affected by the situation.

The Welfare department resolved to move the children from the building to different shelters around the city. In response, the children dug in their heels and refused to leave their home, a home in which they were free and to all intents and purposes relatively safe. They had a roof over their heads and a sense of control of their very out-of-control lives.

Street kids have a tendency to behave badly. Because they have been subjected to abuse and abusive language for most of their lives, it is second nature to them and they often act violently towards others. Their free use of abusive language makes it very difficult to place them. To boot, most of them are abusing one or more substances – ranging from glue to heroin. It is extremely tricky to find schools that are prepared to accommodate these children. Because of their vast life experience they have very special needs and may well even pose a danger to their classmates.

Nesta provided for Jeannine as best she could. Thanks to her, Jeannine did not have to hit the streets to beg for money. Although she smoked a lot of marijuana, she remained largely free of hard drugs. She stopped prostituting herself largely because Nesta forbade it. She couldn't bare the thought of any man's hands on her 12-year-old girlfriend.

Like most street kids, Jeannine was terrified of the South African Police. Whenever they heard sirens, the children would run out of the building and scatter in all directions in order to avoid being caught. Jeannine was so afraid of the police that there were occasions that her fears completely overtook her. While she and Nesta ran for safety, Jeannine would often faint and fall. Nesta would pick her up, throw her over her shoulder and hoof it down the road with Jeannine bouncing around like a rag doll. When she felt it was safe, she would coax Jeannine to wake up, assuring her that she was safe and that she would always look after her. Jeannine would regain consciousness, but the fear would only leave her big blue eyes much later in the day.

Jeannine never really spoke to Nesta about her mother or the circumstances that had led to her ending up on the street. When she did, it ended in tears, with Jeannine sobbing uncontrollably. The street kids seemed to live according to their own code. When something was too difficult to talk about, it simply was not addressed. You didn't want to scratch around in other people's pain, to keep opening wounds that were festering.

They did visit the home of Marie du Plessis on two occasions. These visits ended badly with Jeannine running from the house in tears. This woman had *"thrown away her child"* – she did not want her and made her feelings abundantly clear to her daughter. It would often take Jeannine weeks to recover from these visits. She would become very depressed and withdrawn for long periods after seeing her mother.

In 2002, the media got involved in the De Villiershof saga, resulting in headlines such as: *"Street kids stick to squalor," "A haven of hell for homeless kids," "Building in Sunnyside tells the story of youngsters' desperation," "Messy Building Missing owner,"* and eventually *"Kids, out of hovel, run off."* Journalist Carol Hills wrote the story of how street children fled the faeces- and blood-stained corridors of the disused building in Sunnyside for the second time in two weeks when they were tipped off that welfare officers were coming to forcibly remove them from the premises.

At the time, the building was home to 35 to 40 children. To them, this building was their haven of safety, they had nowhere else to go and anything was better than being separated and locked up in drug-infested places of safety.

All that Pretoria's Chief Social Worker, Gerda du Toit, could do was to appeal to Sue and her husband Marius to try and prepare the children to cooperate and leave the premises. A shocked provincial official conceded that Welfare had lost the battle in trying to negotiate with the children.

With all the hype surrounding the growing problem in the De Villiershof building, Cézanne Visser became aware of the situation.

She approached Sue and offered her assistance, free of charge. Sue was overjoyed and introduced Visser to the children as someone that they could trust – an advocate who could assist them with their legal troubles, and someone who would protect them.

During one of her consultations with Sue, Visser was introduced to Jeannine. She was fascinated by the tall blonde, obviously wealthy advocate. In fact, Jeannine was a little in awe of the woman. Since the initial contact with Sue, Visser appeared regularly, offering aid and legal services. She and Prinsloo invited Sue to their home to discuss legal strategies, but Sue realised that legal action would only buy a little time before they would be successfully evicted.

She was grateful for the offer, however, and agreed to meet Cézanne and Dirk at their home in Raslouw. Overwhelmed by the opulence, Sue said the place *"made her feel small."* One can only imagine how in awe of the extravagant setting a homeless child would have been.

With mounting pressure from Welfare and the Police, plans were again taking shape to move the children to various places of safety. The children ran away from De Villiershof after being tipped off that Welfare officials would again attempt to evict them and they ended up back on the streets, exactly where they had been a year before.

Jeannine encountered Visser on a few more occasions. Every time that she saw the beautiful advocate her fascination grew. She saw her as a role model and a possible saviour. All she wanted was to escape the life that she had been forced into – and she saw in Visser, if not a way to achieve that dream, a pretty powerful inspiration for doing so. A pretty child, she must have immediately caught the eye of Visser – who was, by her own admission, permanently on the hunt for fresh meat to take home to her lover.

Jeannine and the little band of street kids moved in with an unemployed man and his family who were living in the building next to De Villiershof. According to Nesta, it was here that Jeannine began to use drugs – and before long, she started using heroin. Her drug use quickly escalated and she became hopelessly addicted. Nesta went to visit her as often as she was able to, but things were much more difficult for them now. They could no longer live together as they had at de Villiershof and Nesta, who was back living with her parents, had to cycle long distances to see Jeannine.

During one such visit, Nesta was shocked by Jeannine's condition. Completely stoned, she just sat there smiling, incapable of conversation and apparently oblivious to her surroundings. She was so high that she had no idea who she was or where she was. In cases like these, Nesta would run a bath for her and sit with her for long hours before Jeannine became even vaguely aware of her surroundings.

The situation was deteriorating by the day, forcing Nesta into one of the most difficult decisions of her entire young life – a decision that would haunt her for many years to come. She knew that she could not handle the world of drug abuse that Jeannine had now entered. She had to walk away but she prayed that Jeannine would be okay, that she would survive, that she would have the strength to conquer her heroin addiction.

As Nesta walked away, another chapter closed on Jeannine's life. Nesta never looked back, she didn't dare to, and Jeannine never had another lesbian relationship after her.

Jeannine's personality began to change at this point. She became more prone to aggression, even going as far as pushing Sue's daughter down the stairs in a fit of anger when Sue told her that she was going on holiday to the coast but could not take her along. Her inappropriate reaction at the time was possibly exacerbated by her drug use.

A month or two later, Jeannine returned to Sue's care and made a concerted effort to turn her life around. She managed to get off the heroin after a stint in rehab. She was now thirteen.

Jeannine returned to school where she actually took herself – and everyone around her – by surprise. It had taken some persuasion to get her back into school in grade eight at Hendrik Verwoerd, where they did their best to accommodate children with special needs. When she got her school uniform she was so proud she had to go and show her mom straight away, desperate for approval. She looked like any normal schoolgirl and she was pleased to be fitting in.

Although Jeannine struggled, she worked really hard. She desperately wanted to turn her life around and was doing her best to conform and fit in at school. She wanted stability and was managing to put the pieces of her life back together with the help of Sue and even her mother. For the first time in a long time, Jeannine had hope for the future. Hope that things would improve for her and even hope for a normal life.

Sue remembers: *"She really was starting to get her life on track and seeing more of her mother again."* Marie was also on the mend and working at Dolphin House – a halfway house for street kids. Eventually, Jeannine moved in with her mom for about three months. She was so excited when her hard work started paying off. Her first report card showed that she had passed all her subjects. For someone who hadn't been to school since grade six this was a remarkable accomplishment.

On a bright sunny morning, Marie went out to do some grocery shopping. When she returned she found Visser waiting for them at Dolphin House. She claimed that she was visiting in order to offer help and sponsorship and that she was interested in taking the children to her home on weekends in order to spoil them.

12.
SUFFER THE CHILDREN

With child prostitutes now a regular fixture on the smorgasbord of sexual experimentation served up in the Prinsloo home, the challenge to find increasingly younger girls fell squarely on Visser's shoulders. It's unclear exactly which of the two decided that it would be easier to get their playmates by deception rather than just paying the ones who were more than willing to play along – as they are the only two who know the truth and neither want to admit it. It appears Visser soon starts to hunt exclusively for under-aged girls and in this quest she turns her attention to at least four child-care facilities in Pretoria.

Visser arrives at Sue's home one afternoon, looking for some young women to participate in a lingerie party that the Prinsloos are hosting at their home. The kids don't know her, but when they see her they run inside, babbling animatedly about the 'beautiful woman' waiting outside. The advocate explains that they are having a lingerie sale and she needs some models. The girls go along excitedly, dressed in nothing but their best underwear and their dressing gowns. They're thrilled at the prospect of getting their hands on some new expensive undies after they had modelled.

As they leave the house, Sue calls out to the youngsters to be good. Visser replies mischievously that they are definitely not going to be good... In retrospect, one shudders at the sinister implication of this statement.

The group of 'models' includes the red-haired girls, Monja and Marzanne, who would later feature naked on a photo giving foot rubs to an equally naked Visser and Prinsloo, while the latter appears to be masturbating. At the time, the pair was working in the Water Street brothel where Visser was a regular visitor to trawl for prostitutes. According to the girls, they enjoyed visiting the Prinsloos as they paid well and expected less than some of their more eccentric or perverse clients.

After she is turned away by one of the other homes, Visser zooms in on the Bramley Children's Home. She pays it several visits and offers to take some of the girls for weekends. Perhaps a part of the interest she shows is genuine – but she feigns enough to convince the management of Bramley that she and her husband would make ideal weekend parents for the children. Visser, who has gained much publicity following her appearance on *Idols*, is seen as a potential role model and offers to help the girls with grooming and subject choices.

Because of the couple's professional standing – and after Visser applies some pressure – Bramley allows them to take two girls, aged 15 and 11, home for the weekend on different occasions. The pair, Anja van Zyl and Charmaine Stander, would, years later, still pay dearly for this mistake…

13.
A TRIAL RUN
ANJA VAN ZYL'S STORY

Anja[1] was 13 years old when she came to live at Bramley House – a place she would call home until the end of 2002 or the beginning of 2003 when she was 15. She was not isolated from her family and remained in contact with them, often returning to visit them over weekends. In February 2002, Bramley's Social Worker, Marlene Malan, called her in and introduced her to Advocate Cézanne Prinsloo. Malan told Anja that Visser was an advocate, who was married to a fellow advocate by the name of Dirk Prinsloo. She was also informed that Visser was a model who had just entered the South African *Idols* competition.

Visser told Anja that she wanted to offer a young girl the opportunity of spending weekends with her at the home she shared with her husband in Raslouw. Keen on entering the legal profession herself, Anja was eager to spend a weekend with the advocate couple. Marlene thought Anja was a beautiful girl and felt that she might benefit from guidance and exposure to the modelling industry – a world in which Cézanne seemed to be very comfortable.

Shortly after that meeting Prinsloo arrived to fetch Anja from Bramley. He was alone and, as required by Bramley House policies, he signed her out that afternoon. Visser did not accompany him as she was participating in the *Idols* competition that day.

En route home, Dirk stopped at a wholesaler to buy groceries. Anja

---

1 Not her real name.

found him charming and they chatted in general in the car and while they were shopping. Prinsloo bought her some shampoo and body lotion, and she was deeply impressed with his generosity. To her, he seemed like a sweet man and she was grateful for the opportunity to spend time with the two advocates. She had a lot of questions about the legal profession and was hoping to learn from them that weekend. She did learn a lot that weekend but, ironically, it had very little to do with the legal profession.

When he reached the car and started packing the groceries, Dirk realised that he had forgotten a bottle of oil in the store and sent Anja back to collect it. Eager to please, she ran inside and then ran back to the car proudly presenting it to him. Taking the oil from her, Dirk smilingly commented that she looked very sexy when she ran. The remark made the young teenager blush and immediately little warning bells began to sound in her head. She thought that this was a really strange comment for the advocate to make. *"Everybody ran. How could one person look sexy as she ran and another not? Maybe he was a tad weird!"* Anja did not pursue the matter – she kept quiet and left it at that, determined to enjoy her weekend and learn the answers to her many questions.

Hopping back into the car for the last leg of their journey, Dirk enquired about her views regarding sex before marriage – asking her if she would sleep with someone before she was married. She told him that she would much rather be wed before engaging in sexual activities. He then asked her if she took exception to the idea of having sex before one was married. Anja replied that she did not disapprove but that she personally would rather wait for her wedding night before she lost her virginity. Dirk said that in his opinion, it was not necessary to be married before engaging in sexual relations.

Anja was greatly relieved when they arrived at the plot because it effectively brought to an end what she regarded as an inappropriate and embarrassing conversation. By now she had reached the conclusion that he was definitely weird, very weird.

When they arrived at the house, Visser was not there yet. Anja helped Dirk carry the groceries into the kitchen. The first thing she noticed was a trophy on the kitchen counter inscribed with the words *"Best Fucker."* With the trophy was a piece of paper containing a handwritten message to Dirk in which the author had addressed him as *"God."* Anja assumed the message was from Visser. Once again her red flags went up, sending chills down her spine. She was shocked that anyone would have such a disgusting trophy in their home – and saw the note as blasphemous and offensive. She was deeply religious and found the idea that a mere mortal – and a slightly disgusting one at that – could be likened to the Creator.

Later that evening Visser returned from her *Idols* audition. She seemed excited by the fact that she had made it through the first few rounds. They began unpacking groceries and most of the food supplies went into a huge pantry just off the kitchen. Walking down the passage, Anja noticed that the advocates' home was lavishly decorated. It was beautiful, opulent and luxurious. Nothing was out of place and the home was a testimony to their success. She had noticed that the grounds were immaculately kept when driving up the driveway, with even a springbok walking around outside under the trees. The large dam on the property sported an array of wildlife, including a pair of beautiful swans.

Outwardly, the Prinsloo's home was a paradise. Anja was really impressed by what she saw. Her admiration was dampened when she entered her hosts' bedroom. The teenager was confronted by a sea of pornographic magazines lying all over the couple's bedroom. They were scattered on the bed, on the ground and even on the Jacuzzi, in fact, everywhere she looked. The images were very explicit and showed women exposing their genitalia. The magazines also contained photographs of men – leaving nothing to the imagination.

Anja was shocked at the sight, feeling disgusted and a little nauseous. She had no idea how to deal with the situation. She was genuinely frightened and wondered whether she was going to make it through the weekend. The advocates with whom she had been sent to spend the weekend were obviously perverts. From what she had experienced so far their lives seem to revolve around sex – which seemed to be all that they thought about.

Later, while watching television in the lounge, the girl heard movement next to her. She turned to see what was happening and was confronted by the sight of Prinsloo's exposed penis, although he was still dressed. What she had heard was Visser removing her clothing. In a few seconds the busty blonde was completely naked. She then sidled up to her lover before turning to the teenager and telling her to watch carefully as she would learn how "*it*" was done. Prinsloo told the girl that she didn't have to stay and watch if she didn't want to. Visser then promptly proceeded to demonstrate her aptitude for delivering blow jobs.

Anja stood up and fled, relieved to have escaped the show the couple was sure to be putting on in her absence. Shocked and afraid she ran into the bedroom and began to pray. She asked the Lord for assistance and protection to get through the weekend safely. Anja could not believe that two adults, both learned and professional people – advocates – could behave in such a shocking manner in front of her. To the teenager they were quite obviously depraved sex maniacs.

Later that evening, after concluding her performance in the

lounge, Visser went to the girl's room and apologised to her for her lewd behaviour. She obviously realised that what she was putting the girl through was both wrong and unacceptable – but her apology was nothing more than lip service as she certainly did not curtail her behaviour.

Visser informed Anja that she could go and take a bath, which she did; grateful for the privacy the bathroom afforded her. After retiring for the evening, Anja struggled to sleep, wondering what the next day would bring. She was very worried that her hosts' behaviour would escalate and that she would find herself in real danger.

On Saturday morning the blonde woman woke Anja and declared that she was taking her shopping. Visser decided that Anja needed some new clothing. As they tried on several garments in the change rooms at Mr Price, Visser showed the girl the piercings in her labia and clitoris as well as her belly-ring and her numerous tattoos. Anja was unimpressed, to say the least.

Visser bought her a pair of jeans and a revealing top which was way too small for her. Even though Anja had informed her that she usually wore a size medium, Visser insisted on buying an extra-small top. When she continued to question the advocate's decision, Visser told her that it was *"better to show what you had because it entices people. It grabs people's attention when you wear clothing that is too small for you, as it is revealing and a great turn-on for men."*

Anja did not pursue the matter, wondering why on earth the woman was fixated on turning men on and getting attention. Didn't she have enough to handle in her obviously besotted and sex-addicted husband?

After the shopping expedition, Cézanne headed for the beauty salon for her usual Brazilian wax. Anja sat in the cubicle and watched while Cézanne had her pubic area and genitals waxed. She recommended that Anja do the same, offering to pay for the procedure. Anja declined, saying that she was just fine the way she was. It looked really painful and she really didn't want to owe this woman anything. Fortunately for Anja Visser did not insist and, after concluding her business at the salon, they bought a few more odds and ends before heading back home.

Later that afternoon the woman took her guest with her on another trip – this time to a plastic surgeon who was going to perform a procedure on Visser's lips in order to enhance them. They would suck fat out of her bum and inject the fat into her lips to enlarge them. To the teenage girl, Visser looked like a blowfish after the procedure and she thought about the different procedures that she had seen the blonde endure that day.

Anja hoped that it was not going to be necessary, one day, to endure all this just to keep her man. It really was all a little ridiculous to her and she wondered if any man could possibly be worth all this fuss.

That evening the advocates went out, leaving their young guest alone in their home. She found this frightening and disturbing to say the least. Before they left, Prinsloo suggested that she watch the video that had been left in the machine for her. What he failed to tell her, however, was that it was a porn video. He pressed the start button and the tape began to play. Anja was horrified and removed it from the player. Of course, the cover sported images of a man and a woman having sex and she hurriedly dropped the cassette. Anja told Dirk Prinsloo that she would much rather just watch TV. The teenager went to bed before the couple returned home, nervous but thankful for the reprieve the evening had given her.

The next morning, a stark naked Visser invited Anja to take a swim in the large swimming pool next to the entertainment area. Visser was sunbathing next to the pool. Although Anja was wearing her swimming costume, the older woman asked her if she wouldn't prefer to remove it and swim naked. Anja struggled to contain her emotions as she informed her host that bathing suits were there for a reason, which was so that one could wear them to swim in. She flatly refused to take hers off and wondered what it was with these people that they wanted to run around naked all day.

Anja spent the entire morning at the pool with her female host. Apparently Prinsloo was sleeping as he did not emerge until much later. Close to noon, the woman and child decided to move indoors to escape the sun that was beating down on them.

When Prinsloo finally made an appearance, the couple decided to eat outside under the lapa in the scenic front garden. There were many pornographic magazines on display on the table under the lapa and Dirk paged through them continuously like an addict focused on getting his daily fix. It seemed that he just could not leave them alone.

The teenager found it strange that, even while he was eating, he continued to page through the magazines. He temporarily lifted his gaze off the magazine to ask Anja how she washed her genitals. Anja at this point thought that he had totally lost his faculties and she refused to answer him – becoming more and more uncomfortable at his inappropriate questions.

He then changed course and began questioning Anja about Charmaine Stander, an 11-year-old girl who also resided at the Children's Home. Anja could not answer many of his questions as she did not reside in the same house as Charmaine and barely knew her. During the entire conversation, the couple tried to get Anja to confirm if Charmaine had been the victim of rape or sexual abuse before arriving at Bramley. She had no knowledge of Charmaine's history prior to her arrival at the home and couldn't tell them anything.

Later, while sitting in the lounge, Anja witnessed Visser rubbing a hand over Prinsloo's crotch. When the busty woman caught the teenager's eye, she declared that when her lover's penis was erect, she would satisfy him immediately at any time and that it made no difference to her if they were out partying or if there were other people present. His sexual pleasure was her priority. As if their lewd behaviour wasn't enough, Prinsloo turned to the young woman and asked her if she was becoming sexually aroused by their overtly sexual behaviour. Of course, Anja said that she was not.

Later that afternoon, Visser offered to colour Anja's hair and, excited by the offer, the girl agreed. During the procedure the conversation inevitably turned sexual in nature. The advocate explained how a man really enjoyed it when his penis was inserted deep into a woman's mouth, adding that if Anja wanted to give pleasure to a man she should learn how to perform fellatio really well. It is unclear whether she repeated her offer to teach her by demonstrating the process on the ever-willing or should we say Prinsloo.

Once her hair was coloured, it was time for Anja to go back to the children's home. Visser dropped her off without Prinsloo. After stopping outside the home, the advocate instructs Anja not to talk to anyone about the events that had occurred during her visit to the Prinsloo home. Afraid and confused by the events that had transpired over the weekend – and well aware that both Prinsloo and Visser were advocates and therefore people in powerful positions – Anja didn't know what to do. She was afraid of what they would do to her if she told anybody about her strange experience. She didn't want to tell her House Mother about what had happened to her, fearing that she would tell the Children's Home's manager, Martie Booyse.

Oddly, Anja was afraid of Martie's possible negative reaction and what she would do if news of her experience at the hands of the Prinsloos were brought to her attention. Anja was also terrified at the prospect of having to tell her story in a court of law. After all, it would be only her word against that of two legal professionals. She decided to keep quiet and to not tell a soul about what had happened. Instead, she decided, she would just refuse to go back there if she was asked again. Anja thought to herself that although the weekend had been disturbing and uncomfortable, she was unscathed – for which she was very grateful.

A few weeks later, Anja was called to the office and told that Martie and Marlene wished to speak to her immediately. She was further informed that Charmaine Stander had spent the weekend with Dirk and Cézanne Prinsloo at their home in Raslouw and events that had transpired there during the weekend had deeply traumatised Charmaine.

It was at this meeting that Anja finally revealed the shocking facts of what had happened. By her own admission, she did not tell them everything, only revealing the events that she had experienced as the most traumatising.

Both Bramley staff members did their best to comfort and reassure Anja that she had done the right thing disclosing her experiences – but she was not so sure of that herself. She was embarrassed by the events and did not want to be involved in a prolonged court case. Anja felt, for the most part, relieved when the administrative staff of the children's home decided not to pursue the matter through the South African Police Services – although she did want the Prinsloos to be punished for what they had done to her and Charmaine.

Ironically, Malan tried to justify their questionable decisions when she testified in court years later. In her evidence she tried to explain the lax policies that were in place for screening people who requested access to the children.

Firstly, she explained that it was not the policy of the children's home to do background checks on prospective weekend parents. Incredulously, kids were sent out to spend weekends with any Tom, Dick or Harry, without doing so much as a background check or surprise home visit to the premises where the children would staying. The question remains as to what these so-called professionals were thinking – or rather not thinking. How many other children have they managed to place at risk with this policy and how were they planning to handle the consequences of this very risky policy?

Secondly, Malan stated: *"If (Cézanne Visser) had said they were not married we would have had a conversation with them to tell them to keep their sex lives private."* And this conversation would have been taken to heart by alleged paedophile, sexual sadist and rapist Dirk Prinsloo and his sex-slave Visser? Why did these Bramley staff members regard married people as virtuous – believing that only unmarried couples needed the talk?

Thirdly, both Anja and Charmaine were identified solely on their looks for placement with the advocate couple. Did nobody in this facility bother to think that in numerous cases children are targeted for sex trafficking and sexual abuse because of their physical attributes – being attractive, young and not able to defend themselves?

Finally, Bramley staff admitted that Visser pressurised them into letting her take Charmaine home with her for the weekend. Visser, who was aware that Malan was against the visits, because she believed that Charmaine was not ready for weekend visits, slyly applied pressure on the staff to establish when Malan would be away in order to side-step her. This reinforces how calculating Visser was in pursuit of her goal to obtain vulnerable children for the sole purpose of sexual exploitation. She insisted in court that she did not know what Prinsloo had planned for the girls – but in the words of Talk Radio 702's morning host, John Robbie: *"pull the other one."*

After listening to Charmaine's horrifying story, Malan and Booyse apologised to her and Anja for sending them to Visser and Prinsloo's home. Incredibly, they also promised the girls that they would not send them there again. One wonders wonder if they were actually considering it?

They did mull over the possibility of going to the Child Protection

Unit, but decided against it. Malan stated under oath: *"…it was a very difficult decision for me and Mrs Booyse, in the light of the fact that we were dealing with high profile people who were trained in the law. By the nature of our work we have a service motive and we are not well versed in legal aspects. We didn't want to put the children through, you know, court cases and stuff and it was a very difficult decision for us. We didn't want to traumatise them any further. We decided, yes, that … if we could perhaps bring the case to the attention of the Commissioner of the Children's Court, they could maybe call these two people in on a legal level … to explain to them that the matter has been reported to them and they should stop this practice, you know, of taking children from other children's homes."*

Have these two so-called professionals never heard of attorneys who can be consulted for legal advice in situations like the one they faced? Surely the National Prosecuting Authority would have been only too happy to advise them on the best way to handle such incidents. Had they considered that seeing the perpetrators punished for what they had done may in itself have been healing for the children – allowing them to feel safe again, knowing that justice had been done and affording them closure. Was turning a blind eye and doing absolutely nothing not a greater failure than seeking justice? The statement about asking the Children's Court to instruct Prinsloo and Visser to stop their activities, is nothing short of ridiculous. Prinsloo showed complete disregard for any kind of authority.

If Prinsloo was in fact the sexual sadist he was portrayed to be during the trial, he would have, in all likelihood, continued to feed his fantasies – which would probably have escalated until he really hurt someone. The apathetic decisions and lack of proactive thought processes and procedures demonstrated above contribute to innocent children being abused, raped and ultimately murdered in this country.

South African social welfare organisations are way overdue for policy review in my opinion and social workers should be far more vigilant than they were in the cases of the girls they 'loaned out' to Visser and Prinsloo.

To their credit, however, according to Malan: *"Other children's homes were contacted to tell them that if these people came to them for children, this was the situation we experienced and they should stop it."* When the social worker spoke to Jacaranda Children's Home about the incidents, they told her that Visser had already tried to take children from them in December 2001, before the school holidays, but that their holiday arrangements had already been made and they couldn't help her.

She goes on to state: *"I withdrew because I felt it was the manager's responsibility to take the matter further, I didn't follow up with her, you know, how far the case is now, etc."* Now this is dedication for you – allow a situation to occur, pass the buck, don't follow up, and make it someone else's responsibility. One shudders to think how many orphaned and vulnerable children are put at risk on a daily basis with such ineffective policies and procedures. It would be interesting to see if and how systems have been brought into place in the ten years since the incidents occurred to prevent a repeat. The case remained in limbo with no one lifting so much as a finger, until Malan received information that Visser had approached another children's home in Pretoria West for access to children. She stated: *"There and then I decided it couldn't continue like this, it must stop somewhere. I made a call to the Children's Court."* Finally, a sensible decision had been made in this case.

Approximately a year later, Captain Carel Cornelius of the Child Protection Unit approached Anja, requesting that she provide him with a detailed statement about what had transpired at the Prinsloo home. It was only when she was interviewed by the detective that Anja told her story in detail for the first time. She knew that this was the beginning of what was going to be a very long and painful battle for justice. That fight continues in her attempt to recover R600 000 in damages from Visser in a pending high court action. She is relieved that the criminal prosecution was successful and is reassured by the fact that Visser and Prinsloo are exactly where they deserve to be, securely behind bars.

14.
BREAKING THE SILENCE
CHARMAINE STANDER'S STORY

Charmaine Stander had faced and survived much trauma in her home environment by the time she was placed in Bramley at age 11. Although she was a petite child she was well-developed for her age and immediately caught the eye of "Advocate Barbie" in her pursuit of finding easy prey. She set out remorselessly and systematically to acquire the girl for just this purpose.

From the outset, Charmaine resisted Visser's invitation to visit the advocate couple at their home on weekends. She was traumatised and withdrawn when she arrived at Bramley a few weeks prior to Visser's first visit. The girl had no sense of security and the thought of visiting strangers at their home terrified her. She was terribly afraid of going anywhere unknown.

Shortly after Anja's ordeal, Visser arrived at the children's home to collect Charmaine for a similar 'treat'. Visser was scantily clad in ski-pants – which were too tight and pulling up between her buttock cheeks – and a bikini top. She told the young girl that they were going to the gym before going to *Inner Circle Castle*. Visser was accompanied by her lover who waited in the car while she collected Charmaine. The young girl saw Prinsloo for the first time when she approached the car. He, too, was barely clothed and sported only Lycra shorts. Prinsloo was naked from the waist up, exposing his muscular frame to the child. Charmaine was very nervous as she tentatively climbed into the car. She said a silent prayer that nothing would go wrong.

Driving to the gymnasium in Centurion, Prinsloo told the young girl that he had purchased ski-pants for her and that she was to put them on. Charmaine said that she didn't want to wear them. Visser then insisted that she wear the pants because, she said, people did not wear ordinary clothing at the gym. Under duress, the little girl pulled the ski pants on under her own clothing, careful not to expose herself to the leering stares from the two adults.

Arriving at the gym, the couple set about their usual workout routine, leaving Charmaine to wander around alone. Prinsloo pushed his girlfriend hard, working her to the point of near exhaustion. He loved to watch her strain and sweat to reach the goals that he set for her each day.

It took about an hour for the pair to finish their training and collect their weekend guest on their way out.

The magnificence and tranquillity of the *Inner Circle Castle* grounds fascinated the young girl as it did most visitors to the Centurion property.

Charmaine began to relax, thinking that nothing bad could happen in such beautiful surroundings. Upon entering the opulent home, Prinsloo headed for the couch in front of the TV where he plonked himself down, waiting to be served his after-gym beverage. Visser in turn, dutifully made protein shakes for both her lover and herself and a milkshake for Charmaine, which they drank before she took the girl down the passage to the main bedroom in order to change.

Nothing in her short life could have prepared Charmaine for the sight that would meet her when she entered the room. The unsuspecting child was frightened out of her wits when she saw masks, some of which appeared to be covered in blood. Added to this there were several vibrators lying scattered on the floor. A pile of clothes hung over a chair and on a table in the room, a number of pornographic magazines were on display. Some of the books were open displaying graphic images, while others were stacked in piles. A door behind the couple's bed led to a walk-in closet that housed hordes of X-rated videos. The sheer volume of pornographic material in the room overwhelmed and frightened the little girl.

Visser stripped in front of the child, stooped and picked up one of the vibrators from the floor, lay down on the bed and – in front of the bewildered girl – proceeded to insert the vibrator into her vagina, demonstrating how to use it. After completing her demonstration she turned to the child and told her to do the same. Horrified and terrified by what she had just witnessed, Charmaine refused. Visser also showed the child the rings she had had inserted through her labia, her clitoris and her nipples. While Charmaine stood watching the lewd display in absolute horror, she couldn't help but notice that Visser had the name "Dirk" tattooed on her pubic area. The woman ordered her young guest to take off her clothes. When the girl refused, Visser reinserted the vibrator into her vagina, turned it on and then reached out and fondled the child between her legs where she stood terrified and rooted to the floor next to the bed.

Charmaine pleaded with her tormentor to stop touching her, saying over and over that she didn't want to do that – her pleas fell on deaf ears. Visser had gone to a lot of effort to gain access to the pretty, well-developed 11-year-old and she was not going to give up on her grooming mission quite so easily.

After concluding her outrageous demonstration, Visser invited Charmaine to choose a video from the huge selection. She was unable to object and with trembling hands selected a tape – barely registering the pornographic nature of the imagery on the cover of the cassette. A nude Visser then marched Charmaine off to join Prinsloo in front of the television.

While trailing down the passage Charmaine noticed that, in addition to the tattoo she observed earlier, Visser had inked her lover's name on her lower back. When she caught sight of Prinsloo she was shocked to find him naked on the couch – his penis visible and erect. To the little girl it seemed excessively large and intimidating. Charmaine averted her eyes. She was dreadfully embarrassed. She had no idea how to deal with the situation.

Visser placed the cassette in the video machine, pressed play and sat down beside Prinsloo. The child was directed to a nearby chair. From where she sat, she had a clear view of the couple on the couch. At the tender age of 11, Charmaine Stander was forced to watch her first pornographic movie. As the film ended Visser fetched another one.

While the second video played, Prinsloo and Visser proceeded to imitate every explicit deed, including the act of copulation, with the child looking on in disbelief. The sex marathon continued for an hour and a half – the entire duration of the movie. Prinsloo's staying power is remarkable – possibly fuelled by "a little blue pill."

Charmaine was put to bed straight after dinner – a short while later Prinsloo appeared. Standing over her, he attempted to fondle and kiss her. Revolted and terrified, she turned her head away, praying that he would leave her alone. It felt like hours before she heard him finally leave her room. Later, after her racing heart had quietened down and the tension in her muscles had relaxed, she felt herself fade into a troubled sleep.

The next morning, Charmaine was woken by Visser who told her to go outside to the entertainment area for breakfast. The girl got dressed – fearing what the day might bring – and headed outside. After she had finished her morning meal, she looked up and saw Visser approaching. Once again, Visser was not wearing a shred of clothing, and commanded her guest to undress and join her for a swim. Reluctantly, Charmaine took her clothes off, desperately trying to shield her naked body from Visser's appraising stare. Suddenly, the woman grasped her firmly by the hand and she felt herself being dragged towards the pool. She waited until Visser released her hand before running back into the house to grab a towel which she wrapped around her bare body.

When Visser tired of swimming she climbed out of the pool and draped herself onto one of the deckchairs to suntan. She suggested to the girl that she should also have a swim, which she reluctantly did. Charmaine placed the towel alongside the pool and slipped into the water. She swam and played in the water for a while until Prinsloo made his appearance at the poolside.

As soon as she caught sight of him, Charmaine quickly got out of the pool, wrapping herself in the towel. The last thing Charmaine wanted was to be naked in his presence. She moved quickly out of his way and onto a chair at the corner of the pool. Charmaine stared vacantly into the blue sky as Prinsloo dived naked into the pool.

Meanwhile, Visser, still naked, sat filing and painting her nails on the deckchair. It always took a fair amount of time for her to complete her manicure as she painted each nail on her fingers and toes a different colour. After Prinsloo had finished his swim and Visser had completed her grooming routine, she took Charmaine to her bedroom and told her to change into the clothes that hung over the chair in the couple's bedroom.

Charmaine did not want to wear the ensemble picked out for her as she thought it too revealing and inappropriate. Although Charmaine voiced her opinion, Visser eventually convinced her to at least try on the clothes that had been bought especially for her. Similar in style to that of Visser's own outfits, the threads did not cover very much. Charmaine felt very exposed in the revealing outfits and quickly undressed, putting her own clothes back on.

Before long, Prinsloo arrived in the master bedroom as his mistress ran a hot bath in their oversized tub and ordered Charmaine to get into the bath with the man. Absolutely mortified at the idea of climbing into a bath with anyone – let alone a man she had every reason to mistrust, Charmaine backed away and flatly refused to get in. Visser finally gave up and got into the bath herself where, in full view of the child, she and Prinsloo began to fondle each other. The girl quietly slipped out of the room and hid behind a wall. From where she now stood she could no longer see them but could hear everything that was going on in the bath. She just stood staring at the couple's bed, too afraid to run away, wondering when her nightmare was going to end.

When Prinsloo had finally finished playing with his girlfriend, he got out of the bath, dried himself off and sauntered back to the lounge where he once-again positioned himself on the couch in front of the TV and his apparently unlimited porn collection.

Visser then called Charmaine to sit next to her while she finished her bath. Too scared to refuse, Charmaine did as she was told. The older woman then grabbed hold of the child's leg and began shaving it. The girl was horrified, knowing that this was against the rules of the Children's Home. She begged the advocate to stop as she would get into trouble at the Home. Visser simply ignored her pleas and continued. Charmaine fled the bathroom as soon as she could.

The rest of the evening was uneventful – she had dinner with the couple and quickly disappeared to her room and went to sleep, thinking that she only had to get through one more day in that dreadful house. With any luck, she would soon be safely back at Bramley.

The Sunday morning Visser woke Charmaine up and joined her for breakfast. At some point during the meal she told the girl that she was to tell no one what had happened at the home during the weekend. The frightened child promised to keep the events of the weekend secret.

Shortly after this conversation, the couple took Charmaine back to the home where she was handed over to the house mother, Veronica Shepard. As was the case with Anja before her, the child was so traumatised by the events of the weekend, that all she could do was cry. She sobbed her little heart out. When questioned by her house mother, Charmaine told her that the weekend had been good and that she was just glad to be back.

She managed to hide the truth from Veronica until the next morning, when she could no longer contain her pent-up emotions and they bubbled over like a brook bursting its banks. In tears and between sobs she blurted out the entire tale. Veronica was taken aback by what she heard from the child and immediately informed her supervisor, Martie Booyse, of Charmaine's claims.

Charmaine was required to retell her tale. It was then that she finally told both Martie and Veronica how terribly scared she had felt all weekend at the Prinsloo home. Many years later, Charmaine would testify again of the overwhelming terror that she had experienced during her weekend at the Prinsloos. She stated that the advocate couple had instilled a deep and all-consuming fear in her. She had been terrified to go near either one of them. She was petrified that they would do to her what she had witnessed them doing to each other.

After the incident, Charmaine received intensive therapy in an attempt to help her deal with the traumatic events. She was supported by numerous social workers and psychologists in the time leading up to and during the trial. She is doing her best to move on with her life in the most positive way that she can.

Like Anja, Charmaine is finally fighting back. In order to gain a measure of justice for herself, she is claiming R600 000 in damages from Visser for the harm that she suffered at her hands. The case is ongoing.

15.
THE ULTIMATE BETRAYAL
JEANNINE'S STORY
PART II

Jeannine du Plessis was doing her best to be a normal 13-year-old girl but her home life was still rocky at the best of times. There were no luxuries and most months they struggled to make ends meet – relying heavily on donations from sponsors. Visser befriended the youngster with promises of gifts and the opportunity of a better life. Like all teenagers, Jeannine was entering a rebellious phase. She was fascinated with the voluptuous advocate and yearned for the high life. She didn't want to remain where she was, with her poor and, for the most part, uneducated mother. She believed that her new friend could assist her in realising her dreams.

When Visser indicated that she would like to take Jeannine out shopping, Marie was reluctant to let her child Rumours had reached Marie's ears about Visser sexually abusing girls from Bramley. Most of the institutions accommodating vulnerable children had been warned not to allow their children anywhere near the Prinsloos. When Marie confronted Visser with the rumours, the advocate told her that there was absolutely no basis for the stories that were being spread around by the staff of Bramley. She did, however, admit that there were pornographic magazines in their home but assured Marie that these were confined to their bedroom and that she would never show them to children.

Visser assured Marie that there was absolutely no chance that either her or her husband would, under any circumstances, harm any child as they both loved kids and were doing everything in their power to improve the lives of children in need. She added that they really wanted to give back to society for the privileged lives they were enjoying. They both felt, she said, that they would be offering children in need opportunities that would otherwise never be open to them. Marie accepted the advocate's version and was completely convinced that there was absolutely nothing amiss at the home she shared with Dirk Prinsloo.

Unlike her mother, Jeannine was overjoyed and excited by the idea of spending time with her new friend. She begged her mother to be allowed to go out and spend the afternoon with Visser at Menlyn Park shopping centre. Eventually, Marie gave in, allowing her to go with the blonde advocate.

When Jeannine returned from the outing, she raved about what a fantastic afternoon she had spent with Visser, who had taken her shopping and bought her a few items of clothing and hair gel. She had even offered to buy some food for Jeannine's cat and had taken the young teenager out to eat at a fast food restaurant. Marie was relieved when her daughter returned unharmed as, despite the assurances that she had received from Mrs Prinsloo, she claimed that, as a mother, she was still concerned for her daughter's safety.

On another occasion Visser took Jeannine out, they stopped at the plot for a while on the way back to Dolphin House. She showed the young teenager where she lived with her husband and introduced her to their secretary, Riana. Never before had Jeannine seen such an opulent home and she was seduced by the obvious wealth of the advocate couple. They gave her some *Milo* and snacks and she was eager to return. Visser had been pleasant and even caring and Jeannine felt herself beginning to trust her.

She desperately wanted to believe that these were good people who could change her life, a life that had been fraught with danger and despair. On her return to Dolphin House, Jeannine now told her mother how amazing the home was where the couple lived – she couldn't wait to go back and see them again.

By this time, Marie's fears had been completely allayed and she was unconcerned when Visser invited Jeannine to spend the weekend of her 14th birthday. The only thing that troubled Marie was that she wanted to spend at least part of her daughter's birthday with her. When she mentioned this to the other woman, she was assured that Jeannine would be home early on Sunday morning so that she could spend time celebrating her birthday with her family. Satisfied with the arrangement, Marie agreed to let her daughter spend the weekend with the Prinsloos.

When Jeannine left her home that weekend she was no stranger to adult experiences. She had a boyfriend with whom she was sexually active and had been prostituting herself on and off on the streets of Sunnyside for the last five years. She admitted openly to drinking alcohol and smoked marijuana on a regular basis.

Jeannine worshipped Visser and wanted to be just like her when she grew up. Beautiful, successful and, above all, wealthy. She had everything that Jeannine desired, a man who adored her, a beautiful home and – in Jeannine's eyes – she was famous. What amazed the girl even more was that this gorgeous creature was interested in her and wanted to spend time with her. And spending time with her was so much fun as she was often given presents. Jeannine hoped she would get the cell phone they had promised her for her birthday…

Visser picked Jeannine up, dropped her belongings off at home and then left for the gym. When they returned an hour later, the older woman made her way into the kitchen with Jeannine to start dinner. While they were preparing the food Jeannine was given two shooters and two tots of vodka. Although she was used to consuming alcohol, she felt jubilant and perhaps a little tipsy.

They served Prinsloo his dinner in the lounge. After finishing his meal, he sent his mistress to the kitchen to fetch Jeannine some *Milo*. Shortly afterwards, she began to feel sleepy. As Visser locked the house, Prinsloo carried the child to their bedroom.

Jeannine was wearing a white jersey that belonged to Visser and a black-and-white bikini bottom when Prinsloo took her off to bed. She had very little recollection about what actually happened to her after she fell asleep but the flashes that she did remember included her feeling almost paralysed. She also recalled being unable to move. Another thing she vividly remembered seeing were bright flashes of light, which she thought was the flash of a camera.

During an interview with Laurie weeks before her death, Jeannine claimed she had vague memories of Dirk's penis inside her and that she remembered feeling Visser penetrate her, using her fingers. These details were never verified though as she failed to mention them in her testimony before the high court.

According to Visser's evidence in court, she found Prinsloo on top of the naked child after she had returned from securing the house. He had ejaculated all over the child's stomach – presumably after raping her – careful to avoid her falling pregnant. Prinsloo instructed his ever-willing servant to clean up the child when he was done with her – which, of course, she did. As soon as she was done, she and Prinsloo retired to bed where they had a steamy encounter before falling asleep.

Jeannine felt heavy and very tired as she awoke the next morning. She could barely move and just wanted to sleep. She could not understand what had happened to her and why she felt so dreadful. She had never experienced this particular feeling in her life before – not even when she had used alcohol or had smoked marijuana. The symptoms she described were consistent with those caused by the date rape drug *Rohypnol*, found in the Prinsloo home when it was finally searched by the Police after the couple's arrest. In all probability the *Milo* that she had been given to drink the evening before had been laced with this drug.

Shortly after she woke up, Visser asked Jeannine if she knew how to *douche*. Jeannine had no idea what the woman was talking about, but Visser insisted on helping her to rinse out her vagina, removing any possible DNA evidence that might have been left behind.

Meanwhile, Marie began to worry when her daughter was not returned to her early on Sunday morning as Visser had promised. She dialled the advocate's cell phone to enquire when her child would be returned – but all her calls were rejected. When Visser eventually dumped Jeannine on Marie's doorstep, the teen was still wearing her pyjamas. She could barely keep her eyes open. She was obviously still under the influence of the drugs that had been administered to her the previous evening. Marie was shocked at Jeannine's appearance. She put her to bed and the girl slept virtually the entire afternoon.

Beside herself with worry about her child's physical state, Marie continued to question her until she finally spilt the beans. A third party overheard the conversation and through her interference, the 14-year-old girl was convinced to set aside her fear of police and open a criminal case.

Eventually, when Jeannine testified in Visser's trial she recalled the devastation that the experiences on the weekend of her 14th birthday had created in her life. In court she admitted to being HIV-positive, as well as being a full-blown heroin addict. Jeannine also conceded that she had been addicted to many other drugs through the years, following the abuse at the hands of people she had idolised saying, *"I turned to drugs time and again in order to escape the memories, patchy as they are."*

Because of her incomplete memories, she was unable to work through the events of that evening and she suffered constant flashbacks. Every time another memory surfaced, she found herself propelled back to the Prinsloo home and – to her mind – the rape that had occurred there.

Ironically, had the couple offered Jeannine the cell phone that she wanted or some sort of payment, she would most probably have participated quite willingly in their games. She was upset by the fact that they had drugged her and had used her without her permission.

16.
EXPOSED: INVESTIGATION AND ARREST

The celebrity advocate couple's bizarre sex life does not go unnoticed. The Afrikaans newspaper, *Rapport*, publishes several articles on some of their tamer sex escapades. When the paper wants to publish nude photos of them – which it apparently got from some schoolchildren who were distributing the pictures on the playground – Prinsloo and Visser turn to the Pretoria High Court to obtain a gagging order. The images are never published, but the interdict and subsequent media reports start to focus unwanted attention on them – the "no smoke without fire" adage being bandied about in an apparent smear campaign weeks before their arrest.

Investigating officer, Captain Carel Cornelius, first hears the rumours that two prominent advocates are molesting children from a colleague. He goes to the Commissioner of the Children's Court to enquire if any cases have been opened against Prinsloo and Visser, but – ostensibly due to the sensitivity of the Commissioner's own probe – cannot find anything concrete to start an actual criminal investigation. He learns, however, that a third girl, who was not one of Bramley's wards, had also lodged a complaint. As any good detective will tell you – the harder it is to find information, the more determined you become. Cornelius finally learns the name of this third girl and visits her.

Initially, Jeannine is reluctant to make a declaration under oath. Cornelius, with the help of a female Metro Police officer, eventually coaxes a statement out of her. Finally he has something more than rumours to work with and the investigation begins. Based solely on Jeannine's statement, Cornelius convinces a magistrate to issue a search warrant – which is executed the week before Christmas 2002. The raid takes more than ten hours to complete and a team of police officers goes through *Inner Circle Castle* with a fine tooth comb. Every nook and cranny of the house is searched in the hope of finding evidence to support Jeannine's claims.

Throughout the raid, Prinsloo is full of bravado – threatening law suits against the South African Police Service in general and Cornelius in particular. He also maligns Jeannine, calling her a little bitch and a thief. He claims she stole some of Visser's jewellery and is taking revenge against the couple for laying criminal charges against her. It is only when officials demand he opens the safe that Prinsloo's blustering attitude changes. Inside, the investigating team strikes pay dirt. Not only do they find prescription drugs known to have been used in date rapes, they also find a photo album – which would come to play a crucial role in the trial. A small amount of dagga and several *Viagra* tablets complete the contents of the safe.

When the raid is finally over, police officers leave *Inner Circle Castle* with two computers, bags and bags of pornography, the drugs, and what would become known as the infamous Red Photo Album. Visser and Prinsloo are arrested and taken away to separate police stations for questioning. Cornelius now has some physical evidence, but the real work of building a case against the couple has only just begun.

"Advocate Barbie's" arrest makes big headlines. The story would have received a lot of media attention in any case – but news is notoriously thin over the December holidays. Newshounds relish hauling out photographs of Visser taken during her tenure as *Idols* contestant and sex kitten.

When the Commissioner of the Children's Court becomes aware of the SAPS investigation, she is less averse to sharing the information received from the two children. Cornelius now has three statements in the bag. Media reports prompt more women to come forward with claims that they had fallen victim to the couple – until Cornelius has seven statements and seven witnesses.

While they are in custody, investigators try to convince Visser to turn State Witness against Prinsloo. Even before she knew that the police are not only investigating Jeannine's claims, but had reason to believe there were several more victims, Visser tells Cornelius that Prinsloo manipulated her into committing crimes – giving an indication that she not only knew that their actions were criminal, but also that she was aware of more victims other than Jeannine. The slew of police officials visiting her in the holding cells – urging her to turn against her lover – spooks Visser to such an extent that she writes a letter to Prinsloo, breaking off their relationship. This letter, which never reaches Prinsloo, is intercepted by police.

Ultimately, however, Visser decides to stand by her lover – continuing the pattern exhibited by the majority of battered women: protecting the aggressor. She would later explain that her motivation for not turning State Witness was a mixture of fear and adoration.

The media has a field day with rumours that "Advocate Barbie" is turning against her lover. When the two appear in the Pretoria Magistrate's Court for their bail application, they leave hand in hand, with Prinsloo putting up an entire production to demonstrate to journalists and photographers how much he loves his girlfriend. The performance is short-lived though, as they leave in separate cars. As part of her bail conditions, Visser has to stay with her mother. The couple is also forbidden from having contact with each other – fuelling their fantasy that they are living out a Shakespearian tragedy.

While in the relative safety of her mother's home – and acting out the "Damsel in Distress" role – Visser breaks off the relationship with Prinsloo. During their next court appearance, her lawyers ask the magistrate to retain the ban on contact between them, saying she wants nothing to do with her co-accused. Prinsloo, in turn, tells the court that it is unconstitutional to prevent spouses from having contact with each other. Despite the court order, Prinsloo incessantly calls Visser's mother in an attempt to reconcile with his mistress.

Worried that his co-accused might take up the offer to turn State Witness against him, Prinsloo threatens to kill Susan or her only child – making it clear that he would leave the other one alive to suffer. Fearing that he might make good on his threat, Visser moves back in with Prinsloo to assure him of her *bona fides*.

Partly due to this badgering and partly because of the sway he holds over her, Visser gives in just days after the court appearance and a passionate reconciliation follows on Valentine's Day, with Prinsloo sending his mistress a huge bouquet of flowers in an expensive crystal vase. The reunion sends Susan into a rage and an almighty fight between mother and daughter sees the vase shattered and the younger woman applying for another family protection order.

During his attempts to win her back, Prinsloo promises Visser the sun, the moon and the stars – or rather, he reiterates his promises to make a star out of her – and swears that things will be different between them. Desperately wanting to believe him – and completely buying into the idea that their love is a quasi-drama playing off against a backdrop of malicious prosecution and Romeo-and-Juliet-style parental interference – Visser chooses to ignore her mother's advice and takes him back unreservedly. The prohibition against contact between the two love birds is lifted after a court application and they put up a united front during their next appearance. The temporary impasse in their relationship has only served to add an extra sense of drama to their already stormy affair.

Despite Prinsloo's enmity, Visser's mother refuses to give up on her only child. In order to endear herself to her daughter's lover, Susan turns a blind eye to the blatant sexual advances he makes towards her. Having been reconciled with her daughter – and as far as she could stomach it, with Prinsloo – Susan becomes a regular visitor at *Inner Circle Castle*. Her behaviour towards Prinsloo convinces him that his "mother-in-law" has had a change of heart about him.

He even allows his lover to go to Cape Town with her – on condition that she convinces the older woman to have sex with him. On his instructions, Visser has to coach her mother on the finer aspects of sex and has to take her to adult shops to open her mind a bit. Visser, who has never questioned her "god's" orders, cannot bring herself so far as to raise the issue with her mother. When the two women return from their holiday, Prinsloo picks them up at the then Johannesburg International Airport.

While driving home, he unzips his pants and forces Visser's head down on him. She gives him a blow job while Susan sits in the back seat with a jacket pulled over her head – trying to control her revulsion at the scene playing itself off in the front seat. Yet, whether she's repeating old patterns or is afraid to lose contact with her child again, she never discusses the issue with her daughter.

During one of Susan's visits, while mother and daughter unwind at the swimming pool, Prinsloo brings them each a smoothie. When the two women start to feel a bit drowsy, he helps them into the house and tells them to relax in the living room. Visser helps her mother to the bathroom when she feels a bit nauseous – but leaves to answer the phone when it rings in Prinsloo's office. When she returns from his office and goes to her bedroom, she finds her naked lover on top of her equally naked mother. The issue is never discussed by the two women. Visser also never questions Prinsloo. A few hours after this incident, she drives her mother home, drops her off and returns to the house in Raslouw.

When Prinsloo sells *Inner Circle Castle* and buys a small farm outside Bela-Bela, the couple temporarily move in with Susan. One night, the younger woman wakes up to go to the bathroom when she hears panting from the guest bedroom where her mother is sleeping. Susan has been suffering from insomnia for years and routinely takes sleeping pills. When Visser looks into the room, she finds her boyfriend having sex with her sleeping mother. Shocked, she walks out of the room and goes back to bed. When Prinsloo joins her, she asks him to leave the premises. He begs her forgiveness – claiming he did nothing wrong as there are no rules in his life. Angry at her lover, Visser spends the night on the couch. The next morning, her mother dresses and goes to work without saying a word about the night before – the incident swept under the rug with the rest of the abuse and degradation. The message drilled into Visser from childhood is reinforced when her mother – for reasons unknown – decides not to press criminal charges.

As the two advocates continue to pander to the media, posing for photos and decrying their innocence, Captain Cornelius tries furiously to strengthen the case against them, but the process of piecing the puzzle together is a slow and laborious one. When the state asks for another postponement, Magistrate Bernard Swart refuses, saying a further postponement would unfairly prejudice the couple. Prosecutor André Fourie tells the court that he has no option but to withdraw the charges against the accused – which does not mean they are off the hook. When charges are withdrawn, the State reserves the right to charge them again.

The two beleaguered advocates shed tears of relief as they leave the courthouse – with Prinsloo telling reporters that it is a pity that children's rights are being used to wage a vendetta against him. He claims the charges against them are trumped up because his crusade for justice has made him a thorn in the side of Government for years. A red-haired Visser clings to her god, telling the throng of reporters that she has changed her mind about testifying against him.

Cornelius fears that the couple, and Prinsloo in particular, will try to interfere with state witnesses – and that they will be intimidated and discouraged even before a trial date is set. The clock is ticking and with the charges against the suspects withdrawn, there is nothing he can do to prevent them from approaching their accusers. His fears are not baseless – as Prinsloo tries to convince Jeannine to withdraw her case and press charges of his own against Riana Burger after sending 'Norman' and 'Robert' to interview her. Despite the gloomy outlook, Cornelius slogs away until he feels he has enough evidence to secure a conviction.

17.
THE AFTERMATH
JEANNINE'S STORY
PART III

Shortly after her experience at *Inner Circle Castle*, Jeannine ran away again, returning to the streets. Eventually, she moved back in with Sue but never stayed very long. Jeannine considered Sue a trusted friend and always turned to her in times of great need. During this time, Sue took Jeannine to see a few lawyers who had offered their assistance. Unknown to her, one of these attorneys was acting on behalf of Dirk Prinsloo. Jeannine described him as tall with brown hair but was unable to recall his name.

While in his office, Jeannine was given a document which she was asked to read and sign. She was told that if there was anything in any statement that she did not agree with she could simply draw a line through the text that she disputed and they would remove it from the statement. This document would years later be handed in as an exhibit in court and Jeannine's evidence about it would take up 32 pages in the court record.

In the affidavit, Jeannine admitted that she had opened the case against the Prinsloos to blackmail them – as she (according to the document) previously had done to other couples. She supposedly thought the case against the Prinsloos would be over soon because they would pay her off to save themselves the embarrassment of a trial, as they were professionals and in the public eye. In the affidavit, the teenager admitted to stealing jewellery and clothing from Visser while visiting the Prinsloo home. The document also stated that Captain Cornelius pressurised Jeannine to open the case against the Prinsloos, as he wanted to *"sink"* the couple.

The pre-prepared statement went on to claim that the investigating officer had made several threats to force her to help him – including that he would have her sent to a place of safety or locked up on charges of prostitution. The help he had wanted included that she had to convince other girls and women to open criminal cases of sexual misconduct against the couple. She also had to make sure that all the stories matched up and corroborated each other. It claimed Cornelius also replaced her original affidavit with a backdated falsified affidavit which he had forced her to sign. His plans to *"sink the Prinsloos"* had since evolved and the original statement contradicted some of the new developments. These included that Jeannine would get one of her fellow child prostitutes to open a case against the couple. The document makes several allegations of malicious prosecution and cover-ups against both the SAPS and the NPA.

Jeannine deleted several of the paragraphs in the document, scratched out certain sections and made changes to others. When she returned a few days later, Jeannine signed the supposedly corrected version of her statement without reading it, as she was high on heroin. Unbeknownst to her the changes she insisted on were never made. In effect, she had signed a blatantly falsified declaration that made her look like a pawn in Cornelius' so-called attempts to destroy the Prinsloos.

Fortunately, because Jeannine did not trust the attorney, she asked for a copy of the corrected statement. Jeannine wanted to have the changes with her in case the lawyers did not adjust the document as she had asked them to do.

She visited her mother in order to discuss the events that had transpired in Prinsloo's attorney's office because she knew that her mother would disapprove of her withdrawing the charges against the couple. While she was there, Jeannine gave the copies of the statement that she had received from the attorney to her mother for safekeeping.

The young girl who had wanted to become a judge, had instead become very disillusioned with the legal profession. Life on the street had made her a good judge of character and, if she had had the education, she could have been an asset to the bench. For her age, Jeannine had a very mature way of thinking about things and of expressing herself.

When Prinsloo failed to get what he wanted from Jeannine he turned to Sue, requesting her to provide him with an affidavit portraying Jeannine as a prostitute, drug addict and person with questionable morals. Sue refused to sign a statement to this effect, as she knew that Jeannine was many things, but not a liar. The girl would always tell the truth, even if it were at a cost to her. If Jeannine ever stole things from Sue she would admit it, despite knowing that she would end up out on the streets for a few weeks. Jeannine could handle the consequences of her actions and she did not shirk responsibility.

Prinsloo then approached Roelien for an affidavit – essentially to discredit her sister. It seems that Roelien, after receiving a bribe from Prinsloo, agreed to assist him and made a statement at the Sunnyside Police Station in which she maligned her sister's character – a true case of the pot calling the kettle black. After a while, however, she regretted lying under oath in order to assist Prinsloo and attempted to withdraw her statement.

Meanwhile, Jeannine had been living with a young Nigerian man in Sunnyside shortly before learning that she was HIV-positive. Although Casey was good to her and seemed to love her, he gave her drugs and prostituted her. Jeannine was visiting Sue on the day that she tested positive for HIV. When Sue asked Jeannine about the results, she looked out the window and said: *"The woman says I am positive."* They drove all the way home in relative silence and, upon arriving home, Jeannine went to the room and threw herself on her bed. Although unsure of how to approach her, Sue knew that they had to talk about the situation.

When Sue walked into the bedroom, she found Jeannine staring out of the window. She was not sobbing, but tears were flowing unchecked down her little face. In order to fight back her own tears, Sue became confrontational, telling the child: *"You cannot expect to stand in the middle of a highway every day of your life and not get hit by a bus! Eventually it was going to happen. You have done everything in the book in order to get yourself HIV-positive. How can you expect to be negative?"*

Jeannine then began to sob uncontrollably. Obviously remorseful for lashing out, Sue explained that it was not the end of the world, but that Jeannine would have to make drastic changes if she wanted to live. She would need special food, special healthcare, no longer leave her razor on the bed and she could no longer cook other people's food.

Jeannine did not take the news of her status well and did everything in her power to die and to let others die with her. She would sleep with all and sundry and, asked why she was being so self-destructive, she would reply: *"If they are stupid enough to sleep with me without using protection then they deserve to die."* Jeannine was angry and out for revenge. The situation was bad and talking to her didn't help. She was lashing out at the world around her.

When Roelien fell pregnant with her first child in 2005, Jeannine's self-destructive behaviour escalated. Suddenly, and for no obvious reason, she began to use copious amounts of heroin. As soon as she came down from a high she would spike again, becoming terribly depressed.

It seemed she was spiralling out of control, deteriorating visibly by the day. Later that year, a pregnant Roelien got married without inviting her sister or even telling her about the ceremony. Jeannine went berserk when she heard the news - she put a rope around her neck and tried to hang herself. She was supposed to go to a rehabilitation facility but wouldn't co-operate since she had apparently stopped caring.

Sue had reached breaking point with Jeannine. Dealing with her daily histrionics was becoming increasingly impossible and, she said, *"the responsibility of Jeannine was overwhelming."* She had managed to secure an interview with a rehab facility for the troubled teen – you have to be approved because of long waiting lists and because the institution did not want to waste time with unwilling applicants. On the day of the interview, Jeannine was so high that she fell off her chair, breaking a glass. Sue could tell she wasn't pretending but was genuinely really high. The older woman sat with her through the interview, praying that they would accept her, which they finally agreed to do. She was supposed to report two days later.

The next day when Sue had to go to work and worried about Jeannine's suicidal frame of mind, she approached the SAPS for assistance with the girl. They told her there was nothing they could do to assist and Sue had to abandon her work and stay with Jeannine until she could take her to rehab once again.

Of course, the stresses linked to the Prinsloo/Visser case were constantly part of Jeannine's existence. She was afraid of having to testify about the experiences but not for reasons one would have anticipated. The exposure that the case brought to her own life and the lives of her parents was a constant stressor to her. She desperately tried to prevent her parents from being exposed for what they really were. Whenever a court date was set for her to appear at the trial she would disappear, usually leaving a letter explaining her actions. These letters would usually contain wording along the lines of: *"The case is tomorrow, I am not going to be there, I do not want my parents to go through this."*

For all her faults, Jeannine had a very kind and forgiving nature. She never held a grudge against anyone for long, including Visser and Prinsloo. She forgave easily and readily. Her mother, however, continued to tell people that she was very angry and could not forgive *"Barbie"* for what had happened to her daughter. It appears Marie had found a scapegoat in Visser – someone who could be blamed for all the injustices and abuse the teenager had suffered in her life.

Jeannine was always very straightforward and not shy or afraid to admit it when she had transgressed. She openly admitted to stealing Visser's jewellery and clothing. In addition, she admitted to stealing a little doll from the older woman – she though it was beautiful and she wanted it. Amusingly, she always referred to Visser as "Barbie" after her arrest – openly displaying her contempt for the woman she once idolised. Jeannine told Laurie shortly before her death that she held Visser responsible for what had happened to her but never attributed much blame to Prinsloo, saying: *"He was just a man, doing what men do… Barbie should have known better."*

18.
BETRAYAL
LAURIE'S STORY
PART II

I heard through the grapevine that Dirk and Cézanne had been arrested, but I had no idea what the charges were against them. On a number of occasions Dirk had expressed an interest in obtaining cocaine for recreational use, so I presumed that the charges were most probably narcotics-related. In addition, I knew that his brother smoked dagga, as I had witnessed him doing so while staying with Dirk. I know it is wrong, but musicians and drugs have stereotypically had a long relationship, so I cannot say I was surprised.

A couple of weeks went by before I saw either Dirk or Cézanne again. By then, she was pathetically thin and looked terrible – I knew that she had been through quite an ordeal when she and Dirk had been arrested and incarcerated. Somehow I suspected that there was probably more to the story than had originally met the eye. I asked her how she was doing and, in typical Cézanne fashion, she said that she was fine. I told her that if she ever needed any help in getting away from Dirk all she had to do was ask. I had many friends in the Military and Police and told her they would be more than happy to assist should she feel that there was a need to call in the reserves. I also made it clear that she could come and stay with me if she had nowhere else to go. In addition, I added, no matter what she thought or felt, her mother loved her dearly and would never turn her back on her. Cézanne just needed to reach out and ask, and help would have been there for her.

She just smiled, telling me that she was fine, that she loved Dirk and could not or would not desert him. Cézanne added that no one could understand what he meant to her and what he gave her, describing him as amazing and providing the best sex she ever had. She added that no other man would ever be able to give her what he gave her or satisfy her the way Dirk did. It wasn't the right time to pursue the issue and I told her to keep in mind that she had several people to turn to if she ever was in need of assistance. Unfortunately for Cézanne, that time never came – at least not when there was still some chance of salvaging things.

A few weeks later Dirk contacted me again. They had moved to Bela-Bela and had discovered an underground water spring on the property. Dirk described the water quality as "unparalleled" and he had decided to bottle and sell it. Dirk called his company KS and was planning to market two brands - KS Liqua and KS Cool Cave. I was asked to design a corporate identity and draw up a business plan. Many hours were spent putting together the corporate identity for KS. The graphics that he chose were fairly intricate and had to have a 'liquid' feel. In typical fashion, Dirk insisted on an image of a naked woman in a provocative pose.

Dirk and Cézanne arrived at my home one evening with a box of pizza and two bottles of red wine for dinner. He demanded that I finish the documentation that evening. He indicated that he would supply all the text on disc and that all I would need to do was copy, paste and format the document – but this failed to materialise and I was expected to type the content as he dictated it. I was not impressed, to say the least. With a lot of coffee and no sleep, the document was completed on time. He and Cézanne were forced to spend the entire evening in my home in order to accomplish this task.

Before going to bed, my mother threw two old and rather tatty dressing gowns at Dirk and Cézanne, saying that if they were going to stay over they should dress before coming downstairs to use the bathroom as she had heard stories and would not tolerate lewd behaviour or naked people running around in our home. I think that both Dirk and Cézanne were a little taken aback by my mom's directness. My mother was not big on diplomacy when it came to Dirk Prinsloo as she really didn't like him very much. She found him to be arrogant and abrasive and he cooked his goose when he told her that she was very sexy for her age. The next morning, Dirk and Cézanne rushed off to their meeting and I didn't see them again for a week or two. Then, one morning, I received a number of calls from Dirk. Although I did not want to speak to him, Dirk drove to the complex where I lived with my mom, and without so much as a knock on the door, he barged into the house and made up the stairs to where my office and bedroom were. My mother heard the ruckus, and caught him half way up the stairs. She asked him what he thought he was doing. He angrily replied that I was ignoring his phone calls and that he was going upstairs to speak to me.

With that, my mother told him in no uncertain terms that this was her home and that he should have the courtesy to knock at the door before entering. She then calmly told him to leave as I was not at home and it really wouldn't help him to look for me upstairs.

Dirk then began shouting at my mother, asking her where "*the hell*" I was and demanded that she call me immediately as I was not responding to his calls. My mother told him that if I was not taking his calls, then I obviously did not wish to speak to him. She suggested that he should leave a message, saying I would return his call when I had the time. Finally, she informed him that his bullying and abrasive behaviour would not be tolerated. Dirk was obviously not used to being scolded in this fashion, and promptly stormed out of the house, apologising for the invasion.

As it turned out, he needed a flyer for his business venture, which I agreed to do for a R450 design fee. Later, after completing the job, I went downstairs for a cup of coffee, leaving Dirk by the railing at the top of the stairs. He proceeded to count out the money and threw the cash down the stairs, telling me to catch it as the notes floated to the floor. My mother and I were completely gob-smacked at Dirk's behaviour. He really seemed to enjoy the sight of me running around, trying to pick up the cash, obviously deriving pleasure from his attempt at belittling me. Smiling, he then collected his goods and left, looking immensely self-satisfied.

A week or so later, Dirk arrived at my home for a chat, appearing sad and almost defeated. Prinsloo then told me how a young teenager, Jeannine du Plessis, who was an orphan and whom he and Cézanne had taken under their wing, had stolen Cézanne's jewellery and other items. He claimed that they had taken Jeannine home over weekends and had even offered to pay for her education. Apparently the girl had wanted a cell phone and that she had opened a case of rape against him when he refused to buy her the phone.

According to Dirk, he was at his wit's end because the Police – in particular Superintendent Daleen du Plessis, whom he violently detested – was going all out to persecute him and was intent on destroying his life. He claimed that all the evidence had been *"manufactured"* by *"corrupt"* officers at the Wierda Bridge Police Station and that they had planted *Rohypnol*, marijuana and other drugs in his home. Prinsloo also insisted that the Police had put pornographic photographs of young naked children on his computer's hard drive, which they had then confiscated and sent to their *"complicit"* colleagues for analysis, resulting in a charge of manufacturing and possession of child pornography.

Referring to the growing number of newspaper reports, Dirk said these were all lies fed to the media by the officers at Wierda Bridge. He claimed these officers were part of a conspiracy against him. Behind this conspiracy, he said, was Superintendent Daleen du Plessis. My own experiences with Wierda Bridge had been less than favourable, to say the least, and I was aware of corruption and incompetence at the Station. Dirk's story seemed almost plausible at the time. I understand now that Dirk was a master manipulator of the truth, who blended fact with falsehood until the two were so well merged that it was almost impossible to tell which was which.

Having heard Prinsloo's tale of woe and part of me believing him, I was still wondering what he wanted from me. Was it just an ear, someone to listen to? I doubted this, as Dirk had never struck me as a person who did anything without an ulterior motive. I soon realised what he wanted – an affidavit to serve as a character witness statement in his upcoming court case.

I had never had a major problem with Dirk. Yes, he was a bully at times, aggressive, rude and certainly narcissistic, as well as extremely selfish, but he had never harmed me. In fact, when I needed him and had asked for his help in a custody matter, he had been very supportive and had gone out of his way to assist me. There was a part of me that admired his self-confidence and his assertive manner. When you felt hopeless and helpless, Dirk could be relied on to take control, kick your butt and motivate you to take control of your life. On hearing his request, I was quite happy to oblige him and told him to go home, type up what he needed and when it was ready to give me a call and

I would sign it. I jokingly added that he should just make sure that he stuck to the truth. I would not lie under oath.

The following day he called me to make sure that I was at home, saying that he would send Cézanne over with the affidavit. A few minutes later she arrived with the document.

What I read shocked me to the core and ended, in an instant, any illusions of friendship that I thought had existed between Dirk, Cézanne and myself. I told Cézanne that the affidavit was a pack of lies and pure perjury. She indicated that Dirk had given her a disc with the document saved on it so that I could make any changes that I felt necessary. I took the disc from her, saying I would think about it and asked her to leave.

I was totally enraged at Dirk Prinsloo's audacity for even considering that I would sign the document. I was hurt and disgusted and felt totally betrayed by both Dirk Prinsloo and Cézanne Visser. I thought of all the hours that I spent working on their projects, at no charge, often right through the night. Dirk who, despite my instincts to the contrary, had almost convinced me he was a person who valued loyalty above all else and who, in a time of crisis, could be trusted.

What a joke. I felt like an idiot. What a fool I had been for even thinking I could trust him for a minute. I felt that Cézanne was just as despicable and I hoped that one day they would get their just deserts.

To this day, I have no idea what Prinsloo's motive was for writing certain paragraphs of this affidavit while, on the other hand, his motives for the inclusion of other paragraphs are crystal clear and rather frightening. Nevertheless, what this affidavit did make unequivocally clear is the extent to which Dirk Prinsloo and Cézanne Visser would stoop in order to clear their own names. Because of the contents and their implications, this affidavit was the primary reason that I became involved in the Prinsloo/Visser case. Later on, as the trial unfolded, my motives for staying involved may have changed, but this document was definitely the catalyst.

The opening lines were fairly standard and even though I had been acquainted with Dirk Prinsloo for almost eighteen months by this time, he had still managed to misspell my name, which was rather insulting.

After stating that I knew what I was saying, was doing it voluntarily and swearing under oath that the content of the document would be the truth. the document goes on to say:

"I know Advocate Prinsloo since I worked for him as a personal assistant in 2001 for about six months. I started working for him on the expressed arrangement that I am looking to expand my horizons despite the fact that I have my graphic design business on the side. To find my feet after I had to sell my previous business, it was expressly agreed between advocates Prinsloo and myself that as soon as I have an opportunity again to work full-time in my business I would be allowed to leave without animosity."

I had worked for Dirk and Cézanne for some five weeks. *"Expanding my horizons"* and resuming my studies was true, but at no stage did I sell or contemplate selling my graphics design business, as it was doing fairly well. I had no idea what Dirk Prinsloo was hoping to attain with this statement.

Acknowledging that I had been in his employ for six months would have, in essence, meant that I had been in the office during a period that I was not there. Either my employ would have overlapped with that of Riana Brink or with Mercia Jacobs, who had been employed by Prinsloo until just before I started working there. The reason for this statement is also unclear, unless it was an attempt to implicate me in some other criminal or shady event that occurred before or after I was employed there.

"I was happy working for advocates (sic) Prinsloo and found him to be very self-assured, effective, firm but fair. He is one of the few people whose word is actually his honour."

I was not unhappy working for the Prinsloos, but their lewd behaviour was difficult to stomach at times and had made me incredibly uncomfortable. Dirk was a bully and a control freak with an extremely narcissistic personality, but I never felt that I could not stand up to him. Of course, the *"word is his honour"* bit is a joke. I'm assuming that his motive was to present himself as an honourable, firm and fair employer. Of course, this too is a bit of a stretch and was obviously not the case – as shown by the high staff turnover of his practice. Few decent people would describe the work environment at the Prinsloo home as healthy.

"I have been to the premises at various times of day and night since my employment there and even after that and there has never been any pornography lying around in the house war (sic) office areas."

In the entire time that I associated with Dirk and Cézanne, they invited me to their home once for dinner. At the time, I really didn't want to be in their home alone and asked my mother to call me during the evening to tell me there was something amiss with my son and that I must come home urgently. They served a wonderful meal but I had a very uneasy feeling – as if was in a highly predatorial environment. I was mindful of what I ate and drank and was very happy to leave when my mother called. On that particular evening, numerous pornographic magazines were all over the place, as well as pornographic videos.

"Advocates (sic) Prinsloo, his ex-wife and later Cézanne were all good to me and no sexual advances by any of them had been made to me (or any of the clients)."

Again, this paragraph is a mystery to me. I had never met Elsie

Prinsloo and why Dirk would want to allege this is still beyond me. Cézanne had, indeed, always been good to me and I was really quite fond of her – while Dirk, with his chameleon-like personality, had also been very good to me at times. On other occasions, he was a total bastard. Dirk was prone to have wandering hands which often found themselves in highly inappropriate places. In fairness, he never pushed the issue when corrected. I had never seen either Dirk or Cézanne behave in a sexually inappropriate way with any client.

"I confirm the fact that ad hoc labour consultants had 24 hour access to the office area and the Internet."

I had never even seen an *ad hoc* labour consultant on the premises. In fact, I had never even spoken to one on the telephone. The computer used to access the internet was situated in the office next to the reception area in which I worked. This was also the office in which most of the files were stored. Only Cézanne and Dirk were allowed to touch this computer and they were extremely cagy about this particular computer and its contents. In the entire time that I worked for Dirk Prinsloo I never, at any stage, touched that computer and didn't even know the password. I found out later that it was "*Slet100.*"

I believe that the only reason for adding this paragraph, was to establish a base from which to argue that he and Cézanne were not the only persons with access to the computer on which the pornographic material and child pornography had been downloaded and then stored. Perhaps some other "*ad hoc person*" or previous employee had downloaded and stored or placed the material on his computer.

"I actually met Riana Brink on my occasional visits in 2002 and she was always very happy working for Advocate Prinsloo. It came as a surprise to me when Advocate Prinsloo told me that she resigned and claimed constructive dismissal against him at the end of October 2002.

I never had any contact with her after that."

In fact, I spoke to Riana on two separate occasions. She had contacted me in connection with the location of files and other work-related matters. To this day, I have never met Riana Brink. I would therefore have no idea whether Riana Brink was happy working for the Prinsloos or not. From her testimony in court it is easy to deduce that she was deeply unhappy when she was working for Dirk Prinsloo. Obviously, he had wanted to use me to discredit Riana Brink.

"Advocate Prinsloo never used Riana's two computers (confirmed by her to me in our chats) i.e. the Internet's (sic) computer and the computer at her desk (which computers were "my" and their consultant's computers when I worked at Riana's office)"

Dirk Prinsloo and Cézanne Visser were the only two people whom I ever witnessed using the Internet-linked computer. By adding this paragraph, Dirk Prinsloo was effectively pointing the finger at both Riana Brink and me for the downloading of pornographic material, including the child pornography. If we were the only people, together with Cézanne and the *ad hoc labour consultants*," who used the computer – and Dirk could falsify evidence that he was computer illiterate – it would be very difficult, if not impossible, for the State to prove its case against him in respect of the pornography.

"It was a constant office joke and irritation to myself (when I worked there) that advocate Prinsloo never bothered, had time or wanted to learn anything about the Internet, and Riana (despite the fact that Cézanne was able to work on the Internet as well) had to use the Internet computer when the Internet had to be used for something."

There was no joke and no irritation to me with regards to Dirk Prinsloo's computer literacy issues. I knew he could receive and send e-mails quite competently. He was also quite able to search the Internet for information should he need it for any reason and to access that information. I really had absolutely no interest in Prinsloo's computer literacy skills and cannot really comment, apart from stating that he was quite capable of typing his own affidavits and the documentation that he needed in order to work. Cézanne Visser was also quite capable of doing the same. Prinsloo's only motive for this paragraph would have been to portray himself as computer illiterate as well as being incapable of using internet-related programmes, thereby placing some distance between himself and any Internet-related criminal act.

When Cézanne delivered this affidavit to me I had no inclination to become in any way involved in the Prinsloo/Visser trial. I was relieved that I had managed, for the most part, to extricate myself from the situation in time. My instincts to resign had been proven right and I had been careful to make sure that my dealings with Dirk Prinsloo, after my resignation, had been well-managed and conducted primarily in my home with either my mother or my grandmother present.

I was a single mother of a fairly young child at the time – my son means everything to me. By asking me to sign an affidavit of this nature, Dirk Prinsloo and Cézanne Visser were trying to play Russian roulette with my life.

I was really angry at the brazen, calculated attempt at manipulating me into a potentially precarious position. Cézanne was no angel in this endeavour. I pointed out very clearly to her how dishonest this affidavit was and asked her, as an advocate and an officer of the court, how she could ask me to sign a document that was so flawed. I told her that I would be committing perjury if I signed it. She replied that she was just the messenger.

This was absolute rubbish, as my signing the statement would have assisted her as much as it would have assisted Dirk. As an advocate, she had to be well aware of that fact. I did not believe that Cézanne was just the messenger, as she looked very guilty when I called their bluff. I will be the first to concede that every person is entitled to a defence. However, one reaches a moral limit when you are prepared to sacrifice another to protect yourself.

If I had been prosecuted for perjury – which in South Africa can carry a heavy penalty – my child would have grown up without a mother. I thought about the possible fallout as I discussed the situation with my mom and she encouraged me to report what had transpired. I really didn't want to speak to the Wierda Bridge Police Station detectives and decided to call the National Prosecuting Authority, to give them the perjurous statement as well as the disc. I hoped that Cézanne would tell Dirk what I had said, and prayed that I wouldn't hear from him again.

My mother sat with me as I made the call to the NPA – I was really nervous. To say there were butterflies in my stomach would be an understatement – more like swarms of really angry wasps. When the call was answered and I asked if I could speak to the person in charge of the Prinsloo/Visser case, I was immediately transferred to Advocate Retha Meintjies. I outlined the situation and she was really kind, patient and understanding. She asked for my number and said Advocate André Fourie, the Lead Council for the Prosecution, would give me a call. She assured me that I had done the right thing and thanked me for contacting her.

The phone rang within five minutes. It was Advocate Fourie and he wanted to see me as soon as possible. He asked me for my address, told me to sit tight and said that he and Inspector Benade of the SAPS would be at my home as soon as they could get there. I was quite surprised by the prompt and efficient reaction by the State Advocate. This was the first time that I realised that the charges against Dirk and Cézanne were much more serious than I had been led to believe. I told my mom what was about to happen and begged her to wait with me for their arrival.

I was relieved when they finally arrived. I had not met either of them before and André Fourie introduced himself first, then Inspector Benade, a member of the Child Protection Unit. André asked me to show him the statement. After reading it he handed it to Inspector Benade to read. He asked me about my history with Dirk and Cézanne and I told him exactly how I had met Dirk, worked for him and continued to do odd jobs for them after I terminated my employ there. I told him that I had regarded them as friends but, looking at the document delivered to me that afternoon by Cézanne, I had obviously been mistaken.

Advocate Fourie then asked me to give him a statement regarding the statement that Dirk Prinsloo had wanted me to sign. Fourie asked me if I would mind showing them the photographs that had been given to me by Dirk and Cézanne. I was more than happy to hand over the disc. Inspector Benade asked if I had ever seen any children at the Prinsloo home during the time that I had been employed there. I said that I had not.

I asked the advocate and the detective what the crimes were that the Prinsloos had been charged with. Without revealing too much of the State's case, he outlined the basic charges against Dirk and Cézanne. These included multiple counts of indecent assault, rape, possession of illegal substances, manufacture and possession of child pornography and fraud. I could hardly believe what I was hearing and felt the bile rise in my throat. The waves of nausea eventually subsided and Fourie and Benade prepared to leave.

The two men promised to be back with a statement for me to sign regarding the events that had led up to me handing them the perjurous statement and the disc with images. As they were leaving, I asked Advocate Fourie what the consequences would have been had I signed the document. He looked me straight in the eye and said it would have been one of the biggest mistakes of my entire life and that he would have put me on the stand, discredited me as a witness and most probably charged me with both perjury and attempting to defeat the ends of justice. I shivered at the realisation of my close call at the hands of Dirk Prinsloo. I thank God to this day for the keen instincts that I have and for the fact that on that day I had the courage and conviction to act on my instincts to call the NPA.

I hope that this chapter has underscored the dangers of signing any false statement. I trust that after reading this you will have the courage and the moral conviction to say no to any person asking you to make or sign a false statement. The consequences of dishonesty can be dire, but more importantly they can be unforeseen, unpredictable and unmanageable.

19.
PROSECUTION

The two alleged sex offenders' joy and relief at being freed is cut short when the State reopens its case a day after it was withdrawn. Prosecutors request them, via their lawyers, to report to the Pretoria Regional Court – with the warning that, should they fail to appear, they will be arrested.

The State requests for the matter to be referred to the High Court in Pretoria because it can hand down longer jail terms. From the start, Fourie had no doubt in his mind – he was not going to settle for anything less than seeing "Advocate Barbie" and her lover behind bars. Visser is charged with 14 counts – including fraud and indecent assault, while Prinsloo has to answer to 15 charges – the additional charge being one of assault.

When the trial day in the High Court arrives, Prinsloo immediately applies for a postponement – saying they could not prepare their defence as the State had not supplied them with the entire docket. The Prosecution had decided not to include the list of witnesses in the documents handed to the couple, as they feared they – and especially Prinsloo – would try to intimidate the women and girls who were meant to testify. This fear seems to have been justified. When he eventually learns the identities of the other two minors accusing him of molesting them, Prinsloo launches an urgent court application – this time asking for access to the two girls' Children's Home files.

In court papers he argues that Bramley Children's Home seem to have experienced problems with the *sexual deviancy* of one of the girls. The court hears from Prinsloo's lawyers that the defence wants to establish whether any of the two girls had laid similar charges against other persons – insinuating that either one, or both of the girls had had an ulterior motive for laying criminal charges against the couple. This tactic is similar to the attack on Jeannine, with Prinsloo seemingly hell-bent on discrediting his accusers before they can testify.

While he is trying to interfere with and discredit the girls and women who accused him, Prinsloo accuses them of conducting a trial by media and of intimidation. The application for access to the girls' files is turned down. The trial is set to start in 2005 – more than two years after their arrest.

When the date finally arrives, Prosecutor André Fourie and his assistant prosecutor, Advocate Jennifer Cronjé, are chomping at the bit – convinced that they will secure a successful conviction. Cronjé, in particular, has no sympathy for Visser – and would often say that, as a woman, Visser should have known better.

As expected, the two advocates' appearance in the dock draws a lot of media attention and the pair pleads not guilty to all the charges against them in a courtroom packed to the rafters with newshounds, other advocates and case-chasers.

In the final charge sheet, Visser has to answer to 15 charges and Prinsloo to 16:

The pair stands accused of raping a child and a woman on different occasions – in each case allegedly drugging their victim first.

There are three charges of soliciting a 15-year-old girl to commit indecent acts on different occasions. Alternatively, they are charged with exposing themselves to the girl and/or performing sexual acts in front of her and/or showing her pornographic material.

The couple is also charged with paying another minor to perform a variety of sexual acts – including having intercourse with Prinsloo.

There are four counts of indecent assault – two of them involving an 11-year-old girl and the others involving two different women.

It is alleged they had shown the child pornographic films, exposed themselves to her, and had sexual intercourse and performed other sexual acts in front of her. They also allegedly forced her to walk around naked at their home.

The State claims the couple committed fraud by pretending to be married for the purposes of obtaining temporary supervision over minors from a children's home, in order to abuse them.

Other charges include one of possessing child pornography, two of manufacturing such materials and one of possessing dagga.

Prinsloo is furthermore charged with assaulting a complainant in one of the indecent assault charges – a former employee.

In detailed plea explanations, the pair denies guilt on any of the charges – with Prinsloo stating that one count of indecent assault refers to an incident in which the adult complainant willingly performed oral sex on him in the presence of – and with the help of – Visser.

Judge Essop Patel, a devout Muslim, must have been just a tad apprehensive about the case before him. Not only were the charges sleazy and salacious at the very least, but the two accused before him were officers of the court – his colleagues in upholding and protecting the law. Looking like a character out of Star Wars, his red-robed presence commanded respect – even when, later in the trial, he clearly battled to contain his frustration with Prinsloo and his antics.

A champion for human rights – and especially the rights of women and children – Patel specialised in civil matters, but his ability to fairly dispense justice in this trial was beyond reproof, to anyone but Prinsloo.

Outside the courtroom, Prinsloo and Visser sit hand in hand, alternating between smiling and taking swipes at reporters covering the case. Dressed in a tight-fitting outfit, wearing heavy make up and her hair – blonde again after the quick flirtation with the red hair dye – tied up in a high pony tail, Visser looks every bit the part of "Advocate Barbie." But other than the plastic doll, this advocate was on the wrong side of the law. Prinsloo sits very close to Visser as the two of them hold hands and listen intently to proceedings.

Cornelius is the first witness to take the stand. His shy smile belies the steely determination he has shown in building the case against Prinsloo and Visser. That side of him is only suggested by the cropped grey haircut and the appraising stare in his dark brown eyes. Cornelius testifies in detail about the raid on *Inner Circle Castle*.

The court hears that pictures of naked children, footage of bestiality and the date-rape drug *Rohypnol* were among items found during the search. He describes the masses of pornographic magazines exhibited throughout the house and tells the court how Prinsloo had tried to prevent police from finding the Red Album – the photo album containing about 300 pornographic photos. The Album, which would be kept under lock and key during the trial, contains damning evidence against the pair and would play an integral part in the trial.

During Cornelius' testimony, some of the accused in the so-called Boeremag treason trial sit in the gallery, curious about the first trial in years to command as much, if not more, media attention than their own, long-running case. The 21 men are on trial on an array of charges pertaining to a failed plot to overthrow the Government. Some of the bizarre evidence coming out of their case includes an Afrikaner breeding camp, where pure-bred Afrikaner women would be kept in a facility for the sole purpose of having babies. I'm still not sure what a pure-bred Afrikaner is – seeing as the cultural group is made up of the progeny of several different nationalities.

Soon after Cornelius starts giving evidence, the Defence objects to the State's use of the Red Album as an exhibit – arguing that save for 12 photographs, the other images bear no relevance to the case. This turns into a heated argument – the first of many – and a considerable delay in Cornelius' testimony. When the Defence's argument is overruled and Judge Patel decides that the Red Album in its entirety is regarded as an exhibit, he also rules that the album is not deemed fit for any eyes apart from the Defence, the State and the Bench. It would be locked away in the Registrar's office and would only be hauled out if and when necessary.

Prinsloo jumps up several times during Cornelius' testimony, giving notes to his lawyers, or gesturing to them – prompting judge Patel to issue him a stern warning.

When Cornelius is questioned during cross examination, the first indication emerges of what would become a pattern. The Prinsloos' advocates use the opportunity to grill the Investigating Officer about the reason why the case is being heard in the High Court and not the Regional Court. Piet Coetzee, for Prinsloo, hypothesises that the matter was brought before the High Court in order to create maximum embarrassment for the accused and to sensationalise the case. Cornelius has nothing to do with the placement of the trial and Fourie objects to the question – an objection which is sustained by Patel. The next attack on the State witness is based on the fact that he is perspiring – a fact which Coetzee says proves that Cornelius is not comfortable. Although he does not go as far as to actually say it, he seems to be insinuating that the investigating officer is lying.

The Defence directly accuses Cornelius of lying in the affidavit used to obtain the search warrant. In a tirade against the investigating officer, Coetzee accuses him of bungling the case, overstepping his powers and feeding information to the media in an attempt to sensationalise the case and vilify Prinsloo and Visser. Judge Patel eventually has to step in – warning Coetzee that he will not allow the trial to be used as a forum to discredit the police. Patel points out that there are other avenues to follow if the accused really have a problem with the police's conduct – including a trial within a trial.

Coetzee then attacks Jeannine's integrity and credibility – asking Cornelius if he is aware that she had, on a previous occasion, pressed charges against another couple and later admitted she had done so to blackmail them. He also asks the investigating officer if he knew of Jeannine's alleged involvement in child prostitution, claiming that she had abused drugs and had displayed behavioural problems. Cornelius replies that he had heard such rumours but that he had no factual knowledge of the claims. Visser's lawyer, Gerhard Botha, accuses Cornelius of trying to trick her into turning State witness against Prinsloo.

The next witness to take the stand is Senior Superintendent Rudi van Olst – a career policeman with a no-nonsense approach. Although very courteous, Van Olst has never, in all the years I've known him, given the media the slightest morsel of information – despite my best efforts at coaxing even the seemingly most insignificant confirmation out of him. His integrity and reputation ensured him a plum job in the private sector after he left the SAPS.

Van Olst testifies about the day of the raid on Prinsloo's home. To the scribes in the public gallery, his evidence is not exactly riveting – but building a case in court is about meticulous attention to detail, something that includes the less interesting aspects of an investigation.

Despite his rather boring testimony, the Defence guns for him – making a big fuss about the police's supposed violation of Prinsloo and Visser's rights. Prinsloo's advocate accuses police of tipping off reporters – a point which Van Olst had to concede, probably much to his own chagrin, considering his less than fraternal relationship with the media. Coetzee also suggests – although once again he would not say it outright – that the police could have planted evidence on the scene. He points out to Van Olst that there is no video footage of the period when officers found the dagga confiscated from Prinsloo's home.

Upon Coetzee's insistence, cross-examination is halted in order for the Court to watch the almost eight hour-long video footage of the raid. He is trying to point out what the Defence considers to be discrepancies in the SAPS' procedural behaviour on the day of the couple's arrest. Judge Patel, his assessors, the prosecution and defence teams, the two advocates in the dock and the assortment of people in the public gallery sit through eight hour-long video tapes – not exactly riveting stuff – with some of the 'highlights' in the video portraying police officials guffawing and snickering like teenage boys over the piles of openly displayed porn in the house.

Although not altogether the epitome of professionalism, I think their reaction was the result of shock rather than pubescent excitement at the find. Prinsloo is shown tagging after the policemen throughout the search in his shorts and a T-shirt, grumbling from time to time. At one point he can be heard tearing into Jeannine, at others he's silencing his dog, Boesman.

Visser keeps her eyes downcast as the camera zooms in on the hordes of open porn magazines in their bedroom. She appears to be making notes when the hordes of pornographic magazines are shown. During the most explicit parts of the footage, Susan abruptly leaves the courtroom with two other women who had been sitting by her side.

Despite the fact that the videos are shown at the Defence's insistence, Coetzee objects to the screening of footage taken during the confiscation of the Red Album. Judge Patel lambastes him for his audacity to object to an exhibit he himself had introduced, while Fourie can hardly contain his delight as he tells the court that *"the Defence had gone on a fishing trip and, now that they had caught a shark, they are complaining."*

Patel overrules the objection – but when the footage in question is shown, the media contingent strains fruitlessly to make out the images. The shots were taken from so far away and scanned over the album so quickly, that no detail is discernible.

Before the court wades through the last three hours of the footage,

Judge Patel orders the police witnesses who would still be called, to watch it in their own time – saying *"It would be like watching the movie Titanic 20 times over"* if the exercise had to be repeated. He wipes aside the Defence's protest that it would be unprocedural for the witnesses to be shown the tapes without an attorney being present – saying he would not allow the Court to be dictated to. Patel makes it clear that he wants the trial sped up and will tolerate no more delays.

Shortly after this stern warning, it becomes evident that more time would be needed to complete the hearing. At the time, though, it is thought that three months would be sufficient.

Superintendent Daleen du Plessis is the next State Witness to be called. Prinsloo and Du Plessis have had altercations in the past, with the advocate laying a complaint against the policewoman, resulting in departmental charges being brought against her. The complaint related to a disagreement they had had when Prinsloo was not satisfied with the outcome of investigations into criminal charges he had registered at the police station where Du Plessis headed the detective unit.

Du Plessis is a fascinating woman. Like Visser she is blonde, tall, slim and attractive. In contrast to Visser, however, she is a woman of extremely good moral character with very strong opinions of right and wrong. She is a stickler for procedure and tends to follow it without compromise. She has an uncanny ability to see right through people – which contributes to her being an exceptional interrogator – and is extremely difficult to manipulate. This is, in all probability, the reason why Prinsloo perceived her as a threat. Laurie says of Du Plessis: *"In all the time I have known Daleen I have never known her to tolerate any form of nonsense from anyone, and although her attitudes have not made her popular they have earned her my respect. She would have been more than a match for Prinsloo at any level."*

Coetzee informs the policewoman under cross-examination that Prinsloo will testify that she had begged him to withdraw the complaint as it hampered her promotion – a statement she vehemently denies. Coetzee then accuses her of re-opening an attempted murder investigation against Prinsloo out of spite – which she also denies.

Next in the State's arsenal of witnesses is Captain Nicolas Coetser, a narcotics investigator, followed by computer expert Danny Myburgh. Apart from a very detailed description of the forensic investigation conduced to extract evidence from the computers confiscated at Prinsloo's home, the only aspects of interest in Myburgh's testimony are the 177 e-mail messages to porn sites – saved under the file *"naughty mails"* – and the array of porn websites accessed from one of the computers. These included *"Lolita's Sex Portal," "Best Links To Real Free Photos," "Bestiality Live," "Banned Illegal Porn Site"* and *"Cannabise's Pamela Anderson-Lee Website."* Myburgh also testifies that the computer had been used on more than one occasion to visit websites apparently containing child pornography. The principal registered user of the computer was "Dirk."

It is a *Beeld* newspaper columnist who is responsible for the next delay in the case. Both the Defence and the State object to the opinion piece – but for different reasons. Visser's advocate, Gerhard Botha, complains about the *"Advocate Barbie"* nickname, saying his client objected to being likened to the busty blonde plastic doll. He also protests about the comparison between Visser and Sara Baartman – the Khoi woman forced into display in Europe for her physical appearance. Botha says his client has adopted a fatalistic approach to the media coverage of the trial, saying she is used to being persecuted by journalists. I could comment on how she adored the media before their arrest, but I will leave it to the readers to draw their own conclusions.

Fourie objects to the column, saying it amounts to contempt of court. He complains about references in the newspaper piece about Visser being handcuffed in court, which is not true. There is also an incorrect mention of *"pornographic videos"* being shown in court daily. The author, Jeanne Goosen, a freelance columnist, refers to a 14-year-old girl (Jeannine) allegedly raped by Visser and Prinsloo – saying the girl had had a history of prostitution and drug abuse. Fourie argues that this is an attack on the character of a witness and implies that it is acceptable for a 14-year-old to be sexually molested if she is a prostitute or drug addict. Goosen refers to the trial as a medieval funfair where perverts could indulge their fantasies *ad infinitum* – which Fourie feels is a direct reflection on the Court.

Judge Patel orders Goosen and *Beeld* editor, Peet Kruger, to appear in court to explain the article – and the wrong information it contains. He also orders the police to investigate a charge of contempt of court against the columnist and the newspaper. The paper's lawyers contest the congruency of the summons – which they interpret as a summary inquiry – together with the criminal investigation, saying there is no provision under the law for a person to be subjected to both on the same charge. Goosen and Kruger invoke their right to silence, requesting Patel to leave the matter in the hands of the prosecuting authority. Fourie agrees that a summary enquiry is not the correct way in which to deal with the issue – but says that Patel should at least admonish the two newspaper hacks.

Less than a day later, the media is in the dock again – this time due to the publication of a nude picture of Prinsloo and Visser in the tabloid *Die Son*. The picture on page three shows the two naked, with Prinsloo leaning his head against Visser's surgically enhanced bosom while clutching her buttocks. The Defence urges the Court to summons the publication and order it to reveal its source – intimating that the State had leaked the photo to the media.

Prosecutor Jennifer Cronjé has a field day with this claim – saying the two advocates have themselves widely distributed the photo in question as well as several others and are now trying to pretend that they were victimised by the State. When the Defence wants to withdraw its application to force *Die Son* to reveal its source, the Court hears that an out-of-court settlement has been reached with the publication.

The trial is postponed to later in the year and the six-month break brings big changes in the two lovebirds' relationship. Visser apparently finds a long black hair on her lover's pillow at his home in Bela-Bela. Despite the fact that he regularly had sex with other women and that she more often than not provided the third parties, this evidence of infidelity seemingly upsets her to such an extent that she breaks off the liaison.

Having rid herself of her co-accused and lover, Visser does what most women in her situation do – she cuts her hair. She also has her surgically enhanced bosom deflated and starts the long, expensive and laborious process to have, at least some, of her tattoo's removed. She now lives permanently with her mother, who helps her find the courage to stand up to Prinsloo – who alternates between pleas and threats in his attempts to win her back.

When the case resumes, the split is immediately obvious. The two former lovers arrive at court separately and sit metres apart in the dock – in sharp contrast to their earlier appearances when they sat huddled closely together and could often be seen whispering to each other. The break also sees the accused both appoint new lawyers. Prinsloo is no longer paying Visser's legal bills and has appointed an advocate from Bloemfontein, Philip Loubser, to represent him.

When the trial resumes after the break, social worker Marlene Malan tells the Court exactly how traumatised the two Bramley girls were after their respective visits to the Prinsloos. She confirms that Visser, who introduced herself as "Mrs Prinsloo," pretended to be married in order to gain access to the two children.

The Court hears that the two girls were identified for placement with the advocate couple based purely on their physical appearance and that Visser was not interested in providing any assistance other than having the girls stay for weekends at her and Prinsloo's home.

Malan says the pair never invited 15-year-old Anja back and pressurised Bramley officials to release the younger girl into their care. The older girl did not report anything untoward until asked about her weekend after 11-year-old Charmaine had reported her experiences. The social worker tells the Court that Bramley officials reported the matter to the Commissioner of the Children's Court and warned other children's homes not to allow the two advocates access to the children in their care. Malan says she was wary of reporting the couple to the Child Protection Unit because of their high profiles and legal knowledge. She also did not want to subject the children to the trauma of testifying – but, she says, when it later emerged that Visser had apparently also approached other children's homes and a place of safety for girls to take home, she realised she had to do something.

During cross-examination, Prinsloo's legal team again questions the integrity of the two girls – but this is quickly nipped in the bud by the Judge, who also refuses permission when the Defence again requests access to the girls' personal files. Prinsloo argues the files are of crucial importance as they might verify his claim that Charmaine had previously accused other people of similar crimes.

Patel tears into Prinsloo – saying he is embarking on a fishing expedition. The Judge also lashes out at him for not disclosing where he heard rumours of the previous charges the girl had opened – saying the Defence is tarnishing the children's reputation even before they had given evidence.

Malan's evidence is corroborated by Bramley house mother, Veronica Sheppard, and the children's home manager, Martie Booyse, who both tell the Court how, first Charmaine and then Anja broke down and told them about their experiences at the Prinsloo home. Booyse also gives evidence that Visser confessed after she was confronted with the children's accusations – testimony which goes unchallenged by Visser's advocate, Casper Badenhorst.

His former mistress' failure to challenge this apparent damning evidence against her, prompts Prinsloo to apply to have their trials separated. He argues that she is in effect pleading guilty, to the detriment of his own defence. He also accuses Visser of trying to implicate him because of her own *"ulterior motives."* Prinsloo then wants to take the stand to present evidence about the break-up between himself and Visser.

When Judge Patel questions the prudence of such a move, Loubser tells the Court that when Visser ended her relationship with Prinsloo she accused him of abuse, intimidation and harassment – and demanded a substantial amount of money from him.

Patel turns down Prinsloo's application to have his trial separated from Visser's – saying it would be a waste of time, talent and resources and would be onerous and burdensome to the witnesses, who would have to testify twice. Loubser insists on a special entry into the record, claiming that the finding is irregular and not according to law. Such a special entry paves the way to an appeal – and, had things worked out differently, Prinsloo would undoubtedly have tried to use it in an appeal, had he been convicted. However, Patel refuses the special entry – and lambasts Prinsloo for abusing the legal process. The small man in the red robes accuses Prinsloo of impeding the trial with frivolous applications, saying it illustrates his bad intentions (*mala fides*).

Outside the courtroom, Visser's every move is being monitored by newshounds. Sunday newspaper *Rapport* is left with egg on its face after it publishes an article, romantically linking her to a man who turns out to be her church minister. The paper publishes a picture of Visser and the *"mystery blond man"* walking together, saying they were cooing intimately and smiling lovingly at each other in court. In response to the article, the Dutch Reformed Church rushes to her (and

Dominee Johan Claasen's) defence in a media statement, saying that Claasen is assisting Visser on a spiritual level with the full knowledge and support of his wife and colleagues.

The next witness to take the stand is Riana Brink. She's allowed to testify in camera because of the sexual nature of her complaint against them.

Fourie takes Riana through her evidence, starting from the day she met Prinsloo and Visser and what her job entailed. The woman tells the Court how Prinsloo helped her win a nasty custody battle – and how, once he started to get abusive, she couldn't leave as being employed was one of the prerequisites of her being granted custody of her daughter. The woman describes how Visser took her to have her private parts waxed and told Prinsloo, upon their arrival back home, that he should see the results of the treatment. She also went to great lengths to explain the impact Prinsloo's violent behaviour towards her had had on her.

While their former secretary is testifying, Prinsloo apparently runs out of money and indicates that he wants to apply for Legal Aid Board representation. He asks that he be allowed to bring this application behind closed doors but Patel turns the application down, saying he will not be party to a media gag. Reporters, who were hanging around the courtroom for any scrap of news, file in and Prinsloo has no choice but to tell an open court that he can no longer afford his legal bills. Visser also applies for Legal Aid before the case continues behind closed doors again as the cross-examination of the complainant is resumed.

Prinsloo pulls no punches when he cross-examines his former secretary – and often has to be reined in by the Judge. When her evidence is complete and the court is opened to the public – and the media – again, the advocate applies to have the rest of the trial be heard in camera, claiming he is being subjected to *"emotional turmoil and defamation by the media."* He claims media reporting had influenced witnesses, led to gossip among Pretoria advocates and turned *"judicial sentiment"* against him. Prinsloo complains about the presence of the Press pack in court, accusing the State of being *"in cahoots"* with journalists and of tipping off reporters about developments in the case.

When the State objects to the trial continuing behind closed doors, an increasingly animated and agitated Prinsloo claims his right to dignity is being trampled on and says he has not received a fair hearing so far. Again, Judge Patel turns down his application – saying he cannot prevent journalists from doing their jobs. The only exception to this would remain the evidence of the victims – who would continue to testify behind closed doors.

It is during this time in the trial when Prinsloo explodes one day and has a screaming match with Fourie. The incident is sparked when Prinsloo's Legal Aid Board-appointed advocate, Pieter Moolman – his fourth since the trial began – refuses to continue with the case. At the same time, the social worker testifies that one of the teenage witnesses was so traumatised by her experiences and the delays in the trial that she did not want to come to court. Fourie and Prinsloo exchange harsh words before Moolman's announcement that he'd had enough. The stand-off leads to an adjournment and in the passageway outside court an angry exchange could be heard, followed by a call from Fourie to a court orderly to remove Prinsloo.

Patel returns to the bench as the angry parties storm in with Prinsloo, standing in the dock, telling the court he wants to place it on record that Fourie said to him: *"I am tired of your fucking shit"* and *"You will not tell me which fucking witnesses to call."* Patel admonishes Prinsloo for swearing – but it takes three attempts from the Judge before it dawns on Prinsloo that he is being reprimanded for using foul language. Patel tries to calm down tempers in the courtroom but Prinsloo refuses to accept Fourie's apology – repeating his view that he is being persecuted and not prosecuted.

After the court closes for the December recess, Prinsloo brings an urgent application before Acting Judge Mahomed Ishmael to amend his bail conditions. Moolman – who is somehow convinced to continue representing Prinsloo – tells the court that his client wants permission to go to Russia on a business trip. As part of his argument, Moolman states – much to the surprise of both the Prosecution and the Police – that Prinsloo has already been abroad twice that year and has returned to stand trial on both occasions. When Ishmael questions where the money for Prinsloo's trips came from – after the advocate has pleaded poverty and applied for Legal Aid – Moolman tells him Prinsloo's father paid for the tickets to Russia and the Ukraine to help his son explore business opportunities.

Fourie vehemently opposes the application – telling the court that Prinsloo, who recently sold his property in Bela-Bela, no longer has any ties to South Africa, except the trial hanging over his head. Prinsloo again protests his innocence and tells the Court that he will definitely return to South Africa to stand trial, as he was wrongfully accused and wants to clear his name. The Judge decries the apparent abuse of the Legal Aid Board but – despite the State's vehement opposition – grants Prinsloo's request and increases his bail from R4 000 to R20 000.

During the break – and with Prinsloo now completely out of her life – Visser resumes her efforts to get her life back on track. Her mother contacts a sexologist to treat her warped sense of what normal sexuality entails – and soon a relationship between the older woman and the self-proclaimed 'sex professor' starts to bloom.

The Legal Aid Board also decides to withdraw its aid to Prinsloo – arguing he is not indigent and therefore does not qualify for State-funded assistance. Prinsloo undertakes another trip to Russia in the meantime, after convincing yet another Judge that he will return to stand trial by claiming that if he should fail to return, it will be an admission of guilt – and seeing as he is innocent, he will not confess to something he didn't do.

When the date for the resumption of the trial arrives, Prinsloo stalls the State in calling one of the teenage girls who was to testify against him. Indicating that he wants to challenge the Legal Aid Board's decision to withdraw its funding, Moolman – who is acting without payment – applies for a postponement.

Prinsloo then questions the objectivity of the Judge and reveals that he will bring an application to have Judge Essop Patel recuse himself. To support this, Moolman presents an affidavit from another High Court Judge, Abraham van Rensburg, in which Van Rensburg states Patel's continued involvement in the trial will be prejudicial to Prinsloo. The resultant legal wrangling leads to another postponement – with Patel making it clear that he is growing increasingly frustrated with the slow pace of the case. He accuses Prinsloo of using delaying tactics and issues a warning that he will not tolerate any further delays.

Two weeks later, complete pandemonium breaks out in court when Prinsloo fails to show up. While the Defence and Prosecution confer, Visser paces up and down outside the courtroom, shaking her head and looking clearly upset.

Moolman tells the court that he received a phone call from Prinsloo three days ago, informing him that he is in Russia and does not plan to return to South Africa. A shocked Patel issues an order that Prinsloo's bail be forfeited to the State if he does not show up within 14 days – but more importantly, an international arrest warrant is issued by Interpol.

The "wanted person notice" issued by Interpol is upgraded within 48 hours and Prinsloo's name is circulated on the so-called "Red Notice" – which is not exactly an international arrest warrant, but seeks the arrest of wanted persons with a view to extradition. At the time, the police vow to have Prinsloo – whom they describe as a dangerous sex offender – back behind bars soon.

Visser is visibly disturbed by the news that her former lover and "sex god" has left her to face the music alone. Despite her protestations of innocence, she admitted to Cornelius during their initial incarceration that she and Prinsloo had committed crimes – and she was now going to have to stand alone in the dock. The stress and tension of the case, combined with Prinsloo's disappearance, cause Visser to have an emotional breakdown and she is placed on anti-depressants. The trial is adjourned for two weeks to give her time to recover.

When the matter resumes, the case against Prinsloo continues *in absentia*. Anja and Charmaine testify *in camera*, outlining their ordeal at the Prinsloo house. Charmaine tells the court of the pervasive sense of fear she experienced the entire weekend she spent with the couple. Visser insisted on having the pre-pubescent girl over, despite Marlene Malan's reluctance at letting the girl spend a weekend with the advocate couple. Visser had waited until Malan went on holiday and then simply booked the child out for a visit. Anja tells the court in detail how scared she was by the advocate couple's strange questions and sexual behaviour in her presence. She testifies how she ran to the guestroom in shock and prayed for protection against the couple.

Then Samantha Olivier takes the stand. She tells the Court she could only remember flashes after she had been given shooters by Visser.

Then Jeannine has the opportunity to face the woman who betrayed and sexually exploited her. The teenager has been in and out of rehab countless times since her visit to *Inner Circle Castle*. Although Visser and Prinsloo are not solely responsible for Jeannine's spiral into prostitution and drugs, the fact that they were willing to first groom and then drug and possibly rape a girl who had obviously already been through the wringer, illustrates the absolute callousness, contempt and calculated intent with which the couple had treated their victims.

Next up in the witness stand is Marie, Jeannine's mother. She tells the court that she allowed her daughter to go with Visser despite the rumours about pornography at the Prinsloo house and the claims that other girls, who had visited the couple, may have been molested. She says Visser convinced her that there was no truth in the rumours and that the pornography at their home was limited to the bedroom. The court hears how Visser slammed the phone down several times on Marie when she called to find out why her daughter had not been returned the next morning as promised. The woman testifies that when the girl was finally brought home, she was very tired and disoriented and slept the entire day.

After being kept under lock and key since the trial commenced, the Red Album is finally hauled out. A Paediatric endocrinologist is asked to determine the ages of girls depicted in two photographs found in the album as well as ten photos downloaded from the Internet and found on a computer in Prinsloo's office. Dr David Segal, whose field of specialisation includes growth, ageing and development, testifies that some of the photos found in Prinsloo and Visser's possession may have depicted girls as young as five. Segal testifies that both black girls on the photos in the album appear to be under 18, with one of them probably between 12 and 16 and the other in the region of 14 – although, he says, it is possible that she could have been an adult. These two girls were never found, despite Cornelius' best efforts.

While the wheels of justice continue to turn for his former mistress, Prinsloo remains on the run – despite the Interpol arrest warrant.

20.
TAKING A STAND
LAURIE'S STORY
PART III

After the medical expert's evidence, Laurie is called to the stand:
The eight years that it took to secure a conviction against Cézanne Visser would keep me on an emotional rollercoaster ride. I would go through peaks and troughs of sympathising with her and detesting her. I would berate myself for not being a better judge of character and then forgive myself because both Dirk and Cézanne proved themselves to be consummate liars.

Often, I thought back to my initial interview with Dirk and shudder to think about what hidden meanings were behind his question on what I thought about sex. I thought of my 'adults behind closed doors' reply, and remembered that people – including children – had been hurt. I often wondered if there was anything I could have done to prevent or even only minimise the damage wreaked by the sex-crazed advocates.

My interest in human behaviour and, more specifically, criminal behaviour was piqued. I was thrilled when I found out that UNISA was offering a new specialist degree in Offender Profiling. I knew with a certainty that I had never felt before that this was the degree that I wanted to do and signed up in early 2003 – a decision I would never regret. I was fascinated by the subject matter and applied it daily in all my experiences. The news became interesting and not merely depressing. I found myself soaking up knowledge like a sponge. I had never been a great student at school but I had never really been interested in what I was studying. Now I was consumed.

My best friend, Celeste, was studying Psychology at the time and many of our subjects overlapped. As a profiling student I was required to do majors in Psychology and Criminology, with a number of policing and criminal law modules to round off the degree. Celeste and I spent many hours discussing the psychological aspects of the Visser case and neither of us could understand how a woman, least of all an intelligent woman, could do what she had done, especially to little kids. Perhaps it was the fact that we both had young kids that made it even harder for us to understand.

I was terribly nervous when I took the stand to testify against Cézanne for the first time. I had never had to testify about intimate details before. Gritting my teeth, determined to stay calm, I knew what I would have to say would be embarrassing. I would tell the truth, no matter what. The prosecutors had warned me to keep my narrative brief and to speak loudly and clearly. This is not very easy to do when you are so nervous you want to throw up!

To be honest, I barely remember testifying before Judge Patel. It was the most horrible experience of my life. I answered the questions that were thrown at me – most of which revolved around the false affidavit I had been asked to sign and the circumstances around which it had been brought to me to sign. Then there were questions about how Cézanne and Dirk had related to each other and to me while I was employed by them. I was also asked why I had resigned and had to tell the Court about the underwear. It was most embarrassing.

Cézanne remained stone-faced throughout my testimony. She appeared to be disassociated from the proceedings and her expression never changed the whole time I was on the stand. She just stared ahead. I felt really sorry for her; she honestly seemed a bit broken, a far cry from the girl that had been Prinsloo's little *"stukkie"* a few years before. Gone was the vibrant Cézanne Visser "Sex-Goddess" and in her place sat a cold and sad-looking woman who seemed to have been chewed up and spat out by life. Paradoxically, a part of me wanted her to be acquitted but another part wanted justice for the children she had hurt.

I remember the wave of nausea that washed over me when I stepped down from the witness box. The world spun and I realised that I had better get myself to the bathroom in a hurry. Once there, I threw up, thinking that I never ever wanted to do this in my life again. I knew that I had done the right thing, having told the truth. Still, I felt dirty being in the same room with Cézanne, now that I had gained insight into her life. Perhaps, I had wanted her to talk to me – to apologise for what she had tried to do to me. She seemed unapologetic and I came to regard her as being bereft of any conscience.

I returned to my studies and obtained my BA Community Safety and Socio-Legal Studies degree, *cum laude*, with specialisation in Offender Profiling from UNISA in 2006. The following year, I registered for a few law modules because I needed a break from Criminology. The next two years would be spent gaining some experience in the field, applying what I had learned in day-to-day practice. I did a course in Veracity Testing (lie detection) and one in Investigative Body Language and got involved in corporate investigations meeting some wonderful people along the way.

I learned more about human behaviour on a daily basis and it was fascinating. I was picking up on subtle cues that indicated deception, that were not visible to me in the past. Slowly but surely I was becoming more skilled at employing the techniques that I had learned. I enjoyed interviewing and interrogation and took pleasure in my work. It was very satisfying to be able to successfully close many of the cases in which I had been involved.

21.
THE WHEELS OF JUSTICE TURN ... SLOWLY

The last witness to take the stand is Dr De Vos, who was on duty at Wilgers Hospital in October 2001 when Mercia Jacobs was brought to the hospital. After he explains his treatment of and concerns for Mercia after seeing the state she was in emotionally, he tells the court how Prinsloo phoned him and fished for information.

The State then formally withdraws one of the charges against Visser – one of sexually exploiting a minor. It's claimed that the former couple had "hired" the underage girl's sexual services for more than a year and that both Visser and Prinsloo had engaged in sexual encounters with her – including penetration. Fourie decided he could not risk putting her on the stand as she was completely addicted to heroin and would not make a reliable witness.

When the prosecutor closes the State's case, Visser's Legal Aid Board-appointed advocate declines to call any witnesses. Visser does not take the stand as expected and her case, too, is closed – without even the slightest semblance of a defence. The case is postponed for a few weeks to give both parties time to prepare their final arguments. In this time, Visser has a change of heart and fires her legal team. With the financial assistance of her mother, she hires top criminal advocate, Johan Engelbrecht.

Engelbrecht has a reputation for being hard as nails in the courtroom, but he has a softer side – which I've seen manifest in several cases where he appeared *pro bono*. The elderly advocate, however, keeps this side of him completely under wraps when he appears in court. He has the habit of putting on an extremely annoying, nasal voice when he cross examines a witness and one of my earliest memories of him was when he ripped a police official to shreds on the witness stand in a voice which could shatter steel. The official and his colleagues were accused by the Defence of concocting evidence against and assaulting a panel beater who killed his pregnant wife by cutting her throat.

From what I could understand at the time, Engelbrecht waived his fee because he truly believed the man was innocent. The court disagreed and the panel beater was convicted and sentenced to 22 years behind bars. To this day, when I think of Engelbrecht, I can hear the nasal, sarcastic voice he used during his cross-examination. Thankfully, he did not repeat this tactic too often during the sex crimes trial.

When the case resumes for final argument, Engelbrecht is not available, as he is busy with another high profile case – much to the chagrin of Judge Patel. With her hair cut shoulder length and dressed in a businesslike pin-striped trouser suit, Visser – now the picture of sophistication – asks for the matter to stand down. In an affidavit, she gives an inkling of the new strategy she is planning to pursue under Engelbrecht's council, claiming she only danced to Prinsloo's tune regarding her defence because he paid her legal fees.

Until their relationship was terminated in 2005, Visser says, she was forced to abide by Prinsloo's rules and wishes because she was financially dependent on him. She also tells the Court she closed her case on the recommendation of her previous defence team – but that she's unhappy with the Legal Aid Board-appointed advocate and the advice he has given her.

Patel reluctantly allows the matter to stand down to the next day – but makes it clear that Engelbrecht has got off on the wrong foot by failing to appear in court himself. Patel accuses the Defence of again reverting to delay tactics and asks that the Bar Council investigate how Engelbrecht could have accepted a brief from Visser, knowing that he had another matter at the same time.

The next day, Engelbrecht applies for a postponement, saying he needs time to read the record of the proceedings and to obtain reports from experts. He also wants to get hold of evidence in the case, including copies of the Red Album. Engelbrecht indicates that the Defence is to reconsider its position – which could include reopening the case so that Visser could take the stand and tell her side of the story.

Explaining the new approach he intends to pursue, Engelbrecht tells the court the defence intends to rely on the so-called *"Battered Woman Syndrome"* (BWS) to justify the allegations levelled against Visser. This includes calling in a host of expert witnesses on the subject, including psychiatrists, to give the Court insight into the relationship between Visser and Prinsloo. Engelbrecht says everything boils down to the fact that Visser had been totally under Prinsloo's control. Patel questions the validity of such a defence – yet nevertheless postpones the matter to later that month in order for Engelbrecht to convince him to allow it.

Patel also makes a very polite request to the members of the media to stop referring to Visser as an advocate – after he questions whether she could still use the title. Engelbrecht tells him in reply that Visser has had herself removed from the roll of advocates and is no longer an Officer of the Court. Courtroom reporters duly abided by Patel's "request" and stop using the title in their daily accounts of the Court drama – yet the "Advocate Barbie" moniker is impossible to shake. To this day, when someone mentions Visser's name in conversation, people are a bit slow to respond – until they hear "Advocate Barbie." I believe even the warders at the female section of the Pretoria Local prison call Visser "Barbie."

"Advocate Barbie" at a children's prize giving (2002)

Dirk Prinsloo post arrest in Belarus (2009)

Cézanne at her matric farewell (1995)

The happy Prinsloos (2002)

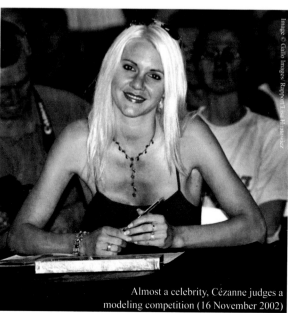

Almost a celebrity, Cézanne judges a modeling competition (16 November 2002)

An emaciated Jeannine du Plessis on another downward spiral (4 August 2005)

Cézanne Visser pouts at Inner Circle Castle (2001)

A cheeky "Advocate Barbie" peeks at the
camera during a modelling photo shoot (2002)

Dirk Prinsloo in his cell in a Belarusian court shortly before
being sentenced to 13 years behind bars for attempted robbery of a bank (2010)

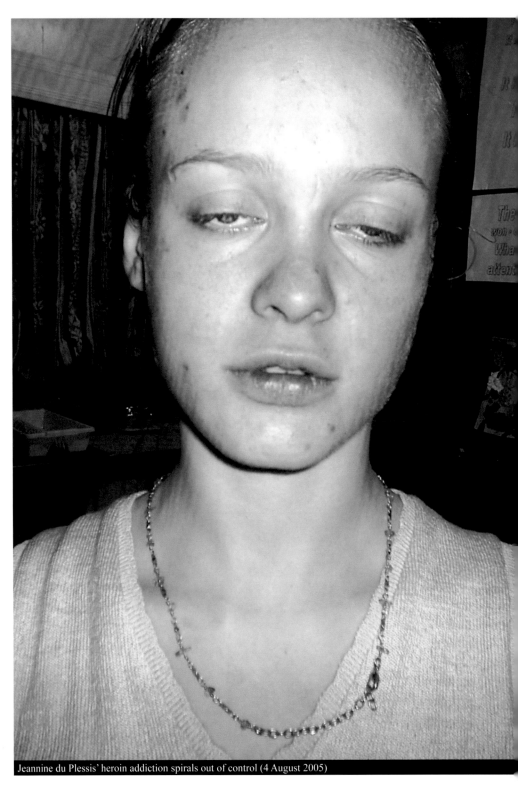

Jeannine du Plessis' heroin addiction spirals out of control (4 August 2005)

Jeannine and her daughter (2009)

Cézanne Visser graduates Cum Laude (2000)

"Advocate Barbie's" poor breast augmentation clearly visible (2002)

"Advocate Barbie" dressed for the dungeon (2002)

The Prinsloos still a confident team outside the Pretoria High Court (10 May 2002)

The quintessential blonde (2002)

Public prosecutor, Andre Fourie, talks to the media after Cézanne's successful prosecution (17 May 2010)

"Innocence" personified (2002)

One of the less dangerous toys that Cézanne played with (2002)

The tearful former advocate in the Pretoria High Court during sentencing procedures (24 February 2010)

When Engelbrecht appears before Patel again, he says after his consultations with Visser he has no doubt that she was the victim of "domestic abuse" and "coercive control" at the hands of Prinsloo. The Defence applies for Visser's trial to be reopened so that she can testify and call expert witnesses to testify on her behalf. Engelbrecht says that if she is allowed to reopen her case and testify, Visser will tell the Court that some of the photos in the Red Album were taken after she had been given a drink by Prinsloo, after which she could not remember anything until the next morning. When she realised she had been beaten, Prinsloo confessed he had inflicted the blows and, when asked why, told her it was because she had been "naughty."

Engelbrecht also tells the Court there were nude photos of two other women in the Red Album, showing similarities to the ones taken of Visser – indicating a pattern of abuse.

The Court hears that although the Supreme Court of Appeal does not regard *Battered Woman Syndrome* as a defence, it is considered to be a mitigating factor. Engelbrecht says there are indications it could be the basis of a proper defence against the charges Visser faced, which *"could result in an acquittal."* Visser's new legal team informs the Court that she has already consulted a psychiatrist and has stopped taking the anti-depressants and tranquillisers prescribed when she had her nervous breakdown after Prinsloo had absconded.

Fourie is not too keen for the Defence to reopen its case, having spent almost two years leading evidence, first against both accused and later against Visser alone. He insists that, if she is adamant to follow her new line of defence, Visser be sent to a State facility for observation. Fourie argues that, as the case relates directly to Visser's criminal capacity and her ability to distinguish between right and wrong, the best way to deal with the matter would be to refer her for a 30-day mental observation period at Pretoria's Weskoppies Psychiatric Hospital.

This, the prosecutor says, could give the Court the opportunity to hear an independent witness, other than the experts consulted by the Defence.

The suggestion of a stay in a State mental hospital seems to upset Visser to such an extent that Judge Patel at one stage warns her to stop grimacing while Fourie makes his submissions. Engelbrecht opposes the State's application, arguing it will serve no purpose to send Visser for observation at this stage, as she has no mental illness. This despite his earlier submissions that she suffers from post-traumatic stress and depression, caused by the domestic abuse and "coercive control" she suffered at the hands of Prinsloo.

Judge Patel grants Visser's application to have her case reopened – but orders her to go to Weskoppies Psychiatric Hospital for a month's mental observation. The Judge overrules the Defence's objections to having her admitted to a government facility, saying the State does not have the resources to appoint its own experts and there is no other mechanism which provides for a balanced observation of an accused by a panel of experts. He says such an inquiry and report will not only be to the benefit of Visser, but also in the interest of justice.

The panel, consisting of a State psychiatrist, two private psychiatrists and a psychologist with experience in the field of domestic abuse, has to determine if Visser is suffering from or had suffered from post-traumatic stress and depression and, if so, what the cause of it was. The experts also have to determine if, and to what extent, Visser had been subjected to domestic abuse and coercive control by her partner, what the impact had been on her and if it had impaired her judgment. The Court also wants them to determine if, at the time of committing the alleged crimes, Visser could not have been criminally responsible for her actions because of abuse, coercive control, post traumatic stress, depression or any other reason. Patel says he hopes the hospital visit will be beneficial to Visser and instructs the facility to maintain her privacy and dignity during her stay.

When she returns to court after her stay at Weskoppies, Visser, who wears a pink suit and pearl necklace, looks relaxed – but noticeably thinner. The hospital indicates the report on her mental state is not ready and psychiatrists need more time to prepare it. Patel grants the hospital 30 days to complete the evaluation but says it's not necessary for Visser to be detained in the facility as the report can be completed in her absence. The matter is postponed to March 2007 and Patel orders that this be the last delay in the matter. Ironically, it would be the last time he postpones the case – but not through any further delays brought on by the defence.

Towards the end of 2006, the Pretoria Society of Advocates brings an application in the High Court in Pretoria to have Prinsloo's name struck from the Roll of Advocates. The Society tells the court Prinsloo should be struck off the Roll because he misled the court, committed perjury, breached his bail conditions and fled the country while standing trial. The court hears that being a fugitive is reason enough to strike Prinsloo from the roll – but his conduct in the past during other cases where he appeared as counsel has contributed to him being regarded as a disgrace to the profession. In one case, he told a female advocate that she must *"go and get stuffed"* (*"gaan vlieg in jou moer in"*). When she became upset about this, he told her she was stupid and that she must *"get over it."* When she informed him she was going to report his conduct, he apparently told her he did not abide by rules.

In the same matter, which was before the Labour Court, Prinsloo apparently grossly overcharged a client to the tune of R1 500 per hour. During the Society's arguments many examples are given, as his peers argue that Prinsloo does not grasp the general rules of the legal profession. It is also brought to the court's attention that Prinsloo, in another matter, had submitted insalubrious and misleading affidavits.

When a colleague accused him of unethical conduct, Prinsloo accused him of being a homosexual – claiming the attorney was attracted to him and that their friendship had soured because he was tired of "*protecting his wickets.*"

Judge Willie van der Merwe grants the application, saying the fact that Prinsloo was an Officer of the Court was probably one of the factors the Court earlier took into consideration in allowing him to leave the country. He also refers to a judgment in the Labour Court in which a judge made comments regarding Prinsloo's conduct. At the time, Judge Landman said: "*He has not yet mastered his craft, although in time he will.*"

When Visser's trial resumes in March 2007, it is immediately postponed to the next month. Judge Essop Patel is battling cancer and is on sick leave. An even more emaciated Visser reports to the court on the due date – but the trial is again adjourned. Patel has still not recovered and the possibility that a new Judge will have to be appointed and the entire matter be heard from scratch is starting to look more and more likely. A day later, Patel dies.

Arrangements have to be made for another Judge to take over the sex crimes trial over which he had presided for more than two years.

In October 2007, a new indictment is served on Visser. Instead of the 15 charges she faced with Prinsloo, she now faces 14 charges, the one charge of rape falling away. The complainant, a prostitute who was only 14 years old when she was regularly hired by the Prinsloos has had a relapse in her drug addiction. Fourie does not want to put her through the ordeal of testifying – and of being subjected to cross examination.

A new trial date is set and it looks like the matter will finally be back on track by August 2008.

On the appointed day, the pattern of repeated delays continues. The court hears that Engelbrecht has been admitted to hospital after developing blood circulation problems. Engelbrecht, who has just concluded a stint in the Cape High Court, defending murder accused Najwa Petersen, would be out of action for six to eight weeks. A provisional date is set for October.

22.
THE SECOND TRIAL

The first time Visser appears before Acting Judge Chris Eksteen, in October 2008, she is wearing a black trouser suit. Eksteen took a tough stance against the sexual abuse of women and children earlier that year when he sentenced an HIV-positive man, who had raped his stepdaughter, to life in prison. He also sentenced seven-year-old Sheldean Human's killer, Andrew Jordaan, to life imprisonment – and has a reputation as a crusader against abuse of any kind, but particularly against the weak and vulnerable. With his bristly moustache and a demeanour to match, Eksteen would be the man to decide Visser's fate. He postpones the case to early in 2009 – making it clear that he will not tolerate any delays.

On 19 February 2009, wearing a striped, silky ivory and black blouse and black trousers, a more sophisticated and slightly plump Visser pleads not guilty to each of the 14 charges read out to her in Court – one charge less to the charge sheet she was served almost five years before.

After entering the same plea she did when she was still sharing the dock with her ex-lover, Visser made an array of admissions, including admitting the authenticity of 12 pictures in which she is posing naked and lasciviously with two girls. In a list of acknowledgments handed to Eksteen, the defence admits Exhibit 1 (the Red Album) and states: *"In 12 of the pictures the accused and two black girls are posing naked in the performance of sexual acts."*

While not admitting that she was aware of the child porn on her former lover's computer, she acknowledges that the Police had seized child porn at their home during their arrest. Other admissions include that the Police seized an array of medication, including *Rohypnol*. Visser also acknowledges that she had made a false statement in which she claimed that she was present when Mercia had oral sex with Prinsloo and that she consented to this. She now confesses she was not present at the time.

Engelbrecht outlines his strategy to the Court saying he will prove that his client was influenced to such an extent that she no longer had a will of her own – adding that her state of mind was not due to one single factor, but rather due to a number of factors. The parties agree that it might not be necessary to recall all the witnesses as Visser has already admitted their evidence. She, however, disputes parts of the testimony of three of the witnesses, including Charmaine and Jeannine.

The disputed evidence means that the two child victims – who are young women by now – would have to be recalled to testify. Charmaine and Jeannine relive their ordeal for a third time as they testify for the second time. Laurie is also recalled to the witness stand by the State. She tells the court that Visser ignored her repeated attempts to convince her to leave Prinsloo, saying she loved him, the sex was amazing and she was happy.

23.
BACK ON THE STAND
LAURIE'S STORY
PART IV

In 2009 I registered for my BA Honours in Criminology. That year, I passed two of the modules with distinction. Little did I realise how useful my newly acquired skills would be when I was called to testify against Cézanne for a second time. This time it was my own doing, I am afraid to say.

The newspapers were reporting that Cézanne was claiming she had been an innocent victim of Dirk Prinsloo and that she could not defend herself against him as she had no will of her own. She also claimed that she was suffering from *Battered Woman Syndrome* at the time that she had committed the crimes of which she stood accused. This, she claimed, was aimed at satisfying Dirk and keeping him happy.

I couldn't believe what I was reading. There had been nothing battered about the young woman whom I had met seven years before. What I saw was a financially motivated girl who enjoyed attention and would do anything to get it. I found it absolutely amazing to see how low this woman would stoop to avoid justice. Her chief motivations had always been fame and finances. What she was attempting was an insult to battered women all over the world. Why couldn't she just admit her crimes, take responsibility accept her punishment, pay her debt to society and move on? There were always excuses for everything she did, always someone else to blame. In my mind, she was no battered woman, she was just a greedy little child molester.

I remember her standing up to Dirk on many occasions. I remember a few serious arguments between the two of them and I distinctly remember her getting into her car right in the middle of one of them – tearing off down the driveway like a crazy person. She had definitely not been very submissive on that particular occasion. The "god" and his "goddess" had had a good go at each other that day and he walked around with a face like thunder for hours after she left, as he couldn't reach her on her cellphone.

BWS is not a defence under South African law, but may be considered in mitigation of sentence. I really couldn't understand why Cézanne, with her law degrees, would resort to such a strange defence, a defence which, in my view, was doomed to fail. Had she turned on Dirk Prinsloo and murdered him, she may have stood a better chance of succeeding. The BWS defence is commonly used in the United States when the abused partner turns on the batterer and either assaults or kills him in self-defence, or to escape the situation.

In contrast, Cézanne Visser went out, day and night, hunting for victims in the form of young women and children for Dirk Prinsloo and herself to abuse and indecently assault. Her actions were all aimed at satisfying and pleasing him.

I was so incensed by what I heard and read in the media that I phoned André Fourie to point out the obvious holes in the Defence's case. He asked me if I would be willing to testify again – and without thinking about it, I agreed.

Before I had to testify for the second time, many questions about Cézanne kept haunting me. Who and what was she really? What kind of person takes a 30-minute drive into town to choose a little girl at a children's home to take home for her partner to rape? How would any sane person manage to decide which child to take, knowing what the child would be put through when she got her home? How did she choose her victim – how could anyone choose? It would take a sick, twisted mind to make promises of fun to a broken little girl in a children's home and then take her home and rape her body and soul. How did one drive the thirty minutes home with that chosen child in the car with you, without turning around and rushing her back to safety? It was all so premeditated and calculated.

My second visit to the witness box was a little less daunting as I knew what to expect. I also knew that I was right – Cézanne Visser had not been a battered woman at the time she had committed the acts of which she stood accused. She was a spoilt young woman, who would do anything to please her lover and who revelled in his money and the gifts that he showered on her for pleasing him.

Cézanne was without morals and boundaries didn't exist for her at the time she committed her crimes. I also believed that she was lying to avoid a prison sentence – one which she richly deserved.

On the stand, I answered Fourie's questions about Cézanne and Dirk's way of relating to each other during the time that I knew them. She had never had a problem standing up to him as far as I could see. She was free to come and go as she pleased – he even provided her with transport. They argued and fought like any other couple. He could be a pain in the neck at times and was a bully with narcissistic traits – yet he knew how far he could push things.

It was very difficult to keep track of my testimony because the new judge, Judge Eksteen, wrote down everything I said. I had to speak very slowly so that he could do this. My nerves made me want to speak quickly so I had to focus on slowing down all the time. It was very funny in an odd way; the internal conflict was quite unsettling. Even though I did my best, there were times when I just had to finish the sentence, terrified I would forget what I was busy saying while the judge wrote down every word. He was very strict, but I liked him. I carefully watched the judge's writing hand, trying to make sure I wouldn't get ahead of him.

When I was finished answering Advocate Fourie's questions, Advocate Engelbrecht, appearing for Cézanne, requested a recess in his very irritating nasal voice. He said, *"My Lord we did not anticipate the nature of the testimony that was given by this witness, we request a recess until 2pm to prepare our cross examination."* I thought he looked a little rattled, but his request was granted and I had two-and-a-half hours to kill before returning to the stand.

Throughout my testimony, Cézanne Visser sat stony-faced, her mother flashing me looks that Medusa would have been proud of. I had probably just become her worst nightmare – someone who told the truth. After my testimony, I was surrounded by the press as soon as I left the building. Fortunately, Captain Cornelius was by my side and I asked him to drop me off at the Magistrate's Court where a friend of mine worked at the Family Court section.

It had been a while since we had seen each other and I really needed to see a friendly face before I had to go back on the stand and face Advocate Engelbrecht.

Talking to John has always had a very calming influence on me; he was just a really good guy and a good cop and always knew exactly how to make me feel better about things. It felt wonderful to have a normal conversation with a normal person in what had been a very abnormal day. He offered to drop me off at the High Court after lunch. As I got out, he wished me luck, telling me to stay strong and just tell the truth – advice I followed to the letter that afternoon.

As I steeled myself for Advocate Engelbrecht's attack, I looked over at Cézanne again. She was still avoiding eye contact and her expression hadn't changed. She looked like an inhuman, emotionless doll. I was looking for a sign of humanity and there just wasn't one. I could visualise this stone creature hurting children because she came across as heartless, totally devoid of emotion.

Advocate Engelbrecht could not have had a more negative effect on me if he had tried. The nasal tone of his voice was hideous, an assault on my eardrums. It was uncomfortable having to listen to him and he irritated every fibre of my being. He droned on and I answered his questions – which weren't really questions at all but rather statements which required yes and no answers such as: *"So, Mr Prinsloo is a narcissist. Is that correct?"* (His actual pronunciation was something like this: *"Saao, Mr Prinsloo is a na-arcisist. Ees that coo-rek?"*) I felt he was trying to intimidate me with his drawn out, nasal intonation as it was not the voice he used to address the Judge.

It seemed as if he wanted me to agree with him, mindless like a puppet on a string. Unfortunately for him I wasn't a puppet and I didn't like his bullying approach. The more he irritated me the more I wanted to stick it to him. I found myself disagreeing with him on principle. Sadly, for his client, he was wrong anyway. The scenarios that he put forward to me were not what I had seen or experienced when it came to the way that Dirk and Cézanne had interacted with each other.

Somewhere during his cross-examination Engelbrecht hauled out a photograph of a naked Cézanne standing next to another woman. I had never seen her before. I was asked if I recognised the people in the photograph. I answered that I recognised Cézanne. He then informed me that the other woman in the picture was Riana Brink. He then went on to read a sentence or two from Riana's testimony in which she said, *"...one never said no to Dirk Prinsloo, no matter what!"* Then he asked me *"If Dirk told you to do something, you just did it. No questions asked? Is that correct?"* I answered, *"Not in my opinion."*

With that, the Judge asked me my opinion. I replied that if Dirk Prinsloo had told me to take my clothes off and pose naked for him to photograph me I would have told him to *"get knotted!"* The Judge, who was not familiar with this expression, asked me to rephrase. I said I would have told him to go and jump in the lake. This he seemed to get and said: *"In other words, Ms Pieters, you would have told him to go to hell?"* To which I answered: *"exactly."* I added then that if one didn't have the strength of character to say no when it was necessary, then eventually one would have to deal with the consequences. Mr Engelbrecht seemed to have nothing left in his arsenal of tricks and retreated to his corner. I was allowed to step down.

I was in court on the day that Cézanne was found guilty of the crimes that she had committed. When the verdict was read she seemed sad, still she showed little emotion save for a tear or two. I was relieved that the trial was almost over.

I went to the bathroom where I was surprised to see Cézanne and her mother. Cézanne walked past me and out the door but Susan, whom I tried to sidestep, flew at me like a banshee. She asked me how I slept at night. I looked her straight in the eye and said that I slept very well every night because, unlike her daughter, I didn't molest little kids.

I braced myself for a slap – instead, she launched into the most illogical, deluded tirade that I had ever heard. She screamed that she knew that I had slept with Dirk Prinsloo and that was why I had testified against her daughter. I was his agent! I smiled as sweetly as I could and told her that sleeping with Dirk Prinsloo seemed to be her family's entertainment, not mine.

The poor woman was just defending her daughter and I pitied her. The last few years must have been terribly difficult for her. But I think that her trying to lay the blame for Cézanne's conviction at my feet was a bit unwarranted. I had been very careful and objective in court, as well as truthful about events as I had witnessed and perceived them.

It is never easy to do the right thing and it usually comes at some personal cost. It is so easy to just stay uninvolved, to say nothing, to do nothing. If everyone in society just took the easy road, where would we be as humanity? I know that my testimony damaged Cézanne's case. I understand that I am partly responsible for her being incarcerated today. This is a burden that I must bear.

Ultimately, however, I believe that Cézanne Visser went to prison because of choices that she had made in her life – and the actions that resulted from them – not because of anything that any one person had done or said.

24.
MY "SEX GOD" MADE ME DO IT
VISSER'S VERSION

Laurie has waylaid the Defence's claims that Prinsloo had controlled Visser's every move. Basically, she painted a picture of a strong-willed woman who chose to stay in a relationship because she had an exhilarating sex life, because she adored her lover and enjoyed living the high life on Prinsloo's account. This was in sharp contrast to the Defence's argument that Visser was a scared, abused little thing with no mind of her own. Laurie did admit, however, that she often had the impression that Visser did certain things she would not have done under different circumstances because she wanted to keep Prinsloo happy.

She conceded that Prinsloo was abusive towards everyone, including Visser, when he could not get his way and regularly called people stupid. When Engelbrecht put it to her that other women had not sent Prinsloo 'to hell,' she replied: *"If they don't have strength of character, then they must live with the consequences"* – a chillingly similar answer to the one Visser gave a reporter years earlier after Prinsloo's ex-wife had made allegations that he had controlled and abused her.

Laurie disputed the notion that one had to go along with Prinsloo when he lost his temper – saying his bark was far worse than his bite. *"I went against him quite often. When I stood up to him, he backed off. He was a bully and a coward. If you stood up to him, he backed away."*

With Charmaine, Jeannine, the investigating officer's and Laurie's evidence done and dusted, the State closed its case – but Fourie indicates that he might apply to re-open the prosecution's case after Visser and the Defence's experts had testified. He says *prima facie* evidence points to voluntary conduct and the onus was on Visser to lay a basis for her defence.

Engelbrecht replies that Visser would vehemently oppose any application for a re-opening of the State's case, because prosecutors have been aware of the nature of her defence all along. He then brings an application for a discharge, which is turned down. Eksteen says it will be premature to make any ruling on the State's intention to re-open its case – saying the matter will be dealt with as and when it comes up.

Contrary to the first trial, when she closed her case without calling any witnesses, Cézanne Visser takes the stand in her own defence.

The evidence she would deliver over the next few weeks would split public opinion right down the middle, with some baying for justice for the victims – especially the children – and others feeling that the abuse and coercion she had suffered at Prinsloo's hands had made her into what she was.

Dressed in a demure ivory-coloured pants suit, Visser twice burst into tears on the first day she starts telling the Court in graphic detail of her relationship with Prinsloo, which started when she was a 24-year-old virgin and ended with her facing 14 criminal charges.

Apart from outlining her life with Prinsloo as described earlier in this book, Visser also tells of a bizarre episode when Prinsloo apparently tried to kill his former wife. She claims he told her he had found out where his ex-wife lived and that he was going to murder her. According to Visser, Prinsloo hired a car and bought outfits to disguise himself. He also bought a body bag before he disappeared for almost a week.

Visser says before he left she had to meet him at a garage in Centurion as he wanted to give her something. A white minibus eventually stopped next to her and someone knocked on her car's window. It was a man in Arabic attire and headgear. He had black hair, dark skin and dark eyes. It was only when he greeted her with one of the many pet names he used for her that she realised it was Dirk. He apparently gave her some documents, before disappearing for several days after he told her he was still the beneficiary of Elsie's life insurance policy and that he was going to kill her. It's unclear exactly what Prinsloo did in the time he disappeared – but it's obvious that he did not murder his former wife, as she is still very much alive.

Prinsloo also apparently told Visser he was a member of the Chinese Triads. The court hears the international fugitive had many Chinese friends who often came to their home. One of the men who was often around Prinsloo, was a big and intimidating Chinese man called Ifwa. Visser tells the court her former lover told her that he only had to click his fingers for the man to "take someone out."

During her testimony, Visser paints a picture of herself as a defenceless, scared and battered woman. She tells the court she did everything she did – even committed crimes – because she loved Prinsloo and feared his punishments if she did not comply with, or sometimes even anticipate his every wish and whim. She testifies that this two-pronged motivation was so strong that she would have committed murder if Prinsloo had wanted her to.

It was one of the most surreal experiences of my life to sit in a courtroom and hear Visser's evidence – at times so shocking that we, as reporters, sometimes battled to come up with sufficient coping mechanisms. I have to admit that humour – and due to the nature of the trial, lewd humour – often became our only defence. I had the immense pleasure of sitting next to one of the funniest men I've ever come across and his very serious, perceptive remarks – of course followed by an hilarious interpretation – not only had us in stitches, but also, I'm convinced, saved our sanity.

I frequently felt sorry for the judge and wondered how a man of his dignity and stature dealt with the sleaze and filth he had to hear day after day as Visser sat in the witness box. I also often cringed on her behalf as she testified about some of the extremely degrading things she did in order to please her man. I squirmed when she told the Court about the genital warts and discharges she suffered as a result of the Human Papiloma Virus she contracted – and when I realised that she would never be able to have children of her own, my heart, as the mother of two beautiful boys, went out to her.

It was more or less during this time that I ran into "Advocate Barbie" at my local supermarket. It was a Saturday and I had my two boys with me. As we both moved towards each other to have a quick conversation, my right arm instinctively went out and I pushed my children behind me. At the time, I felt silly and embarrassed about my behaviour and I self-consciously dropped my arm when I realised what I had done. I did not view the woman in front of me as a paedophile prowling about for victims. In my mind, the actions – the crimes – she committed were not to satisfy herself, but to gratify an apparently insatiable man. In retrospect the incident confirmed to me a mother's inexplicable, intuitive drive to protect her offspring.

It was also with this mother's instinct in mind that I empathised with Susan. Despite her repeated use of the media when she thought it would suit her purposes, Susan – who married the 'sexologist' she had hoped would help her daughter address her skewed sexual experiences – seemed to hate the journalists covering her daughter's trial and would often complain bitterly about their reports. She also had no qualms about phoning an editor and complaining when she did not agree with the reports coming from the courtroom. I decided to see it for what it was – a mother's attempt to protect her only child, even if that child was accused of sexually abusing other people's children.

The court hears that Visser still lives in daily fear for her own and her mother's lives, as she believes it is not beyond her former lover to disguise himself, re-enter the country, wait on top of a high building and shoot one or the other. As Prinsloo is still on the run from Interpol, the idea is not completely foreign. If the man is as vindictive as Visser claims, he might just go to extremes to take his revenge.

While Visser paints herself to be just another of Prinsloo's victims, she does not take responsibility for her role in the sex crimes. She seems to see the trauma inflicted on the victims – especially the children – as more or less on par with her own trauma, if not of lesser intensity. The impression I get is that she is saying "yes, the girls and women were subjected to sexual abuse but they were only subjected to it once, whereas I had to endure it constantly over a number of years." (Not her actual words – my interpretation of what she was saying). This may have been the case, but the little matter of choice is not explained by it. The three women and three teenagers who testified did not have a choice in whether or not they would be sexually assaulted. Visser did have a choice – despite her protestations that she had no mind or will of her own.

As far as I know, the textbook battered woman is subjected to abuse over years before they become "scripted." The relationship between Visser and Prinsloo was not even a year old before she started with criminal sexual activities and much shorter before she gave up – or as she claimed, he seized – control of her body and mind.

Fourie and Cronjé refuse to buy into Visser's story that she had committed the crimes because she was under Prinsloo's spell. Fourie points out several instances in which Visser took the initiative. One such example, he says, was that it was Visser who identified Charmaine. The 11-year-old child was apparently well endowed for her age – and Fourie asks Visser several times whether her physical attributes were the reason she had insisted on taking her home, knowing what would happen once the girl arrived there.

When Susan takes the stand, she testifies that she had always had a good relationship with her only daughter, who was a conservative, loving and respectful child, yet became rebellious and distant after meeting Prinsloo in 2001. She admits that she never approved of her daughter's relationship with Prinsloo, especially as he was still married when she moved in with him.

Susan describes the protection order her daughter had obtained against her as a sham perpetrated by Prinsloo. She blames the Court for what had happened to her and her daughter, as she feels the interdicts had been based on lies and should never have been granted. The distraught mother says she has had little contact with her daughter after the first interdict was granted and was shocked about her child's ill and emaciated appearance during a meeting to discuss the order.

She says Visser looked like a prostitute and acted like a zombie during the meeting and did not say a word – leaving all the talking to an aggressive Prinsloo, who even attacked Susan's attorney.

She says she saw her daughter's tattoos, piercings and "*awful*" breasts for the first time while on holiday in the Cape with Visser. She also heard about the "*awful things*" they did together. She says she asked her daughter why she did not leave Prinsloo, but she replied that she was too afraid of him. The mother testifies that she had been "*very angry*" with her daughter after the two incidents during which Prinsloo had allegedly violated her.

Engelbrecht calls the Head of Clinical Psychology at Weskoppies, Professor Jonathan Scholtz next. He is asked to explain to the Court how Visser, who was known as the Ice Queen among varsity friends and was vehemently opposed to piercings and tattoos, had become the caricature that was known as "Advocate Barbie." Scholtz starts by giving the court a detailed explanation of what BWS entails.

According to Scholtz's explanation, Visser's profile fits this pattern. He says that, while Visser feared Prinsloo, she also felt sorry for him at times, which is illustrated by the emotional dependence she had on him – a common phenomenon among battered women. The psychologist says he finds it significant that, when he asked her whether Prinsloo was a bad person, Visser said what he did was bad, but that he was not necessarily a bad person.

He tells the court that Visser had been *"scripted"* or programmed by Prinsloo to the extent that she did things she would not normally have done. The court hears that her parents' unhappy marriage, the values instilled in her during childhood and her low self-esteem had made Visser the perfect target for Prinsloo and, while she was highly intelligent, she was naïve. Prinsloo had charmed her and treated her like a princess. He, in turn, became her knight in shining armour.

Scholtz explains how Prinsloo systematically pulled her into his web, showing her the pornography he kept scattered around his home to desensitise her before moving on to more and more risqué behaviour. The psychologist says Prinsloo and Visser had never talked about what happened at *Inner Circle Castle* and had an *"us versus them"* mindset. Prinsloo took complete control of Visser – her appearance, what she ate, when she slept and with whom she spoke. Scholtz says Visser's evidence that she would have committed murder for Prinsloo illustrates to what extent she was under his control. It also explained why she at first did nothing after Prinsloo had allegedly sexually molested her own mother. Visser had *"assimilated"* Prinsloo's thoughts and ideas and, although she must have known right from wrong, her will to act accordingly was compromised.

The court hears that Prinsloo is not only a sexual sadist and paedophile, but also suffers from other sexual deviations. Sexual sadists often have numerous disorders, usually collect pornography and have serious personality disorders such as narcissism and psychopathic characteristics. According to him, both traits were present in the Prinsloo case.

The case is postponed to give the State time to consult with its own experts before cross-examining Scholtz.

25.
PRINSLOO RESURFACES

Shortly after Scholtz's evidence-in-chief, Prinsloo resurfaces, writing a series of e-mails to several media organisations as well as the National Prosecuting Authority. After three years on the run, Prinsloo offers to return to South Africa to stand trial – but on his terms.

In the first e-mail, he demands a meeting with then Acting Prosecutions boss, Mokotedi Mpshe, to work out a deal. Prinsloo claims he fled because he feared for the safety of his unborn child and that he is living in exile because he has to face an unfair prosecution. Some of the conditions he wants met before he will return include being allowed to be tried before a judge of his choice and being released on bail. Obviously, both of these conditions are laughable – no accused gets to choose the officer presiding over his or her trial and no judge or magistrate will release him on bail after he had failed to adhere to his previous bail conditions and sent police on a massive manhunt for more than three years.

The e-mail gives the NPA 72 hours to respond to Prinsloo's demands before he will terminate the address from the server he uses – mail2southpole.com. The rest of the letter seems to confirm the picture Visser and the other defence witnesses have painted of him – arrogant and narcissistic – as he berates and belittles authorities for not being able to track him down. He ends by accusing his former mistress of twisting the facts to make him look bad and lashing out at the media for playing an integral part in his *"unfair persecution."*

The next e-mail follows a few days later – and Prinsloo comes out guns blazing against the NPA, which he claims is pretending to negotiate with him in an attempt to track him down. He states that he has closed down the mailbox and tells the NPA to indicate via the media whether it agrees to his demands. The prosecuting authority, which refused to comment on media enquiries regarding the initial e-mail, issues a statement, saying it will not negotiate with fugitives. Prinsloo again berates the SAPS and both Visser and her mother in his correspondence saying *"the only reason her 'theatrical' production in Court had had any impact was because she is a beautiful woman. If a man tried the same stunt he would be laughed off."* Before he signs off, Prinsloo changes tack and starts to sing his former mistress' praises – saying she has a kind heart and would never harm a child.

Whether he is missing the media attention, or is just upset about the fact that Visser – and not him – is dominating the headlines, we'll never know. About ten days after his second e-mail, Prinsloo sends another e-mail to the media saying he feels that his *"end is possibly near."* Unlike the previous two e-mails, which could have been written by someone else, this one is accompanied by a photograph of Prinsloo on horseback.

He writes: *"I write this, possibly my last letter, to the people who made a special and good impact on my life..."* In a message to his brothers, he says: *"The time has arrived where I must deal with a very hard and dangerous project, and it seems that my end is possibly near."* He says this may in fact be very much like in the three films which had made an impact on his life – *Braveheart, Legends of the Fall* and *A River Runs Through It* – once again giving the impression that he views himself as the misunderstood romantic lead in a tearjerker Hollywood movie.

"I have to face an enemy which is stronger than me - not because of their wits, character or skill, but stronger simply because they have guns and numbers and I don't have either..." He writes: *"I showed the world why*

Interpol is an illusion of efficiency and power, and why real criminals will have a picnic to evade all efforts by Interpol to capture and contain any of them."

Prinsloo states in his letter that he is *"very fortunate to have been able to anticipate the end, as many people left life and their loved ones behind without having said important things to them."* In thanking his brother Hannes for *"his unselfish help,"* he tells him to *"be strong"* and to *"find the simple things to make him happy."* Prinsloo muses that *"the biggest pleasure is to be found in simple things, provided you are not attached to earthly fame and fortune."* In thanking his father for his love and support, he writes: *"You never blamed me for the last couple of years' catastrophe which I brought over our family."* The international fugitive concludes his letter by thanking his detractors. *"Thank you to all my enemies who made me realise my own character strength and ability to take loss, destruction, indignation, lies and deceit. Without your help I would never have realised my own personal potential. But, in the end, you failed in your aims, because I proved to be unbreakable..."* In the very last paragraph, Prinsloo mentions he has a daughter and he is watching her and her mother coming out of the sea as he writes.

The idea that the alleged paedophile could have a child of his own – and a daughter to boot – both amused and scared me, although I would not have been surprised if I had been told that the girl did not exist and was another one of Prinsloo's fantasies.

Days before Visser's trial would resume, on a lazy Saturday afternoon, I received a call from Katy Katopodis, the Editor-in-Chief of Primedia Broadcasting's Eyewitness News, who were my employers at the time. When an editor phones an off-duty reporter, it's usually serious stuff – and a list of possibilities ran through my head. The arrest of Dirk Prinsloo, who had been on the run from Interpol for more than three years, was definitely not on that list.

When Katy asked me to confirm a rumour she had heard that Prinsloo had been re-arrested, I first thought she was joking. Although she takes her job extremely seriously and "the news" is no joking matter to Katy, she does have a wicked sense of humour – and I immediately thought she was just testing my responses. Turns out she wasn't. Both the SAPS and Johan Engelbrecht – Visser's advocate – confirmed that they'd been informed by Interpol of Prinsloo's capture.

Two days before he finally met his match, Prinsloo was involved in a failed bank robbery in the city of Baranovichi in the former Soviet State of Belarus. Apparently he tried to rob the bank with two other men – armed with a toy gun and at least one knife. When bank employees refused to co-operate, they were assaulted. One of the women employees managed to press a panic button and the men fled.

Prinsloo's two accomplices were arrested soon afterwards and apparently informed on him. But when the police arrived at his hideout in an industrial area, Prinsloo was nowhere to be found. In the meantime, a boy who saw Prinsloo as he threw down his toy gun and cap outside the bank, gave police a detailed description. By the end of the same day as the foiled heist, investigators were able to identify Prinsloo. Two days later they found him in an internet cafe in Minsk, the capital of Belarus. Prinsloo was reportedly "really shocked," constantly asking how he had been found, and then replying: *"A boy? A little boy?"* – which the Belarusians found quite ironic when they learnt that he was wanted in South Africa for, among other charges, sexual crimes against children.

According to police in Minsk, where he was being held, Prinsloo was an illegal immigrant in Belarus and was apparently travelling on a false passport. The appearance of the man in custody was a far cry from the immaculately groomed Dirk Prinsloo who skipped bail more than three years previously. His hair was darker and longer and unkempt, he had put on weight and was unshaven. It seemed his life on the run was not exactly the glamorous affair he portrayed in the e-mails he had sent only a few months earlier.

Belarusian and South African authorities made it clear that Prinsloo would be dealt with according to the former Soviet State's law before there would be any talk of an extradition. This means that Prinsloo would have to pay for his crimes in Belarus before facing the music in South Africa.

Visser and her mother are hugely relieved at Prinsloo's arrest – saying they could now stop looking over their shoulders. Engelbrecht also makes it clear that the recapture of the man he has been vilifying in Court will have no bearing on his client's case – which continues with the cross-examination of Dr Jonathan Scholtz.

Fourie questions him at length about whether or not Visser had a will of her own. Scholtz agrees that she did have her own will but says her ability to act in accordance with it was severely compromised and curtailed. He explains it by saying that Prinsloo wrote the script and Visser enacted the role he had written for her. Scholtz says Visser wanted to please Prinsloo at all costs – both to avoid being punished as well as to receive recognition in his eyes. This, he says, explains why, in some instances, she appears to have taken the initiative when it came to the child victims being exposed to sexual acts.

According to Fourie, one of the problems the State has with Visser's defence is the fact that Charmaine had testified that Prinsloo was not present when Visser demonstrated the use of a vibrator to her. The prosecutor also points out that it was Visser who went to the children's home and that she was the one who had identified the girls they took home. Scholtz's answer to this is that it all showed that Visser had no boundaries and the examples pointed out by Fourie happened when she was at the height of being under Prinsloo's spell.

After Scholtz, Hendrien Nortjé, a psychiatric social worker at Weskoppies Hospital, takes the stand. Nortjé hands in a report regarding Visser's background and that of her family and what influence that had had on her conduct. The social worker testifies that apart from interviewing Visser, her mother and some of her friends, she also paged through the infamous Red Album. The court hears that Nortjé's first impression when she saw the pictures of Visser in the album was that her eyes appeared to be vacant and dead.

Judge Eksteen gruffly asks her what she means by this statement and what the relevance would be. When Nortjé says that the eyes are an indicator of a person's emotional life, Judge Eksteen asks whether she has studied the art of reading eyes and tells her to stick to her field of expertise.

Susan becomes quite emotional when Nortjé testifies about her daughter's unhappy childhood and the fact that she (Susan) had become pregnant out of wedlock, leading to a forced marriage. The court hears that Visser's father refused to meet Nortjé eye-to-eye for an interview regarding his daughter and said he did not want to be involved, as he now had a new life. Nortjé says the father was neutral in his statements and claimed that he has always been a good father. Susan, however, painted a different picture – describing the marriage as unhappy.

The social worker testifies that Susan's parents were extremely upset with her when she became pregnant, as she had "failed" them. This somehow gave Visser the idea that she was not wanted when she was born and she has spent her life trying to please her parents. This, Nortjé says, was projected onto Prinsloo. She tells the court that Visser kept her problems with Prinsloo to herself in the same way that the problems within the Visser family were kept under wraps at all times. According to the witness, Visser has been described as conservative at school by close friends and also as someone who had never doubted the concept of right and wrong.

Nortjé says it's evident that Prinsloo slowly isolated her from the outside world and broke down her self-confidence. He shaped her into a person who had to address him as her "god." According to the information she has received, Nortjé says, Visser was often *"punished"* by Prinsloo because she had been *"naughty."*

After the social worker's evidence, Engelbrecht closes the case for the Defence. Judge Eksteen postpones the case to later that year for judgement.

26.
JUDGEMENT DAY

When Eksteen starts delivering his judgement in October 2009, Visser – dressed in a baby pink trouser suit – sits in the dock, showing very little emotion. Eksteen first sums up all the evidence for and against Visser. This is a sometimes boring and laborious, but necessary part of the legal process and takes the entire day. Visser leaves the courtroom with uncertainty – but still clings to the hope that she will be acquitted when she returns the next morning.

Her hopes are dashed when judgement resumes and Eksteen completely rejects her defence – saying she had been a willing partner in the sexual abuse of the three women and three girls who had testified against her. He throws out her testimony in its totality – calling it a self-serving pack of lies.

The judge tears into Visser, saying she is always blaming someone else and is conveniently hiding behind Prinsloo – adding that it will be interesting to hear what Prinsloo has to say about being made the scapegoat. Eksteen makes much of Laurie's evidence and refers to her testimony several times during his judgement. He rejects Visser's claims that she had been Prinsloo's pawn and had no will of her own when she committed the deeds – saying her actions throughout had been aimed at the sexual abuse of children and women for the gratification of her own and Prinsloo's sexual needs. The court finds that Visser knew what she had done was wrong, as she had instructed the children not to tell anyone about what had happened to them.

Although she must have known that there is a possibility that the verdict may have gone against her, Visser sits stunned in the dock as Eksteen finds her guilty on 11 of the 14 charges:

Charge 1:

Fraud – pretending to be married in order to take children from the Bramley Children's Home… **Guilty.**

Charges 2, 3 and 4:

Soliciting Anja to commit indecent acts by showing the child her private parts, by showing her pornography and having sexually explicit conversations with her… **Guilty.**

Charge 5:

Indecent assault on Charmaine by showing pornography to her, by demonstrating on herself how a vibrator worked, exposing herself to the child and having sex in front of her… **Guilty.**

Charge 6:

Indecent assault on the Charmaine… **Not Guilty.** The court finds the girl was not forced to take off her clothes at the swimming pool.

Charge 7:

Being a beneficiary to the indecent assault on Mercia by making a false statement to the police that the victim had been a willing partner to oral sex with Prinsloo… **Guilty.**

Charge 8:

Indecent assault on Riana… **Guilty.**

Charge 9:

Indecent assault on Jeannine… **Guilty.** Although the initial charge is rape, Eksteen finds her guilty of indecent assault and not rape.

Charge 10:

Indecent assault on Samantha… **Guilty.**

Charge 11:

Possession of child pornography… **Guilty.**

Charge 12:
Manufacturing child pornography... **Guilty**.
Charge 13:
Possession of 13,2g of dagga... **Not guilty**.
Charge 14:
Manufacturing child pornography relating to Jeannine... **Not guilty**.

The Court concludes that Visser was a willing partner to the sexual activities committed against Charmaine, Jeannine and Anja and that she took the initiative in finding some of the victims. According to Eksteen, her conduct was aimed solely at obtaining children and women to sexually abuse for her and Prinsloo's own gain. He finds that the couple had sex in front of some of the children to solicit them to commit indecent acts and that Visser had been aware of the medication which Prinsloo used to drug some of the victims – and that she knew that their drinks had been spiked.

Eksteen rejects Visser's claims that she was under Prinsloo's control, saying many of the acts against the children were committed in his absence. He says the fact that Visser demonstrated the use of a vibrator on herself in front of Charmaine, fondled the child's private parts, invited her to remove all her clothes and offered to have her private parts waxed all show that Visser took the initiative in some of the indecent assaults. He says Visser was the one who identified Charmaine, without Prinsloo's input and insisted on taking the girl home.

After the damning words by the judge and her conviction, Visser sits stunned for a few seconds before her mother and stepfather rush over to the dock to hug her. The blonde woman holds her composure for several seconds longer – and only allows her tears to flow after making her way to the public toilets outside the courtroom.

The case is postponed to December for sentencing and Visser's bail is extended.

When sentencing proceedings are due to start, Engelbrecht asks for another postponement, saying some of the witnesses the Defence is planning on calling are not yet ready to testify. This delay gives Visser the opportunity to spend one last Christmas with her family before learning her fate.

27.
JUSTICE IN A FAR-AWAY LAND

Meanwhile, police in Belarus are investigating several claims that Prinsloo has repeated the behaviour which had led to his trial in South Africa. Justice is normally dispensed extremely quickly in that country, yet even so, the investigation period is prolonged because of allegations that Prinsloo may have committed sex crimes in Minsk. Belarusian authorities say that some of this information referred to *"sexual perversions with former girlfriends"* – but will not give any further details, despite repeated attempts by several South African reporters.

As part of the investigation into Prinsloo, a special psychological forensic examination is conducted to determine whether he is mentally fit to stand trial on charges of attempted robbery with aggravating circumstances and hooliganism – the latter charge added after it was claimed that he had beaten up a woman in the street while he was running away from the bank. As the probe deepens, it comes to light that Prinsloo has apparently also stolen jewellery belonging to one of his girlfriends.

While incarcerated, Prinsloo writes several letters to a good friend of mine, who was working at the *Pretoria News* at the time. Hanti Otto is perhaps the person who has the most objective insight into Prinsloo – and their correspondence continued well after Prinsloo was convicted and sentenced. Hanti knew Prinsloo long before he started making headlines for all the wrong reasons, as she worked as a Court reporter for many years. Her impressions of him are wide and varied – but she's often told me that he's a charmer of the first order and that she could only get rid of him at court by smoking. An avid health fanatic, Prinsloo detests cigarette smoke. The fact that people continued to smoke outside the courtroom, despite the tough anti-smoking laws, apparently irritates him no end and he would often lecture smokers – myself included.

In his first letter to Hanti, Prinsloo tells her that he wanted to leave Belarus to go to Europe, where he could make money faster – as he planned to return to South Africa a rich man. This plan was apparently scuppered when the mother of his child became fearful that he would leave her or that something might happen to him and begged him to stay. According to Prinsloo, he stayed in the former Soviet State out of loyalty to the woman, whom he called *"Tanya."* Shortly afterwards he was arrested. The former advocate and international fugitive claims he was forced to rob the bank because Tanya had given all their money to a swindler – leaving them bankrupt.

The arrest and subsequent investigation seemingly gives Prinsloo some satisfaction – or as he calls it *"a bitter-sweet victory."* According to him the Belarusian police had *"turned my life upside down, investigating and interrogating every person I ever talked to or met, and, surprise, surprise: NO sex charges, NO paedophilic tendencies or charges and no rape or child porn charges."* He says he hopes that this will cause people to ask about the validity of his South African prosecution – but people back in his home country were far more concerned with the fact that he had been rearrested and that he may have committed more sex crimes while on the run. Prinsloo goes on to bemoan the legal representation he had been afforded in Belarus – complaining about his lawyers' competence and their lack of faith in his innocence. He ends off the letter by asking Hanti to send him warm clothes, vitamins and magazines.

Days before the year 2009 ends, Hanti receives a second letter from

Prinsloo. This time, he obviously has been reminiscing about his life with Visser – whom he describes as an amazing person. Prinsloo writes that he has forgiven his former mistress for concocting *"fairytale facts"* about him. Being incarcerated meant that Prinsloo no longer had internet access – and he is not aware of Visser's conviction until Hanti wrote to him. In his response, after learning that Visser has been found guilty, Prinsloo writes: *"Cézanne is just a good person who chose to try and survive at all costs, no matter on whom she may have to step, or how much she may have to humiliate herself. She was also influenced to adopt her crazy 'defence' by her friends, mother and opportunistic and greedy lawyers."* Prinsloo states that she is innocent, but not for the reasons her defence claimed. He says if Visser had stuck to normal legal principles and defences, the case against her (and him) would have been won *"quite easily."* He also appears to have 'forgiven' Susan. *"I respect her mother's dogged loyalty towards Cézanne. I know she and Cez will easily get through this setback coz (sic) they stand together"* Prinsloo writes.

Referring to his Belarusian case, Prinsloo says he is not expecting a fair trial. He explains that, according to the Belarus system, the judge will receive the entire docket before the trial, including all *"admissible and inadmissible evidence mixed together."* In addition, Prinsloo says, his right of cross-examination – *"being one of my much hailed strong points as an ex-advocate"* – would be *"virtually nullified"* as witnesses may choose not to physically appear in court.

Prinsloo also claims that the South African Intelligence Services are trying to block his support lines (letters and parcels) because he has *"humiliated"* them for many years. According to him the motive is to weaken him to such an extent that he cannot put up a defence in Belarus and will be only too happy to be extradited.

It's hard to keep a straight face as Hanti shares the captured fugitive's ramblings but the best is yet to come. As a postscript, Prinsloo refers to President Jacob Zuma, saying he understands why the ANC leader compared his suffering to that of Jesus during his *"persecution." "The honourable president could hardly have used a better example to convey his pain. I feel the same. The only problem is that my crucifixion had taken almost nine years, and I was not spared an ounce of pain. And while the honourable president had many loyal people to support him, I stand virtually alone and my few allies are intimidated by the collective efforts of the Legion of Liars."*

About two weeks after she received this letter, Hanti is shipped out to Belarus to cover Prinsloo's trial (some would say smuggled out – as she is not allowed to tell even her best friends where she is going). Whatever we in South Africa glean from the Court case is largely thanks to Ms Otto, who is accompanied by photographer Masi Losi. Incidentally, when the pair returned home, Losi has several interesting stories to tell about his experiences as a black man in a country where dark skins are unheard of.

In the High Court in Belarus accused persons appear in a cage, unlike in South Africa where there is no physical restriction, except in extreme circumstances when the suspect is handcuffed or placed in leg irons – the exception being convicted criminals who appear in court under heavy guard with both hand and leg restraints.

When Prinsloo's trial starts in January 2010, he takes his place inside the cage, armed with documents, notes and applications. Among them is a request that the judge and court recuse themselves as they are biased – a delay tactic very similar to the one he used while still on trial in Pretoria. The application is denied and Prinsloo is asked to plead to charges of attempted bank robbery with aggravating circumstances, hooliganism, theft of a former girlfriend's necklace, torture of one of his girlfriends and threats of murder, grievous bodily harm or destruction of property against bank personnel.

(I find the charge of hooliganism strangely appropriate – but shudder to think how overcrowding of prisons would grow exponentially if such a charge was ever to be introduced to the South African legal system).

Prinsloo refuses to enter a plea. It is becoming clear that he is planning to stall and delay the trial as much as possible – a tactic that seemed to have worked to such an extent in South Africa that the trial was not even half way when he skipped bail and fled – almost two years after it had started. Unfortunately for Prinsloo, Judge Vasily Petriv does not have the patience and self-restraint his counterpart in Pretoria, Judge Essop Patel, displayed. While Prinsloo refuses to plead to the charges on the Monday when the trial starts, he changes his tune quickly and *"partially admits guilt"* – a plea option in Belarus – to the attempted robbery charge, saying he was in emotional turmoil at the time because of his financial problems. By the Friday he denies any knowledge of the theft, torture and threat of murder charges.

During the State's case, a little more light is shed on the three years Prinsloo spent on the run from Interpol. The prosecutor calls several witnesses, including three of his ex-girlfriends – one of whom bore him a son while another must have been the "Tanya" from his e-mails, as she is the mother of his daughter. The women all have a chillingly similar tale to tell – not unlike the one another ex-girlfriend, Cézanne Visser, has been telling all along...

According to their testimony, Prinsloo introduced himself as an Australian businessman to all three women, claiming his name was Michael Grant. One of the witnesses, known only as Anastasia to protect her identity, tells the Court that within two weeks from moving in with her, Prinsloo changed from a charming man full of compliments to a sadistic pig who treated her like dirt. She also refers to Prinsloo's "god complex," saying he regarded their liaison as a "god-slave" relationship. The Belarusian woman testifies how Prinsloo severely assaulted her on several occasions. She claims he photographed her face after one such an attack had left her with a broken nose, cut lips and blood on her arms – telling her she looked very nice and that it excited him. He apparently tried to convince her to have her lips and breasts enlarged and persuaded her to have his (real) name tattooed on her private parts and his Interpol website photo inked on her stomach. The court hears that Prinsloo killed Anastasia's dog, threatened to kill her entire family and warned he would cut her up if she told anyone about the torture he inflicted upon her. His apparent obsession with pornography and taking photographs also comes up repeatedly in her testimony.

Under Belarusian law, a witness may not be cross-examined. When Prinsloo challenges some of the statements made by Anastasia, Judge Petriv stops him in his tracks – leading to an outburst from the South African, who angrily tells the court: *"I was hailed in my country as a brilliant cross-examiner. Now I am hampered by you!"* To which Petriv calmly replies: *"I am not interested in what expert you were in South Africa, you are now in Belarus."*

Prinsloo describes his relationship with Anastasia as the worst time of his life. He claims she was an insatiable nymphomaniac who could not get enough of him, even though he was not really interested in having sex with her. He also denies killing her dog – saying her mistaken belief that he was responsible for the animal's death was her motivation for laying false charges against him.

The disgraced former advocate claims he failed to return to South

Africa to stand trial because his first Russian girlfriend, Svetlana Basalai, was scared that he would be killed if he returned. Basalai, the mother of Prinsloo's son, also testifies. She tells the court about a tattoo of Prinsloo's full names, *George Diederik*, on her private parts – reminiscent of the story told by Visser that he regarded her body as his canvas. She alleges Prinsloo had stolen a diamond necklace from her (worth about R15 000) – but he claims it is jewellery he had bought for Visser while he was still in South Africa. He says when the relationship with Svetlana started deteriorating because of the trial in his home country, he decided not to give it to her but to rather sell it – as he was on the brink of bankruptcy due to legal fees.

Prinsloo's last girlfriend, Tatiana Leshko – the mother of his daughter Ksenia – tells the court that he spent hours every day browsing the internet for porn. She testifies that she often came home from work to find Ksenia crying while Prinsloo was surfing for porn. Tatiana only found out the real identity of her baby's father after his arrest.

When Prinsloo brings his application for Petriv to recuse himself – based on the fact that Petriv had access beforehand to all evidence, whether it could be regarded as admissible or not – he antagonizes the presiding officer ever so slightly. That provocation is followed by several outbursts when Petriv overrules his objections and criticises his argumentativeness – leading the judge to warn him on more than one occasion that he could be removed from the Courtroom.

When Prinsloo grills the three female bank employees, who are testifying about events on the day of the foiled heist, tensions in the Courtroom heat up. The women tell the Court how a masked robber, armed with a knife in the one hand and a gun in the other, ordered one of the tellers to give him money. The teller, realising something was amiss, pressed the silent alarm moments earlier. When she froze out of fear, the robber, whom she later identified as Prinsloo, hit her in the face with the handle of the knife. She spent two weeks in hospital. Prinsloo claims Judge Petriv is stopping him from questioning victims after several of his cross-examination-like questions are disallowed. This leads to a squabble between the presiding officer and the former South African advocate who claims that his right to a fair trial is being trampled on.

Eventually, after he has warned Prinsloo for three days, Petriv makes good on that threat and Prinsloo is removed from the courtroom by three policemen. The incident is sparked by an argument over the translation of a witness' statement. Prinsloo insists the woman's statement is different to the one in the docket. He waves around a hand-written note, saying he wants it to form part of the record as it apparently shows that the translation he received was different. The outburst prompts Petriv to adjourn the hearing and Prinsloo is not allowed back in until the witnesses and victims have finished their testimony. An annoyed-looking Prinsloo turns his back on the guards and holds his hands behind him to be cuffed, shaking his head as he is led away.

He is only allowed to return to his cage two days later – when he apologises to South Africa for shaming it. Prinsloo, who obviously decided to eat humble pie rather than further antagonise the judge, also apologised to Belarus and to his victims and the bank. He says he planned the robbery out of desperation, as he could not even afford shoes for Tatiana or Ksenia. He claims the bank employees were injured by accident and that he was planning on handing himself over at the Spanish Embassy after the heist – during which he would have only stolen a few thousand roubles to give to Tatiana.

Prinsloo claims police tortured him during his incarceration and that they coached the witnesses on what to say. Petriv orders an investigation into these allegations and postpones the trial for almost two weeks. When it resumes again, a forensic psychiatric report is read into the Court records. The report was compiled during the assessment on whether Prinsloo would be fit to stand trial. It states, amongst other things, that Prinsloo always wants to be the centre of attention and is excessively self-assured.

No-one is allowed to speak to prisoners on trial in Belarus. Despite this, Hanti is able, over the course of the trial, to ask Prinsloo several questions. The disgraced former advocate is all too happy to see someone from his home country and they have numerous short conversations in Afrikaans. He tells her amongst other things that he didn't plan to flee South Africa – it was a spur of the moment decision after he learnt that Svetlana was pregnant. When their relationship soured and his dreams of having a family of his own were shattered, he thought he could get a second shot at it with Tatiana.

When Hanti asks him why the evidence of the three Belarusian women sounded so similar to the testimony heard in Pretoria, Prinsloo smiles, saying the one woman read the articles about Visser on the Internet and decided to get a similar tattoo. The other, Prinsloo claims, asked if she too was special enough to have the same tattoo as his other lovers. Shortly afterwards she also had one done.

Petriv finds Prinsloo guilty, sentences him to 13 years behind bars and orders him to pay the legal costs of the case and an amount of money to the victims for *"moral and material damage."* Afterwards he tells Hanti and another South African reporter who arrived half way through the trial: *"This is fucking crazy! It is ridiculous. This entire Court case was unfair and illustrates the approval of corruption and Stalinism. It breached just about every human right."* He complains bitterly that he has not been allowed to call any witnesses, to prepare and present the case in his mother tongue and that he could not cross-examine the witnesses – saying these objections would form the basis of his appeal.

28.
FIGHTING TO STAY OUT OF JAIL

A week after her former lover – and the man she blames for leading her down the primrose path – is sentenced, the final chapter in Visser's trial starts. In their sentencing arguments her lawyers try to convince Judge Eksteen that she should not be sent to prison.

Forensic criminologist, Dr Eon Sonnekus, is called to testify in mitigation of sentence. He tells the court that Visser has gained a lot of wisdom in the time between committing the crimes and being convicted. Sonnekus says Visser had undergone a positive change in the more than seven years since she was arrested with Prinsloo. The criminologist claims there is little chance that Visser will commit the same crimes again – and says she will have to live with the consequences of her deeds for the rest of her life. Citing several passages of Visser's testimony, Sonnekus says he has no doubt that she is very sorry for what she had done. He says the remorse she shows indicates that her rehabilitation process has already started – adding that sending her to prison would not contribute to this process.

In a statement which would entertain – and infuriate – South Africans across the country, he suggests either a suspended sentence – or a rigorous correctional supervision programme, which would allow for 12 hours per day at work and 10 hours over weekends for shopping and social interaction. It also includes working eight hours per month in the Pretoria Zoo.

When Judge Eksteen questions the relevance of the zoo in a child molestation case, Sonnekus replies that Visser has become so distrustful of other people that it would be better to let her work with animals – which she loves. Eksteen drily asks if the aim is to make things as easy as possible for Visser. He also questions whether Visser has ever apologised to any of her victims. After a heated debate between the Defence and State about whether or not she has ever apologised, Engelbrecht points at transcripts of Charmaine's testimony behind closed doors – in which it appears that Visser has apologised.

When it's his turn to question Sonnekus, Fourie comes out with guns blazing, slamming the proposed correctional supervision regime. He jokingly says that if being only allowed to go to work, go shopping and go to church is considered to be a punishment, many mothers – who haven't committed any crimes – would be forgiven for thinking they were under house arrest, too. Fourie says remorse denotes repentance, followed by feelings of guilt and accountability, adding Visser has never accepted responsibility for her actions.

Sonnekus says Visser's punishment should not be about retribution – adding that he thinks the correctional supervision programme he suggested is quite rigorous and that he cannot see Fourie's problem with it.

The next witness to testify in mitigation of sentence is clinical psychologist Micki Pistorius. Pistorius shot to fame – or notoriety, depending on who you're talking to – in the nineties when she was the first profiler to be appointed to the South African Police Service. She founded and headed the SAPS' Investigative Psychology Unit and worked on more than 30 serial killer cases. After she left the SAPS, she became a private investigator, presented a television documentary on crime and wrote several books about her experiences as a profiler, including her autobiography: *Catch me a Killer*. She evaluated Visser in 2006 – long before her conviction – at the request of Susan.

Pistorius testifies that while Visser knew she was committing crimes, she continued with the acts because she was 'psychologically imprisoned.' She says Visser is a typical victim of a sexual sadist: *"Ms Visser is a victim of domestic abuse, coercive control and a compliant victim of a sexual sadist at the hands of Mr Prinsloo. Her behaviour was influenced by him."* Pistorius tells the court that the term 'compliant' defines a person who "gave in" and should not be confused with a consenting person who "gave permission." *"Miss Visser was coerced into compliance."* Pistorius says Visser was a sitting duck for someone like Prinsloo and that she had sacrificed her own moral values when she solicited minors and prostitutes and participated in their sexual abuse.

She tells the Court that Visser's judgement was probably impaired by chronic post traumatic stress and depression and that she has since regained her conservative, moral personality. The psychologist also argues against direct imprisonment – instead suggesting extensive therapy. Although Visser is expecting to be punished, Pistorius says, she still has a desire to contribute to society and poses no danger to the community. The court hears that Visser, who has so far kept a tight reign on her emotions, would crack once the trial was over and would need extensive therapy.

It turned out to be prophetic words as Visser has a nervous breakdown that afternoon after returning from the courthouse and is rushed to hospital. The next morning, when final arguments are due to start, a pale, dejected-looking Visser sits in the dock with her mother next to her. Engelbrecht tells the court that the sedatives prescribed by the doctors had caused her to pass out the night before and he could not guarantee that she would be mentally present during the proceedings. He says Visser would be on medication for other two or three weeks.

Judge Eksteen postpones the matter for ten days.

In those ten days, Visser spends time in the *Vista* private psychiatric clinic. When she returns to court on the appointed date, she is dressed in black from head to toe and appears calm and in control.

During his sentencing arguments, Fourie calls for a sentence of between 15 and 20 years' imprisonment, although he leaves it to the court to decide how much of the sentence should be suspended. Engelbrecht suggests a totally suspended sentence, linked to 36 months correctional supervision, community service and counselling at Visser's own cost. Fourie, however, stresses the seriousness of the crimes and the devastating effect they had had on the victims. He says the defence has made much of Prinsloo's influence over Visser, but the court should not lose sight of Visser's own initiating role in the crimes. He concedes that Visser does not have inherent perverse sexual tendencies, but says she had also benefitted from the crimes, which she had committed in order to satisfy Prinsloo.

29.
SENTENCING

Visser has allowed herself a glimmer of hope that she would not be sent to prison. The tension she is feeling is clearly visible on her face when she reports to courtroom GA for the last time. When Judge Eksteen starts handing down his sentence, she sits staring straight ahead of her and remains expressionless throughout his verdict.

Eksteen finds that her remorse is nothing more than lip service – saying that in an orderly community, Visser, with her legal qualifications, could be expected not to sexually abuse women and children. According to the judge, Visser rejected her conservative upbringing in favour of Prinsloo's immoral lifestyle and, in the process, traumatised young girls. He says she tried to justify her actions and blamed Prinsloo for her own actions. *"While the court accepts that she would not commit similar crimes again, it has to take into account the community's abhorrence and righteous indignation about crimes against women and children,"* Eksteen says. He accepts the evidence that Prinsloo is a narcissistic and manipulative man, but stresses that none of the other women in his life committed crimes because of his abuse.

"Although Prinsloo had made Visser his sex slave and had influenced her conduct, she knew the difference between right and wrong and nevertheless decided to satisfy him at the expense of children. Visser knew that a Children's Home would be more likely to allow two married advocates to take out young girls and she had therefore pretended to be married to Prinsloo. Her visits to the Children's Home had been carefully planned and she had taken the initiative to get the children, whose vulnerability she and Prinsloo had exploited.

One shudders at the thought that (Visser) purposely went to fetch children, knowing that they would fall prey to a sexual sadist and that they would be drugged for sexual deeds." Eksteen says Visser's adult victims have also been traumatised.

Taking the mitigating factors into account, he sentences Visser to seven years behind bars.

Visser sits stony faced throughout the entire sentence – but when Eksteen says he had no option than to impose direct imprisonment, a single tear starts running down her cheek. She turns around to her mother and stepfather who are sitting behind her and gives a little smile before she holds out her hands compliantly to a policewoman to be cuffed and led down to the holding cells.

At first Susan, too, puts up a brave face, but after an adjournment she broke down and sobs bitterly. Two days later her reaction to the sentence is published in *Huisgenoot* – which pays her handsomely for the interview.

The court is adjourned for a short while before Engelbrecht brings an application for leave to appeal his client's conviction and sentence. Judge Eksteen turns down this application, saying he doubts another Court would have come to a different conclusion. Nevertheless, he grants her bail, pending the outcome of an application to the Supreme Court of Appeal for leave to appeal. Her bail is increased from R5 000 to R10 000 and she has to hand her passport to Fourie.

In total, Visser spends about 90 minutes in the holding cells before she is released again. After hearing that she will be allowed to go home that day, Visser and her mother hug each other – visibly relieved that their looming parting is once again delayed. Shortly thereafter, Susan pushes a news photographer out of the way – clearly irritated at the media attention.

The news of "Advocate Barbie's" seven-year sentenced is met with mixed reaction. While children's rights groups welcome the fact that she is going to serve time behind bars, several of them bemoan the length of the sentence – saying it should have been much longer. Anja and Charmaine, who have since reached adulthood, are also in Court to hear their molester's fate. While neither would say whether they could ever forgive her, both are adamant that they are happy that she is being sent to jail. The two young women express relief that the trial is finally over and that they no longer have to see Visser's face in the newspapers every day.

Charmaine says the sentence does not compensate for the pain and suffering she had to endure – but expresses the hope that she will be able to finally get closure, saying she was doing her best to handle the pain, which will always be with her. Despite Visser's defence that Prinsloo made her do the things she did, their youngest victim sees them as equally guilty. She says as a result of the two advocate's deeds, she has learnt not to trust anybody. The young woman wants to become a motivational speaker and help other children in the same position.

Anja says she had dreamt of becoming a lawyer. When the couple took her for a weekend visit, she was ecstatic, as she thought they, as advocates, could make her dream come true – but after what they did to her she no longer wanted to be associated with that profession. She says, despite her best efforts to put the matter behind her, she is still being haunted by nightmares about her ordeal.

Jeannine is not in Court to see the woman she had once trusted sent to jail. In fact, she is doing her best to forget Visser, Prinsloo and what had happened to her in *Inner Circle Castle* when she was only 14 years old. The diminutive young woman is completely distraught when she hears the news about Visser's sentence – not because Visser had to go to prison, but the mere mention of "Advocate Barbie" would send Jeannine into a foul mood for days.

30.
A TRAGIC END
JEANNINE'S STORY
PART IV

Jeannine fell pregnant in 2008 and gave birth to a baby girl whom she named Mecayla. She had managed to remain heroin-free during her pregnancy and the baby was healthy. Amazingly the child was born HIV negative and has remained so to date. Mecayla was to become Jeannine's inspiration to once again try to turn her life around.

Jeannine was living with Sue again and one weekend she asked her to drop her and Mecayla off at Roelien's home as she hadn't seen her sister for a while. They were supposed to drop Mecayla off at Marie's home later that afternoon. Unfortunately, Jeannine and Roelien made dagga-cookies that weekend and the baby somehow managed to get hold of them and eat a few. When the girls took the child to Marie she noticed that the baby was behaving strangely and took her to the hospital where she had Mecayla tested for drugs. The result came back positive for marijuana – a fact Marie used to successfully apply for custody of the child.

She contacted Jeannine and told her that she would only allow her to see her baby once a week on a Sunday – and then only for two hours. She told her that she was never allowed to sleep over. Marie also called Sue and informed her of her decision and the conditions that she would allow Jeannine access to the child.

Sue was horrified that she was isolating Jeannine from her child. Jeannine loved her daughter – who was her primary reason for living.

She was HIV positive and very thin, struggling with her demons daily. Sue argued with Marie asking her how she could do this to her daughter, effectively robbing Mecayla of her mother. After all, no-one knew for how much longer Jeannine would survive. AIDS, her drug addiction, her self-mutilation, her depression and her suicidal tendencies could claim her life at any point. Sue begged Marie to let Jeannine see Mecayla as often as she could, to give her at least as much time with her daughter while she was still alive. She said it was shocking and inhuman to take from Mecayla any time, even precious seconds, that she could spend with her mother who, despite her problems, adored her little girl and was desperately trying to get her life on track. Marie would not relent.

Jeannine was extremely concerned for Mecayla's well-being in Marie's care. She was worried about her daughter's welfare in the custody of a woman who had driven her out onto the streets years before. She hoped that her mother would not fail her daughter as she had failed her.

In the last year or so of her life Jeannine met a really sweet guy. The moment he met her, Johan fell hook line and sinker for the troubled young woman. His mission in life was to save her from herself. It was to be an uphill battle for him and he found that he was not winning the war with heroin. Every day he spent with Jeannine was a struggle and every day she broke his heart a little more. However, he was determined to stick it out, hoping that he would win in the end. He took her to several doctors to prescribe medication for her to help her conquer her addiction but nothing worked.

Sue confirmed his story, saying that "...*during the last year of her life Jeannine's drug use was bad, it was really, really bad. She would use multiple bags in a day as she would spike every hour. She would wrap a band around her arm injecting the heroin in a matter of seconds. She was so used to it by that stage. She always took time to prepare the drug, however. The entire preparation was a slow ritual for her, one which she never compromised and it seemed to have an almost calming effect on her. She did not like needles and really didn't like to spike and for a short while, in 2007, she smoked her heroin, but of course the desired effects were not really gained and she soon resorted to spiking again."*

Johan eventually managed to persuade Magaliesoord, a rehab facility outside Pretoria, to give her a bed. True to form, Jeannine ran away. When she realised her mistake she begged them to give her another chance, but they refused. She had just destroyed her final opportunity to beat her heroin addiction and spiralled into a deep depression – one from which only copious amounts of heroin seemed to offer relief.

At the end of her life she was constantly high and if she wasn't high she was terribly depressed. She could not live with herself. The withdrawal was physically excruciating and drove her wild with pain.

Just before her death Jeannine had gone to visit her mother for a week. Marie phoned Sue shortly after Jeannine had returned to her, to complain about how the young mother constantly reprimanded her daughter, stopping her from doing things that she was normally allowed to do. Marie felt that Jeannine was much too strict with little Mecayla.

When Jeannine returned home to Sue, Sue asked her about the conversation that she had had with Marie. Janine was very unhappy and told Sue, *"I cannot touch my child, I cannot do anything for her because my mother just takes over."* She felt totally useless when it came to her daughter because her mother made her feel that everything that she did for Mecayla was wrong. It seemed that she had little part to play in her daughter's life and her role was, in fact, totally inconsequential.

Just after her return from that fateful visit Jeannine sat at the kitchen table, she was preparing her drugs in her usual ritualized manner, rolling and playing with the spoon. She had her back to Sue at the time. Suddenly she broke the silence and said, *"...so, did you miss me?"* and started laughing, her little shoulders shaking uncontrollably. Instead of saying *"yes, I did,"* Sue joked that she was so incredibly busy she had no time to miss anybody. Today she wishes she gave a different response and is haunted by the question of what the outcome would have been had she told her that she did love and miss her. Maybe she would have felt more wanted; maybe she would have stayed at home and not gone to Botswana...

Johan was quite a bit older than Jeannine. On his birthday, Jeannine suddenly started to laugh while talking to him on Skype. When he asked her why, she said "There's no way in hell I'm going to call you *oom* (uncle) from now on, 'cause you don't give me cookies after you've had sex with me." Although her wicked sense of humour is clear from this, when one looks a little deeper at what she says, sex to Jeannine meant the receipt of some kind of favour or reward.

Jeannine sported numerous tattoos which she admitted to having done for the pain that was linked to the procedure. She had a large spider web on her neck, a devil on her arm and many other works of "art." Unlike some of the street kids whose tattoos were linked to their image, Jeannine's were not. She knew exactly who she was and, when she wasn't at war with herself, she liked who she was. When her daughter was born she really wanted to turn her life around and become someone respectable. When Johan came along she loved him and didn't want to lose him. She constantly feared that his family would reject her and that he would eventually abandon her.

Her self-mutilation was escalating again. She slashed her skin open daily with a razor blade, leaving deep and ugly scars as evidence of her emotional pain. Initially she hid the behaviour from Johan, cutting one straight line at a time in places where they would not be visible. This soon turned into serious wounds inflicted all over her body – mainly on her arms, but also on her thighs, high up on her inner thighs and on her calves. It seemed as if she wanted people to see them, wanted people to know her deep pain. Cutting became a weapon in her very large arsenal of tools that she used to manipulate people.

She didn't seem to be able to shake off her old life and her old habits. Her actions were a source of constant pain to Johan who stood stoically at her side while she seemed hell-bent on self destruction. She hated the person that she seemed destined to be – the constant disappointment she was to herself, never mind her loved ones. When Johan invited her to join him on location in Botswana, she jumped at the opportunity to escape her life for a short while.

While in Botswana Jeannine somehow came to the conclusion that she did not have much to live for. She had Johan, she was in the bush and away from her troubles for now, but she knew it would never be enough. She needed the heroin – the physical pain of withdrawal was excruciating; she needed to be a mother to her child – a gift stolen from her by her mother. Everything had finally just become too much for her. She didn't want to live this way anymore but could not see any light at the end of the very dark tunnel which was her life. With Johan working and her usual support system unavailable to her in Botswana, her depression deepened.

One early autumn day in 2010 she took an overdose of pills, picked up a rope and strolled into the Botswana bushveld - intent on ending her life. She found a tree from which she could suspend herself but collapsed at its base as the medication took effect. Clutching the rope she collapsed at the base of the tree where she died much as she had lived – alone.

Johan found her body a day or so later when neighbours told him that they had seen her clutching a rope and disappearing into the bushveld the day before. When he found her, animals had already nibbled on her extremities. Sobbing uncontrollably, he clutched the body of the girl he loved, praying that she had finally found the peace she deserved in death.

Marie, of course, immediately blamed Visser and Prinsloo for Jeannine's death, painting herself as the innocent victim of the "Satan" who was Cézanne Visser!

31.
BEHIND BARS

According to her mother and advocate, Visser is devastated by Jeannine's suicide – but Engelbrecht makes it clear that the young woman's death will not have any impact on their planned appeal.

Their battle to keep her out of jail continues. The arguments used to support the application for leave to appeal are in the same vein as the defence mounted in the High Court in Pretoria. In a 151-page affidavit, Visser states that the court erred in convicting her and did not take into account the severe impact the BWS had on her ability to act independently.

Two Appeal Court Judges – one of them a woman – turn down Visser's application for leave to appeal, thereby squashing her last hope of staying out of prison. Her stepfather tells a newspaper reporter that the legal system has failed her and that she was *"comparable to Nelson Mandela."* He also makes it clear that he has every intention of making sure that Visser enjoys her last weekend at home.

According to her bail conditions, she has to report to authorities to start serving her sentence within 48 hours of being informed of the Supreme Court of Appeal's decision. Since that deadline falls on a Saturday, Visser is given grace until the Monday.

When D-day arrives, Visser shows up at the High Court, carrying a kit bag, turquoise pillow and other bedding.

Although she refuses to comment to journalists as she hurries up the steps to the Courtroom she is scheduled to appear in, I had a few words with her before proceedings started. She was in a far better emotional space than I had seen her in for most of the trial. Her main concern was for her mother, who accompanied her in her final moments before reporting for prison. Visser asked me to take care of Susan – which I tried to do to the best of my abilities.

I visited Cézanne in prison on her birthday in 2010. Due to a misunderstanding, I did not stay long, otherwise Susan would not have been able to see her daughter on her birthday. Sitting opposite from her, divided by a thick glass barrier, we spoke through a telephone-like communication device. "Advocate Barbie" was noticeably slimmer – ascribing it to the poor quality food served in prison. She was doing her best to seem upbeat – but I somehow got the impression that her smile did not reach her eyes. I'll stop that train of thought immediately – before Acting Judge Chris Eksteen asks me, too, if I had had any training in reading someone's expression!

The other thing that struck me during that visit was that some of the prison warders referred to Cézanne by the name she had come to be associated with. I found this deeply disturbing – although I cannot really verbalise why this would bother me. I guess it is perhaps because I feel Cézanne is paying her debt to society and should not have to be reminded daily of why she is in prison. The sad truth is that she will never be rid of that tag – "Advocate Barbie" will lurk in the shadows everywhere Cézanne goes for the rest of her life.

Susan took another desperate stab at trying to get her daughter out of jail by petitioning the Constitutional Court. I battled to understand what the constitutional argument was because, as an observer with only a rudimentary knowledge of the law, I was not able to identify any violation of Cézanne's human rights. Unfortunately for her, the Judges of the Constitutional Court agreed with me – and the last-ditch attempt was also turned down.

Prinsloo's attempts to have his conviction and sentence overturned were also turned down. As far as I know, he is serving the remainder of his 13-year sentence under strict conditions in a penal colony in Belarus. He will be extradited to South Africa once his time is up.

32.
PROFILE OF A BATTERER

If Visser was a battered woman, then Prinsloo should fit the profile of a batterer – and there are strong indications that he was:

There are certain relational factors with a higher incidence of intimate partner violence which include the fact that they tend to get involved quickly. Numerous battered people knew or dated their abuser for less than six months before either moving in with them or getting engaged.

Abusers or batterers tend to be excessively jealous and frequently question their partner on where they have been or who they have been talking to. They also often drop by (or drive by) unexpectedly to check on their partners' activities. Batterers have a propensity to have unrealistic expectations of the person they are involved with, and of the relationship. They expect their partner to be the perfect person – telling them things like *"you are all that I need and I am all that you need."*

They often isolate their partners. The partner frequently has no friends, no car and no access to money and often end up feeling trapped in the relationship with no one to turn to. The batterer has a tendency to blame others for their problems. They perceive life's ordinary setbacks as personal insults and attacks on them. Men who beat their partners/wives have very rigid beliefs regarding the role of women and expect their partners to obey them without question. They resort to "playful" force during sex.

Their post-battering behaviour usually justifies the abuse with the excuse that their partner "caused" the abuse in some way. Verbal threats of violence are often used to assert control over their partner's behaviour. They may say such things as *"I will break your neck, I'll kill you, I'll beat you."* They may also threaten to hurt or kill the partner's loved ones or pets.

Research has identified specific personal, social and relationship risk factors that may serve as predictors of male to female intimate partner violence. Personal characteristics frequently identified in male perpetrators, include that they:

- …have traditional sex role expectations. They are often preoccupied with the macho ideal of manhood. They feel a need to dominate and control women and often feel it is their right and privilege to do so. They are inclined to associate feminine qualities with weakness and fear intimacy, believing it makes them vulnerable.

- …frequently seem to exhibit communication deficits. Batterers are commonly characterised as lacking in assertive communication skills, appearing alternatively passive and aggressive in nature. They are inclined to resolve their problems and emotions through aggressive behaviour and violence, as the male sex role stereotype would suggest. This tendency usually adds to the stress many batterers create for themselves and their families.

- …have poor impulse control. Batterers have higher levels of hostility than non-batterers. Their range of emotions is apt to be reduced to anger, which in turn is expressed primarily through violent behaviour sanctioned by male subcultures. Emotional tensions are typically suppressed until they finally "explode."

- …have low self-esteem. Despite the bravado that many batterers demonstrate, they characteristically suffer from much lower self-esteem than non-batterers. They often feel that they have not lived up to the male sex role stereotype and consequently overcompensate with hyper-masculinity.

- …become emotionally dependent on their partners and consequently become threatened by the possibility of their departure. This is often evident in their excessive jealousy and possessive behaviour.

- …have a higher incidence of alcohol and drug abuse problems. The alcohol lowers inhibitions, and thereby intensifies abusive incidents, but it does not cause the abuse. Most batterers are abusive with or without consuming alcohol or other addictive substances and will continue their abusive behaviour even when sober. Drugs and alcohol may even act as a sedative for the emotional distress most batterers bear in response to their sense of inadequacy, poor communication skills and often abusive childhood.

- …, like the alcoholic, deny that there is a problem and refuse to accept responsibility for the abusive behaviour. They blame everyone else for making them angry, thereby excusing their behaviour.

The majority of male batterers have experienced or witnessed childhood violence that has left them with low self-esteem, inadequate coping skills and other more serious trauma-related personal and social deficits. There are a number of community, cultural and social factors that increase the likelihood that intimate partner violence will occur.

These include: Poverty and factors associated with it like overcrowding; Limited social capital which includes a lack of institutions, relationships and norms that shape the quantity of a community's social interactions. Another huge problem is weak community sanctions against intimate partner violence like the unwillingness of neighbours to intervene in situations where they witness violence.

33.
PERSONALITY DISORDERS AND SYNDROMES

Battered Woman Syndrome (BWS) is a recognised psychological condition used to describe someone who has been the victim of consistent and/or severe domestic violence. It is considered to be a form of post-traumatic stress disorder. Abuse occurs in a repeating pattern of three phases. First the tension-building phase, followed by the explosion or acute battering incident, then the calm, loving respite – often referred to as the honeymoon phase.

In general, the woman believes that it is her fault, that she is solely to blame for the violence and that the abuser is omnipresent and omniscient. BWS is marked by four stages: denial, guilt, enlightenment and responsibility. Firstly, the battered woman denies to others and to herself that there is a problem. Most battered women will make up excuses for their partners' behaviour. They also choose to believe that the violent incidents will not happen again. Then, as the pattern of abuse is repeated, the woman eventually admits that there is a problem in her relationship. She recognises she has been the victim of abuse and that she may be beaten again – yet she blames herself for the conflict and believes the abuse will stop if only she could be a better person. The next stage arrives when the woman starts to lay the blame where it belongs; with her partner. She remains with her abuser, hoping for an improvement in the relationship. Finally, the woman realises that only her partner can solve his problem. She takes responsibility for her own life and leaves the abusive relationship.

It can be argued that instead of the *Battered Woman Syndrome* Visser is said to be suffering from; a more apt diagnosis would be *Dependent Personality Disorder*. We are by no means trying to pretend that we are professionals in the field of psychology – but the literature on Dependent Personality Disorder seems to indicate that this may be a possible explanation for the question that has not been answered satisfactorily by the evidence presented in court, namely: What led an educated, intelligent woman to sink so low that she would sexually abuse children?

Dependent Personality Disorder

Dependent Personality Disorder (DPD) is one of a group of psychological conditions known as *Anxious Personality Disorders*, which are characterised by feelings of nervousness and fear as well as submissiveness, helplessness, a need to be taken care of, needing constant reassurance and an inability to make decisions. All of these traits are highlighted by the various experts who assessed Visser during the course of her trial.

DPD is a frequently diagnosed personality disorder. It seems to occur with equal frequency in both sexes, and onset is usually in early to middle adulthood.

DPD sufferers become emotionally dependent on others, spending vast amounts of energy in trying to please the other person. People with DPD tend to display needy, passive and clinging behaviour and have a deep-seated fear of separation. Visser described herself as always trying to please people, needing Prinsloo's love and affection and being desperately afraid of losing him.

Other frequent characteristics of this personality disorder include:
- Inability to make even everyday decisions without the advice and reassurance of others;

- Avoidance of personal responsibility, positions of responsibility and jobs that require independent functioning;
- Intense fear of abandonment and a sense of helplessness and/ or devastation when relationships end. Unable to cope on their own, they often move immediately into another relationship when one ends;
- Pessimism and lack of self-confidence, which includes a belief that they are unable to care for themselves;
- Over-sensitivity to criticism;
- Aversion of disagreeing with others for fear of losing approval or support;
- Inability to start projects. Procrastination;
- Intense dislike or fear of being alone;
- Willingness to tolerate mistreatment and even abuse from others;
- Placing the needs and wants of their caregivers above their own;
- Tendency to be naïve and to live in a fantasy world.

It is interesting that every single one of the traits listed above was highlighted either by Visser, her mother or one or other of the experts who testified on her behalf either during her trial or the subsequent sentencing proceedings. Yet not one of these experts diagnosed her as suffering from this disorder.

Although the precise cause of Dependent Personality Disorder is unknown, it most likely involves both biological and developmental factors. There are researchers who believe an authoritarian or overprotective parenting style may lead to the development of Dependent Personality traits in people who are susceptible to the disorder. The circumstances under which Visser was raised, appear to be the perfect environment to facilitate the development of Dependent Personality Disorder.

Narcissistic Personality Disorder

The term narcissism describes an extreme admiration of one's self. The word originates from a Greek myth in which a good-looking young man named Narcissus catches sight of his own reflection in a pond of water and falls in love with it.

Narcissistic Personality Disorder falls into a group of conditions known as Dramatic Personality Disorders. People suffering from these disorders have extreme, unstable emotions and a distorted self-image. Narcissistic Personality Disorder is additionally characterised by an abnormal love of self, a preoccupation with success and power and an exaggerated sense of superiority and importance. Nevertheless, these attitudes and behaviours don't reflect real self-confidence but rather conceal a profound sense of insecurity and a fragile self-esteem. People with this personality disorder have a tendency to set unrealistic goals.

Symptoms of Narcissistic Personality Disorder

In many cases, people with Narcissistic Personality Disorder:
- Are boastful and self-centred;
- Seek constant attention;
- Seek continuous admiration;
- Regard themselves as better than others;
- Overstate their talents and achievements;
- Feel that they are entitled to special treatment;
- Are easily hurt but often conceal their feelings;
- May take advantage of others to realise their goals.
- Other traits of NPD include:
- Preoccupation with fantasies that centre on unlimited power, success, intelligence, beauty, or love;

- Conviction that he/she is "special" and "unique," and can only be understood by similar special people;
- Expectation that other people will automatically go along with what he/she requests;
- Inability to recognise or identify with the feelings, desires, needs, and viewpoints of other people;
- Jealousy of others or a certainty that others are envious of him or her;
- Hypersensitivity to insults (real or imagined), criticism, defeat or disapproval, possibly reacting with rage, shame, indignity and humiliation;
- Arrogant attitude and/or behaviour.

The exact cause of Narcissistic Personality Disorder is unknown. Many mental health professionals believe it results from extremes in child-rearing. It may possibly develop as the result of excessive pampering, or a parent's need for their child to be talented or special in order to maintain their own self-esteem. Conversely, it could develop as the result of neglect or abuse and trauma inflicted by parents or other authority figures during childhood. The disorder is usually evident by early adulthood.

Anti-social Personality Disorder

Anti-social Personality Disorder, like other personality disorders, is a long-term pattern of behaviour and experience that impairs everyday functioning and causes distress.

People afflicted with Anti-social Personality Disorder don't abide by society's norms, are deceitful, manipulative and intimidating in relationships. They are largely inconsiderate of the rights of others. They may become involved in criminal activity and if they do, they generally have no remorse for their actions. They can be reckless, impulsive and violent. This disorder is more commonly diagnosed in men.

People with Anti-social Personality Disorder commonly do not value "playing by the rules" – they may do so only if they are threatened with punishment. They have a tendency to exploit those around them and take advantage of the fairness or "soft-heartedness" of others which they interpret as weakness, resulting in their feeling indifferent towards – or even contemptuous of – their victims. They have little, if any, ability to be intimate with other people.

Any long-term relationships are likely to involve abuse or neglect. However, people with this disorder are often charming and can be first-rate actors who use distortion and lies to sustain relationships they feel are of use to them. Some persons afflicted with this disorder have no goal beyond the pleasure and satisfaction derived from deceiving or harming others.

People with Anti-social Personality Disorder are self-absorbed and focused on self-gratification, even at great cost to others. They might be able to understand the emotions of others, but they don't have feelings of shame or guilt about the harm or pain they may be inflicting. They apply their knowledge of others' weaknesses to gain favours or to manipulate an outcome they desire. They usually take no responsibility for their own suffering or the suffering of others. They will often shift blame to a third party when things go badly for them. Their self-defeating behaviour results in their suffering because they live lives devoid of mutual and satisfying relationships.

People suffering from this disorder may have additional problems like chronic boredom or irritability, psychosomatic symptoms, pathological gambling, substance and alcohol abuse and a variety of mood or anxiety disorders. They have a high risk of suicide. Most

Anti-socials would have been diagnosed with some kind of a Conduct Disorder before the age of 15 or have exhibited serious behavioural problems as children.

Anti-social Personality Disorder is probably caused by a combination of reasons, including environmental and genetic or biological factors.

- **The environment.** A chaotic family life with a lack of supervision contributes to the development of this personality disorder.

- **Genetic (inherited) or biological factors.** Researchers have identified physiological responses that may be specific to people with Anti-social Personality Disorder. For example, they have a relatively flat response to stress. They appear to get less anxious than the average person. They seem to have a more difficult time maintaining daytime arousal. They have a weak "startle reflex," the involuntary response to loud noises. This relative insensitivity may affect their ability to learn from reward and punishment. Because of this, they are often able to pass polygraph tests with relative ease.

The frontal lobe, the area of the brain that governs planning and judgment, appears to be different in people with Anti-social Personality Disorder. Researchers have found changes in the number of brain structures that mediate violent behaviour. People with this kind of brain function could thus have greater difficulty in controlling their impulses, which might account for their tendency towards more aggressive behaviour.

Borderline Personality Disorder

A person with a Borderline Personality Disorder may be intelligent and appear warm, friendly and competent. They can maintain this appearance for years until their defence structures crumble, usually under stress such as the breakup of a romantic relationship or the death of a parent. Their relationships with other people are intense, stormy and unstable. The person may manipulate others and frequently has difficulty with trusting others. They often exhibit unpredictable and impulsive behaviour which may include excessive spending, promiscuity, drug or alcohol abuse and they display inappropriate and extreme anger or rage. Additionally, there is a propensity towards extreme feelings and behaviour and in severe cases - under excessive stress - there may be brief psychotic episodes.

Borderline Personality Disorder can be treated by long-term therapy, but this option was not open to Jeannine as she had no money to pay for the treatment, her parents couldn't afford it and the State had basically washed its hands of her.

34.
THE GAMES PEOPLE PLAY
EXTREME SEX

At the risk of sounding like Laurie during her interview with Prinsloo, what consenting adults do behind closed doors is their business. But since this entire book is about extreme sex there are a few concepts that warrant exploration:

The sexual relationship between Visser and Prinsloo could undeniably be categorised as Sado-Masochistic. Sigmund Freud described "Sadism" and "Masochism" in his *Drei Abhandlungen zur Sexualtheorie* ("Three papers on Sexual Theory") as stemming from aberrant psychological development in early childhood. This opinion, combined with Dr Eon Sonnekus' conclusion that Visser's sexuality was not integrated during puberty, confirms that she was sexually immature when she met Prinsloo – which might go some way in explaining why she did not walk out on him after the first indications of S&M behaviour. She simply did not know what was to be expected from a "normal," ordinary sexual relationship. It's also worth noting that Sonnekus also states in his report that this sexual immaturity caused an emotional imbalance in Visser.

From several statements he made regarding Visser, especially after she kicked him out of her mother's home after he had allegedly raped the older woman, I get the impression that Prinsloo regarded himself as somewhat of a Libertine. Libertines are devoid of most moral restraints, which are seen as unnecessary or undesirable. They especially ignore or spurn accepted morals and forms of behaviour sanctioned by larger society. These people only place value on physical pleasures. The Marquis de Sade – the person after whom the term sadism was named – was an infamous Libertine. In his book *120 Days of Sodom* he tells an extremely sadistic tale which starts of with comparatively minor torture and ends in extremely violent murders. Within this philosophy anything goes – the more shocking and perverse the better. A Libertine is defined today as *"a dissolute person; usually a person who is morally unrestrained."*

Sexual Sadism

It is important to distinguish between "Sadism," which is the term used in conjunction with *Sadistic Personality Disorder,* and "Sexual Sadism" which may be associated with SPD yet is classified as one of the paraphilias because of the specific sexual component. The two are most certainly related and an understanding of sadism is paramount to the understanding of sexual sadism but this particular section deals only with the paraphilias of sexual sadism.

Sexual sadism refers to the derivation of sexual pleasure from the infliction of pain, suffering and/or humiliation upon another person. The pain and suffering of the victim, which may be both physical and psychological, is pivotal to sexual arousal and pleasure. The ICD-10 (World Health Organisation, 1992) defines sadism as "preference for sexual activity that involves bondage or infliction of pain or humiliation."

Official Criteria

Current diagnostic criterion requires the following criteria be met:
1. Recurrent, intense sexually arousing fantasies, sexual urges, or behaviours involving acts (real, not simulated) in which the

psychological or physical suffering (including humiliation) of the victim is sexually exciting for the person, and have been present for at least 6 months.

2. The fantasies, sexual urges, or behaviours cause clinically significant stress or impairment in social, occupational or other important areas of function.

   Krafft-Ebing, in his 1886 *Psychopathia Sexualis*, defined sadism as: "The experience of sexual, pleasurable sensations (including orgasm) produced by acts of cruelty, bodily punishment afflicted on one's person or when witnessed in others, be they animals or human beings. It may also consist of an innate desire to humiliate, hurt, wound or even destroy others in order, thereby, to create sexual pleasure in oneself" (p.109).

Types of Sexual Sadism

Krafft-Ebing (1886/1965) sub-classified sexual sadism into several categories including:

1. Lust-murder. Here he included cases in which there was a connection between sexual arousal and killing which may extend to anthropaphagy or cannibalism (eating body parts of the victim). Among examples he included "Jack the Ripper" and similar types of homicide;

2. Mutilation of corpses or necrophilia;

3. Injury to females (stabbing, flagellation etc.);

4. Defilement of women;

5. Other kinds of assaults on women - symbolic sadism in which, for example, the perpetrator cuts the hair of his victim rather than harming them directly;

6. Ideal sadism or sadistic fantasies alone, without acts;

7. Sadism with other objects, for example, whipping of boys;
8. Sadistic acts with animals.

Those eight basic types can be roughly categorized into two main groups of Sexual sadism: Mild sadism in a consensual sexual relationship (e.g. S&M) and the major category involving injury or worse, usually in a non-consensual relationship. In both, the element of pain to the victim is the sexual stimulus.

Mild Sexual Sadism

Mild sadism, referred to as S&M, bondage & discipline, or dominance & submission is a specialized subculture, found mainly in the homosexual community. In large cities networks exist for those who have this interest. It is not, however, limited to this group. Sexual sadists of both sexes often seek out masochistic partners. Sexually sadistic behaviour in these consensual cases may involve:

- role-playing with dominant and submissive roles: master-slave, governess-pupil, etc;
- the dominant partner placing the submissive one in a position of helplessness and then applying some form of discipline or punishment, usually accompanied by verbal degradation;
- use of gags and blindfolds to render the submissive partner helpless and immobile;
- the administration of pain, humiliation or bondage is effected through such acts as whipping or flagellation, usually applied to the buttocks;
- cross-dressing the submissive partner;
- treating the submissive like an animal and/or making him/her crawl;
- confining the submissive to a cage;

- humiliation by being forced to wear a diaper or lick the dominant's boots;
- binding or clamping the breasts/nipples/penis of the submissive;
- urinating or defecating on the submissive and forcing ingestion on the victim.

Major Sexual Sadism

Major sexual sadism, on the other hand, is usually not consensual and involves injury or death to the victim. The element of fear in the victim and complete control of the victim is the major sexual stimuli in major sexual sadism. Some of the more severe activities involved in this behaviour may include:

- severe beatings
- torture
- burning, cutting,
- stabbing in the breast or buttocks (piquerism)
- rape
- murder
- vampirism
- necrophilia

Sexual sadism is found predominately in males and usually onsets with puberty, although sadistic behaviour may be evident earlier in children. In all male cases, it becomes evident by early adulthood. Sexual sadism may begin with fantasies and, in some cases, these may never be acted upon or, be acted out in the more mild forms of consensual relationships. In non-consensual cases, the behaviour usually continues and often escalates over time as the perpetrator experiences a need for increased violence in order to stimulate the sexual response.

In cases of female sexual sadism, onset is often later and often triggered by relationships with men who want to be dominated.

Paradoxically, while sexual sadism is more common in men, there appears to be a predominance of female domatrixes found in sadomasochistic pornography (Weinberg, 1984, 1987).

Sadism is commonly found in association with other paraphilias. Many authors have considered sadism and masochism as complementary anomalies and this is supported by the finding that individuals with masochistic fantasies often have sadistic fantasies as well. Hucker and Blanchard (1992) also found an association between sadism and asphyxiophilia (extreme masochism).

One particularly interesting study on multiple paraphilias found that, on average, paraphiliacs with one diagnosis have two or three others as well, often not initially admitted or recognised. Thus, 18% of sadists were also masochistic, 46% had also engaged in rape, 21% in exhibitionism, 25% each in voyeurism and frottage and 33% in paedophilia (Abel et al., 1988). This study guaranteed the confidentiality of the participants and thus feedback could be considered quite accurate.

Other authors have noted an overlap between sadism, masochism, fetishism and transvestism. Among much more serious sadistic offenders, transvestism and fetishism are strongly represented (Dietz et al., 1990; Prentky et al., 1985).

Sexual sadism, when combined with Anti-Social Personality Disorder, can be particularly dangerous.

Paraphilia
Paraphilia is a medical or behavioural science term for what is also referred to as: sexual deviation, sexual anomaly, sexual perversion or a disorder of sexual preference. It is the repeated, intense sexual arousal

to unconventional (socially deviant) stimuli.

Richard von Krafft-Ebing, a German psychiatrist credited with formally introducing the study of Sexology as a psychiatric phenomenon, identified paraphilias first in his 1886 *Psychopathia Sexualis* (Sexual Psychopathy). This highly influential psychiatric text laid the groundwork for the development of research and treatment that has taken place in this area over the last century.

Paraphilias are found almost exclusively in males. Onset tends to begin during early puberty, reaching full development by the age of 20. They are reported in many cultures and have long been reported or described in history. There is often an overlap of paraphilias, the most common being 2-3 concurrently present although cases of up to 10 have been reported in about 5% of paraphiliacs.

Some of the more common paraphilias are:

- Paedophilia (children)
- Exhibitionism (exposing one's genitals)
- Fetishism (specific objects, e.g. rubber, pantyhose, etc)
- Frotteurism (rubbing against strangers)
- Sexual masochism (pain or humiliation of self), including
- Hypoxyphilia/Autoerotic Asphyxia
- Sexual sadism (pain or humiliation of others)
- Transvestic fetishism (clothing usually worn by the other sex)
- Voyeurism (peeping)
- Paraphilia not otherwise specified:
  - Telephone scatologia (obscene phone calls)
  - Necrophilia (corpses)
  - Partialism (exclusive focus on specific parts of the body)
  - Zoophilia (animals)
  - Coprophilia (faeces)

- Klismaphilia (enemas)
- Urophilia (urine)

Paraphilias and Sex Offenders

Not all paraphilias result in illegal behaviours but some, by their very nature, do. Fetishistic transvestism, for example, is simply the wearing of clothes of the opposite sex for sexual arousal. On the other hand, sexual sadism that involves violence to a victim in a non-consensual relationship or paedophilia that manifests itself in child molestation, are criminal behaviours.

Apart from sexual sadism, at least three paraphilias surfaced during the "Advocate Barbie" trial:

Paedophilia

Paedophilia refers to an <u>adult</u> who is sexually attracted to <u>children</u> who have not reached <u>puberty</u>, or who are not yet fully sexually matured. The common definition also says that a paedophile is at least 5 years older than the victim, and at least 16 years of age. It's worth noting that there are two different categories of paedophiles: those who have sex exclusively with children and those who have sex with children as well as adults.

Coprophilia

Coprophilia, also called scatophilia or scat, is the paraphilia involving sexual pleasure from faeces. Coprophilia can either refer to liking the smell, taste, or feel of faeces in a sexual way. The feeling can be either through touching the skin or through rubbing the penis head against faeces. Enjoyment can also be made from the feeling of faeces passing through the anus.

Eating faeces is also known as coprophagia. A person who eats faeces is at risk of getting sick through hepatitis, infection, and AIDS. Those with a weak immune system should not eat faeces. There are people who make movies involving coprophilia. This is called scatology and is common in German and Japanese sex movies.

Urophilia (urine)

Urolagnia (also urophilia, undinism, golden shower and watersports) is a paraphilia in which sexual excitement is associated with the sight or thought of urine or urination. Those who enjoy urolagnia may enjoy urinating on another person or persons, or being urinated upon. Some participants may drink the urine; this practice is known as urophagia, though *uraphagia* refers to the consumption of urine regardless of whether the context is sexual. These activities are often described with the slang terms *golden showers*, *water sports*, or *piss play*.

Erotic Humiliation

From her description in court it is evident that Visser's sexual relationship with Prinsloo included aspects of the Sadomasochistic practice of Erotic Humiliation.

Erotic Humiliation can be described as the consensual use of both physical and psychological humiliation in a sexual context, whereby the one person gains arousal or erotic excitement from the potent emotions of being humiliated and demeaned, or of humiliating another person – frequently (but not always) in conjunction with sexual stimulation of one or both partners in the activity.

The humiliation need not be sexual in itself – as with numerous other sexual behaviours it is the feelings derived from it which are sought after, regardless of the nature of the actual activity. It can be physical or verbal and can be reasonably private or public. The distinctive difference between humiliation and dominance in an activity such as erotic spanking is that the sought-after effect is first and foremost the humiliation – the activity is just a means of achieving that end.

Fantasy and fascination with erotic humiliation is a prevalent part of Bondage Discipline and Sadomasochistic (BDSM) and other sexual role play. Humiliation play can be taken to a point where it becomes emotionally and psychologically distressing to one partner or the other, particularly if it is public humiliation. Erotic humiliation may become extreme enough to be thought of as a form of "edge" play, which many consider should be approached with advance negotiation and the use of a safe word.

The person being humiliated is frequently called a "bottom," and the person who humiliates them is commonly referred to as the "top." Other names are "slave" or "sub/submissive" for the *bottom*, and "Master/Mistress" or "Dom/Domme" for the *top*.

Humiliation differs from dominance, as the devotee is not necessarily looking to be ordered about. Humiliation manifests itself as a sexual force when the devotee seeks out the humiliation above the means – for example when being spanked is principally valued because of the belittlement involved. It encompasses a range of paraphilias, including body worship, foot or shoe fetish, spanking, bondage and the majority of BDSM styles.

It can be basic and may include something as simple as washing the feet of the dominant partner or it can be complex, involving role play or public displays of subservience. It can also be for a set period of time or as an ongoing facet of a relationship. Many scenarios which may give rise to sexual humiliation may be based on verbal abuse or physical aspects.

Verbal aspects highlighted by Visser include:
- Verbal belittlement, for instance "slave";
- Insults and verbal abuse, such as "dumb," "ugly," "stupid";
- Degrading references, such as "slut," "bitch," and "whore";
- Slighting of body parts or behaviours, such as disparaging or cruel references to breasts, facial appearance, genitalia, bottom, responsiveness, standard of self-care;
- Having to ask permission for everyday activities such as going to the toilet, spending money or eating;
- Small breasts humiliation, where contempt is expressed for the supposed inadequacy of the adult female's breasts, or her inability to please a lover;
- Forced repetition, for instance being obliged to repeat commands to confirm them;
- Forced flattery, for example agreeing that every decision that the dominant makes is wise, correct and justifiable, while additionally praising the dominant's physical and personality traits;
- Mockery, derision, and ridicule;
- Being scolded like a child.
- Physical and tangible aspects highlighted by Visser include:
- Ejaculating, spitting or urinating on the "bottom's" body, especially the face;
- Performance of menial tasks;
- Frequent, compulsory performance of sexual services for the dominant, such as cunnilingus, analingus, fellatio or erotic massage, without expectations of reciprocal acts or intercourse;
- Detailed accountability and control (micro-management) regarding time spent or activities undertaken, as well as lists of

jobs to do, precise directives as to how the housework is to be performed and exactly how to act and behave;

- Specific rituals and affectations to be adopted, including displays of subservience, only speaking when spoken to, eating only what he allows, and a wide variety of body-worship activities such as kissing or licking the dominant's feet, boots, buttocks, anus, vulva, etc. to express acknowledgment, subservience, shame, or even positive emotions such as happiness or excitement;
- Suppressed freedom of movement and/or privacy;
- Detailed punishments for a variety of 'infractions' or misbehaviour, such as flogging or whipping, reduced rations, or forced exercise;
- Spanking, slapping, whipping, restraint or other BDSM activities;
- Prohibitions or restrictions on clothing, even in public. For females a common example is being forced to wear only revealing bikinis or lingerie. Both sexes may be expected to go completely nude, with decorative objects such as collars, diapers, bands, tiaras, or cuffs being the only exceptions;
- Wearing of external signs of "ownership," such as a tattoo;
- Embarrassment;
- Having to ask permission to orgasm during sex or masturbation;
- Forced to wear a gag or restraints on the body;
- Financial domination;
- Forced masturbation in a humiliating manner.

A number of sexually humiliating behaviours involve inflicting pain, but a great deal of it is far more concerned with mocking, ridicule, degradation and embarrassment.

Humiliation generally stimulates the brain regions associated with physical pain, inferring that humans evolved to memorize social rewards and punishments as animals recall physical reward or pain in response to their environment. With any type of pain experimentation in a sexual context, consent and (paradoxically) an elevated degree of awareness and communication are essential to ensure that the result is desirable, rather than abusive. For instance, a submissive might enjoy being insulted in certain ways, but be genuinely hurt and devastated if humiliated in other ways.

While this theory might explain why Visser tolerated the torture and humiliation she claims to have suffered at the hands of her lover, it does not explain why she complied with his alleged demands of involving children in their sex play.

ACKNOWLEDGEMENTS: LAURIE PIETERS

I would like to thank Jennifer Cronjé, André Fourie and Retha Meintjies of the National Prosecuting Authority for their input and valuable advice and for the doors at the NPA that were open to us throughout the process of writing this book.

Lucy Redivo and Sonja Theron of the Child Abuse Action Group for their assistance in and facilitation of the gathering of the true facts regarding Jeannine du Plessis' life. To this end I also need to thank Nesta and Louise for agreeing to talk to me about their experiences with Jeannine and their lives on the street. A big thanks to Sue for agreeing to chat to me as well as for the photographs of Jeannine that she supplied.

I would like to thank my mother, Kathleen Pieters, and my grandmother Muriel Mitchell for their unwavering support during the last eight years which strengthened my resolve to see the case through to the end.

To my friends who stood by me through the trial – a huge thank you. They include Celeste Dennis, as well as Ian van der Nest and Elmarie Myburgh from SAPS and Magistrate Wayne Gibbs, who never failed to give me good advice.

My heartfelt gratitude goes out to the staff of both the Criminology and Psychology departments of UNISA and specifically to Prof Herman Conradie and Prof Anna van der Hoven for their amazing support through all my studies and their unwavering belief in me. I could not have done it without you!

A huge thank you must go to my son, Connor Brown, for giving up his "me" time so that I could write and for his unwavering faith in me. For all the cups of coffee he made while I was tied to my desk. He is the light of my life and a special young man of whom I am truly proud.

My fiancé Laurie James for his love and support and never ending patience. Laurie has been my best friend and my sounding board and almost "counsellor." He spent hours listening to the unedited horror stories of the street kids and helped me to deal with untold amounts of anger, sadness and revulsion at some of the things I heard during the often heartbreaking research for the book. His quiet strength was my emotional respite. He has been my rock through this process.

Finally, I would like to thank Liezl Thom for agreeing to write the story with me. She has become a good friend and has made sure that the book is balanced. I have learned to accept that it's not always good to be too close to one's subject matter.

ACKNOWLEDGEMENTS: LIEZL THOM

Firstly, I'd like to thank my husband David for encouraging me to soar – and for listening to every sordid detail of the court case, many of which I couldn't broadcast. As a mother myself, I often imagined how difficult it must have been for listeners who were driving with kids to listen to my "cleaned up" version of the absolute graphic details heard in court. My boys served as a constant reminder that I had to sanitise my reporting. Unfortunately, my poor husband was not spared the horror as I unloaded every night.

To my two sons, Liam and Ethan, thank you for teaching me about unconditional love.

To my parents and in-laws, Burt and Anchen du Rand and Berna and James Thom, thank you for showing me the way.

My two pillars, Majida and Dawid – I would not be able to weather life's storms without you.

Christine and Rosie – thank you for giving me that most precious of all gifts… time.

My friends and colleagues at Eyewitness News and Primedia Broadcasting – I don't need to tell you that you guys rock, but I'll do so anyway. I'm singling out only a few.

Mandy – thank you for showing me it could be done… You're an inspiration.

Yusuf – thank you for being my friend and confidante over more years than I would care to count.

Katy – thank you for believing in me, even when I didn't.

Benita – I'll resist the temptation to get soppy and just say thank you for getting me to follow my own North Star.

Camilla – for your funny, yet honest advice and support.

Ray – I love working with you!

Kate Turkington – for being marvellously generous with your advice and *j'oie de vivre*.

To the man who turned this pie in the sky dream into a reality: Bernie, thank you for being part of this process even from before it began. I guess this officially makes you the daddy!

Our amazing editor, Bernard Hellberg – we could never repay you for your wisdom, kindness, levelheadedness and sense of humour that sometimes drove us crazy, but mostly kept us from going completely nuts.

To the court crowd: Sandra, Zelda, Hermann, Ilse, Jean-Marie – you guys are superheroes! Thank you for helping me stay (relatively) sane…

Hanti and Hilda, for your friendship and help through the years.

Gideon Scheepers – Thank you for your advice and guidance.

My friends in the SAPS, especially DB, thank you for making the research a little easier.

I'd like to thank my co-author Laurie Pieters for pushing me to put pen to paper to write this book, which I believe - apart from all the sex and scandal - will serve as a warning to all women in abusive relationships that unless they take control, things can go horribly wrong.

GETTING HELP

Child Abuse Action Group
Tel: 011 973 5033
Fax: 012 329 2103
website: www.caag.org.za

Inter Trauma Nexus
Tel: 012 348 0149
Fax: 086 527 2470
E-mail: info@barbaralouw.com

POWA (People Apposing Woman Abuse)
Tel: 011 642 4345/6
Fax: 011 484 3195
E-mail: info@powa.co.za
Web: www.powa.co.za

Childline
Tel: 011 645 2000
Fax: 011 645 2020
Web: www.childline.org.za

LKP Criminological and Profiling Services
For assistance with Domestic Violence Orders, expungement of a criminal record
or other criminological services.
Tel: 012 651 0599
Fax: 012 651 0599
E-mail: lauriep@telkom.co.za
Web: www.lkpcrimserv.com

**If you are aware of any criminal activity you can send an anonymous tip to
Crimeline at 32211 of call the SAPS on 10111.**